Letters to the Medicine Man
An Apprenticeship in Spiritual Intelligence

Best wishes for your spirit journey

Barbara Kerr

D1596743

Letters to the Medicine Man
An Apprenticeship in Spiritual Intelligence

Barbara Kerr
John McAlister

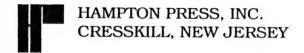

HAMPTON PRESS, INC.
CRESSKILL, NEW JERSEY

Printed in the United States of America

Library of Congress Cataloging-in-Publication Data

Kerr, Barbara A.
    Letters to the medicine man : an apprenticeship in
  spiritual intelligence / Barbara Kerr, John McAlister.
      p. cm.
    Includes bibliographic references.
    ISBN 1-57273-439-6 (pbk. : alk. paper)
     1 Shamanism. 2. Shamans. 3. Healing--Religious aspects.
    I. McAlister, John. II. Title.

    BL2370.S5 K47 2002
    299'.7--dc21

                           2002025007

Cover design: Tom Phon Graphics
Cover art: May S. Cheney

Hampton Press, Inc.
23 Broadway
Cresskill, NJ 07626

Contents

Acknowledgments

FROM BARBARA...

Although much of this book was written in my voice, *Letters to the Medicine Man* is truly the story of a community of loving people. It may take a village to raise a child, but it takes a small city to support a woman who chooses to be a shaman's apprentice. So, here are thanks to just a small number of those people.

My first thanks go to my family, Chuck, Sam, and Grace Claiborn. Chuck has been my best friend for nearly thirty years, and between the lines, the reader will discern that he is the hero of this story, the Odysseus who would have rather stayed home and plowed the fields but went ahead and bore the burden of someone else's battles. There is no greater courage than that which allows the ones we love to seek their own visions, and to support them in the process. For my children, it isn't easy having a mom like me. Nevertheless, over the many years that I was writing this book, Sam grew into the most interesting, most loving, and funniest physicist-writer-rock musician I could imagine. Gracie's wild creativity, limitless energy, and intuitive wisdom challenged me at every step to try to live up to honor of being the mother of a child like her. Throughout this story, you were all here with me, in my heart's core.

I want to thank my mother and father, Doris and Gerrald Kerr, and my sisters, Beverly Schafer and Cindy Kerr. I often felt them watching over me with concern and love.

And then my appreciation turns to that circle of friends who became characters in this story, who read drafts of the tale as it evolved, and who looked on with amusement, protectiveness, love, and loyalty while I thrashed around trying to find my way out of shadows. Sandy Cohn, Roseann Weiss, Harper Barnes, Pipp Piatchek, Delmar Boni, Carl Hammerschlag, Mary Delaney, Susan Lockhart, Esther Ratner, Jim and Maureen Dippold, Nancy and Larry Miller, Susan and Richard Loveless, Michael Young, Leonie Kronborg, Glen Alsop, Jane and Collie Conoley, Cleo and Peter Hardin, Thearon and Vanette McKinney, Mark Pawlowski, Leon Sharpe, Sharon Kurpius, Richard Kinnier, Joe Johnston, Kay Libbus, Bill Bondeson, and so many others: my thanks to you are in this book.

I want to express gratitude to the young people in my life, my students and all the participants in the sweat lodge ceremonies. Thanks to the inspiration of Corissa Chopp Lotta, Nan Benally, Laura Elie, Kara McAlister, Helene Grotans and Shannyn Vicente, who have taught me as much as I have taught them.

Special thanks to Sheila Saunders, who typed the first draft long ago and followed the progress of the book avidly; and to Megan Foley-Nicpon and Camea Gagliardi, who proofread the last draft and gasped in all the right places; and artist May Cheney.

Finally, my thanks to those people who brought this book to fruition. Kathleen Noble, dear friend and author of *Riding the Wind Horse* taught me about spiritual intelligence and led me to our publisher. Barbara Bernstein of Hampton Press, publisher of scholarly books, believed in our effort to bridge science and spirit, and brought our story to light. I will always be grateful.

FROM JOHN . . .

In the traditions of the people that live in the earth it is always good to give thanks. In the process of writing this book many people helped and assisted, in some cases without their knowledge. Their wisdom, knowledge, and meaningful comments have always been appreciated. I wish to thank all of you from the depths of my spirit.

First I would like to acknowledge my daughter Kara, for her beauty inside and out, her courage, intellect and mutual support while we lived through and continue to survive the tragedy of her mother's untimely and early passing into the star nation. She is bright and wonderful and since her earliest steps full of wisdom. She is not only a great daughter, but also a dearest friend. May the blessings of long rainbows guide her through a healthy and prosperous life, rich with experience and love.

I would like to say a heartfelt thank you to my wife Weezee (Virginia Louise Jones McAlister) for her unconditional love, her support and encouragement for me to follow my path, and for twenty-four years of a wonderful marriage. Her willingness to endure my travels, my exploration of the Mystery, and the graciously hosting of the tribes of people constantly visiting our home, is magical. She is and has always been and angel. *For as long as the grass grows, the water flows, and the sky is blue,* Kara and I will love her.

Special mention goes to Blue Otter, Stumbling Deer, Red Crow, Mad Raven, Sage and Thunderwolf for their enduring friendship, the many dances, sweat lodges, ceremonies and miles traveled on the road of life we have shared together.

Mark Pawlowski deserves a medal of honor for his support during the brightest of moments and the darkest of times. He has weathered the storms of life standing like a sentinel, guiding and protecting the future of young people as he continues to do today. His support of this project is appreciated in ways words will not express and in ways he may never truly know.

Many thanks are due my brother Douglas B. McAlister and his wife Nancy. Their excitement about this project, the hours they spent listening to my stories, hosting me in their home, and their invaluable comments after reading one of the final versions of the manuscript can only be appreciated with the highest of regard.

My sister Kate and her husband Michael Kupstas deserve honorable mention for the many nights of hospitality, great food, and tolerance over the four years of development of the manuscript.

I have appreciated the many questions and support from Mary Elizabeth Barnette and Elizabeth (Poppy) Potter. Separately and together they, wittingly and unwittingly helped me hone my thoughts so that I could coherently articulate them in print. Thank you for your love and friendship. You will always be in my heart.

Words will never express my love for my parents C.R. and Mary McAlister who in many ways allowed me to become who I am. They have always encouraged me to be my very best. Though at times I am sure they may have wondered about my directions, interest and activities, they have always supported my efforts to constantly evolve with love. For this I am eternally grateful.

I must not forget my brother Alan K. McAlister and his family. They are just plain wonderful people.

And thank you to my first teacher who taught me the ways of the earth, the sky, and all of creation. Your spirit lives forever in the hearts and minds of all of those with whom you shared your wisdom.

The Great Spirits walks with all of you.

This story is dedicated to the four great Nations of People, and all the ones in each of the Nations who are working diligently to deliver the Spirit of Peace.

It is also dedicated to all of our children. May they long live in harmony and balance, and share the blessings of peace.

Preface

They are referred to as shamans, medicine men and women, curanderas and curanderos, holy people, and by many other names. Throughout most of human history, shamanic healing was the major way in which people were healed of physical and mental illness. Until recently, shamanism as a healing art was in decline throughout the world. Only the few remaining hunter-gatherer societies practiced shamanic healing as their exclusive means of medical and psychological treatment (Frank & Frank, 2000). The power of missionaries and modern medicine was such that many of the most sacred shamanic healing ceremonies, such as the Native American sweat lodge, were outlawed (Bruchac, 1993).

The antagonism of institutionalized religion and medicine to shamanic practitioners is not new. Since the advent of agriculture, the founding of cities, and the rise of priests and kings, shamanic healers have been persecuted as witches and driven to the margins of society (Winkelman, 1992). However, many people continued to seek the services of shamanic healers when their priests and official physicians failed to cure them of their suffering or unhappiness (Hammerschlag, 1989, 1994). Until recently, the occasional tale of a seeker being cured of a long and painful illness by a shamanic healer was regarded as a simple curiosity, an anomalous incident in the otherwise inexorable conquest by science of all mystery. Then, in an astonishing turn of events, Americans lost faith in science, lost faith in medicine, and lost faith in the institutions that had promised them relief from suffering and often failed to deliver. With that loss of faith came an extraordinary growth of interest in alternative medicine. Thirty percent of Americans now use some form of alternative medicine (Gordon, Nienstedt, Gesler, & Gesler, 1998). A rebirth of interest in shamanic healing has focused attention on indigenous people and the shamans who heal them (Moyers, 1993).

Only a few scientific studies of shamanism have been successful in clarifying the nature of the healing and the characteristics of the healers (Frank & Frank, 2000; Kiev, 1964; Winkelman, 2000). Shamans do their work by altering consciousness in the service of another person's healing. The shaman orchestrates consciousness, using meditation, song, dance, drumming, and ceremony to encourage the spirit to travel to a realm where healing takes place. Nobody knows precisely how the actions of the shaman activate the patient's healing response. It seems to work best when both the healer and the patient are in an altered state, when the patient trusts and has faith in the healer's power, and when the healing takes place in a sacred space within the community. Most scientists remain skeptical about the healing mechanisms at work, and the techniques of science, so clearly rooted in ordinary consciousness, do not seem well suited to the study of shamanism. Perhaps the only way of understanding the gift of healing is through intense observation and immersion in the work of the shaman.

Shamanic healers are notoriously difficult to pin down for an interview, and have often given hilariously inaccurate information to anthropologists to distract them from dissecting sacred truths, or just for the fun of it. Too often, the skepticism of the interviewer has kept the shaman dancing in the shadows.

There have been many popular tales of shamanism—Carlos Castenada's (Castenada, Castenada, & Rosenman, 1991) Don Juan stories, *Rolling Thunder* (Boyd, 1974), *Medicine Woman* (Andrews, 1983), and *Mutant Message Down Under* (Morgan & Garrison, 1995)-but unfortunately, all of these seem to be at least partly fictionalized. They follow a general pattern: a skeptical and jaded professional is exposed to a shamanic practitioner whose feats of healing or magic amaze the narrator. A partnership is created, with the shaman quite surprisingly revealing his or her sacred wisdom to the narrator as he or she takes the narrator on an amazing journey to the Spirit World, or the Dreamtime. The hero of the story is changed forever, and becomes a faithful, if not credulous believer, abandoning not only skepticism, but also his or her former way of life. It has been common soon after the publication of these books for the indigenous people who are featured in the narratives to disclaim any knowledge of the narrator or of the events depicted in the story. Once again, the actual shamans seem to be dancing in the shadows, mocking the very people who are earnestly trying to share their wisdom with the world. We are left then with a paradox: shamanism is best understood through immersion in the shamanic journey, rather than from a scientific distance. However, individuals who attempt to communicate the truths learned from the journey may find themselves both discredited by their scientific colleagues for having "lost perspective" and then rejected by their shamanic teachers for divulging sacred ways or engaging in cultural appropriation.

SPIRITUAL INTELLIGENCE

Shamanic healers are individuals who are gifted with spiritual intelligence. Intelligence is the capacity to think, to plan, to create, to adapt to changing circumstances, to find and solve problems, to reflect upon and communicate well with self and others, and to grow from mistakes. Gardner (1983) proposed that there is not one intelligence, but many, and that each intelligence has its own forms of perception, learning, memory, symbol manipulation, and mode of creativity. His theory of multiple intelligences is now well accepted. Spiritual intelligence is a relatively new term for describing a set of abilities that seem to be associated with spiritual experience. Emmons (1999) identified five core characteristics of spiritual intelligence after reviewing the empirical literature in the psychology of religion and spirituality. These were: "the capacity to transcend the physical and material; the ability to experience heightened states of consciousness; the ability to sanctify everyday experiences; the ability to utilize spiritual resources to solve problems; and the capacity to be virtuous (p. 164). Noble's (2001) study of spiritual intelligence led her to describe it as an innate human potential, expressed in various ways and to various degrees throughout the human population. She added two additional, critical abilities to Emmons' list. The first is the conscious recognition that physical reality is embedded within a larger, multidimensional reality with which we interact, consciously and unconsciously, on a moment-to-moment basis. The second is the conscious pursuit of psychological health, not only for oneself but also for the sake of the global community.

Noble wrote:

> Spiritual intelligence is a dynamic and fluid process, not a static product. . . . Although these experiences can be exciting and challenging, they do not automatically bring about psychological growth. In order for them to quicken that growth we must be open to perceiving them, assess their physical, psychological, and interpersonal impact, and integrate them intelligently into our lives. *Intelligence* is the critical part of this equation. This is neither blind nor rigid adherence to a prescribed set of beliefs but a mindset that tolerates uncertainty and paradox as well as the anxiety of "not knowing." Although an individual might choose to practice a particular religion or spiritual discipline, spiritual intelligence is the awareness that the whole is always greater than the sum of its parts, no matter how cherished a part might be. (p. 46)

Shamans, therefore, are people who have developed this attitude as well as who express the capacities of spiritual intelligence. As children, shamans are perceived as different from other children in important ways. Shamans are often orphans or individuals who have suffered significant losses or disabilities such as blindness or lameness. They have more vivid dreams; they see visions; and often, they have epilepsy or another condition that induces seizures and trance states. They are intelligent, possessing great insight and intuition into human motivation and the sources of conflict. They see the world in a larger perspective, because at all times, they have access not only to the ordinary reality but also to a spiritual reality (Frank & Frank, 2000). Noble wrote:

> There are shamans and healers the world over who can perceive subtle energies and control physiological functions in ways that traditional Western sciences cannot explain. There

are individuals who can alter their state of consciousness at will and use their dreams and inner senses to explore both the physical and spiritual realms. There are ordinary people who demonstrate an extraordinary capacity for goodness— what Buddhists call "loving kindness" and Native Americans a "moist heart"—and who use this capacity to serve their own and other species. There are people who endure conditions of incomprehensible trauma and despair, and whose awareness, tolerance, compassion, and resilience are strengthened, not diminished, by those experiences. (p.13)

Shamanic healers learn their vocation through two significant educational experiences: the apprenticeship and the journey into darkness. Without both of these, the creation of the healer is incomplete. During the apprenticeship, the novice learns the spiritual arts and skills of his or her culture; during the journey into darkness, the apprentice becomes transformed through suffering, becoming whole and balanced. Although shamanic skills have great similarity across individuals and across cultures, the journey into darkness is unique to each individual that takes the vocation of the shaman. All shamans seem to agree, however, that without this descent into darkness, the training is incomplete. And all warn of the terrible dangers of that descent. Hoffman (1981) told the tale of the four Jewish sages who found Paradise through their practice of their faith. The first sage was so enraptured by beauty of that realization, that he could not bear to return to physical life, and didn't. The second was psychologically overwhelmed by the experience and lost his mind. The third could not reconcile his experience with his religious training and left his faith to seek answers elsewhere. Only the fourth "ascended and descended in peace." Wade Davis (1998) applied this to the apprenticeship of the shaman, saying that:

Almost invariably, an overwhelming mental crisis is part of the vocational summons. Indeed, for the seeker of shamanic wisdom, it is a fine line between mystical initiation and psychological breakdown. Yet though this crisis may resemble a mental breakdown it cannot be dismissed as one. For it is not a pathological but a normal event for the gifted mind in these societies, the realization and intuition of a level of spiritual depth that gives the world a sacred character. (p. 145)

Noble (2001) described the difference between the shamanic spiritual crisis and spiritual dimentia. Nobody was ever made better or happier by spiritual psychosis. But the shamanic apprentice emerges from the depths healthier, stronger, and clearer than ever before.

THE PLAN OF THE BOOK

This book tells the story of spiritual awakening, shamanic apprenticeship, and the transformation of a helper into a healer. It is shaped, like the year, into seasons, although in the case of this particular story, each "season" lasted a year. For each of these sections of the book, we have written about events that were happening in the ordinary world, and parallel events that occurred in what I called the unconscious and Ten White Bears called the Spirit World. The first part of this book, representig Spring, is called *Letters to the Medicine Man*. It is the story, through letters and narrative, of the awakening of spiritual intelligence. *Letters to the Medicine Man* is the record of a year-long dialogue across the great divide of science and spirituality. It tells how, as an atheistic psychologist, I discovered my own spirit with the help of Ten White Bears, a teacher of Native American traditions. These letters and the narrative between them also tell the story of a growing friendship between a man and a woman. We had little in common except our determination to create a relationship that transcended the boundaries of culture, gender, and custom in order to learn from one another.

The events recounted here began in late summer of 1992. However, they also began in what was for both of us the late summer of our lives. It is at this time in life, the poets and philosophers tell us, that we are most likely to find ourselves unsure of our direction and suddenly doubting the path we had chosen in our youth. Dante Alighieri, the 15th-century poet, wrote at the beginning of *The Divine Comedy*,

Nel mezzo del cammin di nostra vita
mi ritrovai per une selva oscur
che la diritta via era smarrita.

These lines, which begin Dante's tale of his travels from Hell to Heaven, tell us, "Midway in the journey of our life I found myself in a dark wood, for the straight way was lost."

It is during this experience of being lost that the awakening of the spirit is most likely. At that time in my life, in the ordinary world, my intellectual ambition and achievements had led me, for reasons I did not understand, into a state of dissatisfaction and unease. While in that condition, I found the doorway into the Spirit World—through what, at the time, seemed an accidental exposure to Native American spirituality. I participated, unexpectedly, in a Native American ceremony called the sweat lodge, led by Ten White Bears. Accidents like these occur frequently to those who are unhappy and uncertain of their way.

After a profound spiritual experience, many of us want to explain it away. Noble describes all the reasons why people might want to ignore spiritual realities and explain away spiritual events. She tells of the ostracism likely to occur to the academic or the scientist who claims to have had spiritual experiences. She shows how these experiences expose a person's own deepest fears of loss of control over one's own psyche, corporeal existence, and destiny. When I began to write letters to Ten White Bears, I continued, despite extraordinary experiences I had had with him, to attempt to explain my reactions in familiar psychological terms. This was the only language I had for understanding the force that drove me again and again to seek Ten White Bears' knowledge. I tried to use the language of psychology to explain the visions and dreams I had been having since my sweat lodge experience. I struggled to fit these experiences into my scientific paradigm, which only admitted them as hallucinations, post-hypnotic suggestions, and eruptions of an untidy id.

In the ordinary world, I carried on, anxiously fitting and refitting my worldview to a new reality. In the spirit world, I was being prepared for the failure of this attempt. My dreams became more vivid, and the commands of my unconscious more pressing. With continued provocation of the spirit came crisis, and crisis led inexorably to change. My worldview was shattered by a wintertime encounter with Ten White Bears, and my certainties were swept away. It was a time during which I fought to maintain my professional responsibilities and family life while experiencing waking visions and what were, to my mind, unacceptable and terrifying wishes. I found myself having dreams that bore deep significance not only for myself, but also for Ten White Bears. At last, the crisis was resolved in a metamorphosis of my worldview. My old way of thinking and acting assumed that I was separate from other beings and the things of nature. It also assumed that spirit, being essentially indefinable, was irrelevant. With Ten White Bears' help, I simply gave up the struggle to maintain a worldview that was frozen and limiting. It is the crisis of disintegration of the old and the acceptance of the new way of being that marks this tumultuous stage of the journey of the spirit. Religions have many names for this stage: religious conversion, enlightenment, awakening, being born again. For me, it was like finding vibrant life in the midst of winter, where I thought there was only chill and despair.

As critical as the awakening to the Great Spirit is, it is not the end of spiritual transformation. Spiritual awakening brings with it a growing sense of sacredness of all things, of harmony and balance, and of oneness. In the ordinary world—which now didn't seem so ordinary—I explored my new connectedness. I became aware of a new interpersonal power, a capacity to attract, persuade, and teach. Sometimes I stumbled a little in my use of my new abilities; but I also used them to become a more effective teacher and a more capable therapist. As a way of maintaining my awareness of the sacred, I began to practice the traditions of my new spirituality. Reaffirming one's connectedness through daily practice of love, work and meditation brings the ordinary world and the world of the spirit together: we call this *Realization*.

There are many people of many religions who have experienced the realization of their connectedness and the possibility of faith. Shamans, however, are people who have gone beyond realization. Instead of simply living their faith while going about ordinary life, shamans have discovered a vocation for teaching and healing. They go forward to expand the capacities of their spiritual intelligence so that they might help others toward realization and transformation.

The Summer section of this book narrates the story of my apprenticeship with Ten White Bears. In those heady days, I was immersed in the technology of shamanism. The apprenticeship described in this book is clearly an example of the shaping of spiritual intelligence. The words used to describe these skills are unique to

this particular mentor and apprentice; however, the skills themselves are those that are generally acknowledged to be the contents
of shaman's medicine bundle. I don't think I ever made a deliberate
choice to become Ten White Bears' apprentice; he says that I did, but
that I did not express it to myself. In any case, soon I was sitting at
his side in the sweat lodge, learning the songs and stories and
assisting him guiding the young people's prayers. I learned how to
use and care for the sacred pipe; how to build a lodge in the holy
way; how to make medicine bundles and gather herbs. These things
were not difficult to learn. I simply observed what Ten White Bears
did, and imitated him. In fact, throughout much of this time, I was
simply a mimic. I sang the same songs he sang, and built the lodge
exactly as he taught. I was his cub.

However, the art of deliberately altering consciousness, or
"going to the Spirit World" was much more rigorous, because it
could not be learned through imitation. To learn to enter this
realm, it was necessary for Ten White Bears to use a different
learning technology, one that took me unawares and thrust me
wholly into another consciousness. My teacher led me through
experiences that helped me to access the spiritual reality, finding
layers of knowing previously inaccessible to me. It was a long
time before I learned to control the process of shifting consciousness, and to guide myself there and back again. However, in that
time, I was moving beyond mimicry of my teacher and entering
into a more profound relationship that he called shared being.

In the Fall section of this book, I tell how I learned about
the nature of "shared being" through the extraordinary empathy
that emerged between myself and my teacher. A great tragedy in
Ten White Bears' life led him to "go between the wind," which is a
way of describing a condition of mourning that requires the ces-
sation of the practice of medicine ways. This meant that my
instruction of the simple skills of shamanism was over. I could
not ask a grieving man to continue my education in storytelling
and the construction of medicine bundles. However, my apprenticeship did indeed continue, as our relationship entered a new
phase of companionship and peaceful comfort. I visited him in
his den, bringing him warmth and work to do. By day we wrote
and planned our projects; by night, I sat at his side as he struggled in the Spirit World, in a fierce battle against despair. At last I
knew what was meant by the "I–Thou" experience: the meeting of

spirits in the vast oceanic consciousness of the Mystery. I learned the experience of shared being not only with my teacher, but with other living things. As he began to heal, I resumed my education in the use of dreams and visions to guide my own behavior, interpret reality, and to help others. Now, however, I could use these skills reciprocally, helping him as he helped me to understand the symbols and imagery that formed the language of the spirit. I was exposed to healing arts and discovered ways of using these arts to heal my own life-threatening condition. I was encouraged toward personal balance and integration and helped to see ways of living in the world so as to infuse each moment with sacredness. By that time, the most sacred moments seemed to be those I was spending with my teacher.

In the Winter section of this book, the profound attachment I had toward my teacher became the catalyst for my journey into darkness. In this section, the process by which the shamanic spiritual crisis was precipitated by the mentor, was experienced by the apprentice, and was observed by the community is described. In my case, the Mystery provided the exact crisis needed to undo my self-control, to render ineffective all my defenses and coping strategies, and to strip me of all the comfortable roles I had played. One must read ahead to see what the nature of that crisis was. For a time, it looked as though I had lost everything that I valued. I was taken apart so that I could be made whole, in a new way. Winter tells the story of my healing and reintegration. I was to meet new medicine teachers who showed me the way through the darkness. I learned at last that the power of healing and transformation resided not in special teachers, but in all of us.

In the course of writing this book, we have learned about the ways people experience the world of the spirit. We have worked to explain the complex and mysterious process of spiritual awakening, shamanic apprenticeship, and the journey into darkness and return as well as we can in written language. Coming from two very different worldviews, we attempt to show how any person can experience transformation of body, mind, and spirit. It is our belief that the skills and experiences of the shaman are available to everyone who has the courage and desire for transformation. It is one of the strongest messages of this book that even though shamanic healers have great spiritual intelligence, the abilities they manifest are present in everyone.

Our purpose is not to promote Native American traditions as the only path to realization. Rather, it is to show how taking the risk to explore a new worldview can lead to the discovery of the Mystery within and around us, and to an understanding of the transformative power of love.

We recognize that many people are concerned about the inappropriate use of Native American ceremonies and traditions. We have been careful to describe only those spiritual practices that have been published elsewhere. In addition, the names, ancestries, and tribal affiliations of many of the people in this narrative are obscured. Some of these people want to maintain their privacy and do not want to be involved in controversy. We hope readers will understand that the knowledge that Ten White Bears gave to me was freely given, as his teachers freely gave it to him.

We know that it is customary to tell how our book is different from other stories about spiritual transformation. It is really not very different, except that all of it really happened. We had these experiences; we said these words to one another; and we wrote these letters. From the beginning of our dialogue, we both had the sense that what we said and did mattered. Therefore, we each kept copies of our own letters as well as those sent to us, and we each documented in journals many of our experiences together. One of the most interesting aspects of writing the book was coming to agreement about what actually happened, when it happened, and how we felt about it.

It is certainly possible to read our narrative and to explain everything in scientific, naturalistic terms, as I once did. That way, the story becomes an interesting psychological study of a cross-cultural dialogue, as well as a somewhat harrowing description of the shaping of spiritual intelligence. It is also possible just to read our book for the fun of reading other people's letters and narratives. The letters are only lightly edited, and reflect the disjointed and serendipitous nature of any real correspondence. However, we hope that people who read our book will be encouraged to take the risk to expose themselves to new worldviews, to open themselves up to their own spirit, and to find the miracles that lie just below the surface of ordinary life.

Delmar Sings a Spirit Song for Barbara's Coming Together

She came to me with a hurt
Maybe in the heart or spirit
With a woman it's hard to tell.
She said, "The world came apart on me inside Chicago O'Hare."
For me it was inside Wal-mart in southern New Mexico,
My heart heavy with stuff from twenty years worth,
Presented myself to Milford Yazu with eagle plume and yellow
pollen. The blonde woman just cried inside the airport.
Some time passed for both of us.
One day Carl told her to see Delmar.
While doing ceremony in Carefree one day,
Saw her moving about with the desert breeze,
During the four directions part of the ceremony.
Looked to her for a helping hand in the ceremony,
Her response was gentle and kind,
The energy and spirit about her was real loving and gentle,
As the sun began to set the power was strong and comforting,
Her presence around me,

Could feel her dancing with all the people.
Lessons of life and teachings were presented to her,
You could tell by the way she carried herself...
Took her to the desert to be close to the Spirit,
Blew pollen in the four directions,
At the same time sang the song of life to the Creator.
She looks at me as the teacher.
Sometimes I'm the one learning from her.
We all learn from one another
About each other's powers.

Delmar Boni
San Carlos Apache

Spring

You are the Mystery and the Mystery is you.

The East, the Father Sun rises to begin our life. It is here we realize that we are part of the Great Mystery. It is inseparable. This is true of all life. To deny this truth will lead to the illusion of separation from the great spirit. This illusion concludes in disease, imbalance, and chaos. We are the Mystery.
    Ten White Bears

At forty years old I discovered that the strongest feelings I could experience were those of annoyance and fatigue. This came as a surprise, because I thought I had been destined for more dramatic emotions. Having lived life in a headlong rush toward my goals, I suppose I was expecting to feel some kind of wild satisfaction in having achieved them. Instead, I felt like a ball, pitched through the air in a gorgeous, speedy arc, only to fall to the ground, roll a few times, and stop.

I had a friend and colleague for a husband; smart and happy kids; and had work as a professor of psychology that was challenging and useful. Most of my accomplishments, however, were accompanied by a sour twist. By the time my husband Chuck and I clambered, exhausted, over the last barrier to full professor status, there was a widespread suspicion that professors had it too easy. This ensured that we would spend most of our time sitting in meetings discussing the departmental budget rather than sipping coffee in the Faculty Club and discussing ideas. Our family had moved to a sunny place, with palms and a sparkling pool. But the Midwestern winters in four university towns had taken their toll on our health and our spirits; ear infections and pneumonia plagued our children, and my husband and I complained to each other of a hundred symptoms of sleep loss and perceived injustice.

I carried on, at our new university, with a harried, false vivaciousness. The faculty of psychologists and counselors we had joined were angry at each other and obstructive. We knew nobody in the city, and most of these colleagues didn't seem very promising as friends.

My husband, who had been very ill and often unhappy at our last university, did not seem to be improving, which irritated me. I wanted him to hurry up and get happy, so we could get on with our life. He wanted me to get happy first. Chuck and I had been friends from the night we met as psychology majors living on the first coed dorm floor at our college. We started a conversation, as I remember, about Gestalt Therapy, Zen, and J.D. Salinger's *Franny and Zooey*. The conversation kept on going, expanding over thousands of topics of mutual interest, with short breaks for sleep, for twenty years. With our shoulder-length blonde hair, freckled noses, blue eyes, and matching grade point averages, we were called Hansel and Gretel by our professors. However, there was a negative side to being twins. Both of us having avoided traditional sex roles, we found that neither of us could cook or nurture or fix things or take over in a tough situation. So, like children lost in the wood, we alternately stormed at each other or clung to each other through the crises of dual career job hunts, sleepless babies, and editors' deadlines. Now we had been snatched up as a package deal by Arizona State University. We had arrived out of the woods and into the bright desert sunlight—only to find ourselves unable to work and unable to help each other.

My research had always been a breeze for me before the move. The scientific method was a tool I brandished with gusto to answer the questions in which I was passionately interested: What can be done to nurture creativity? How can creative young women be helped to hold on to their goals? How do young people develop a sense of purpose? I formulated hypotheses, analyzed my data, and waited for the printout from the computer center that would deliver that tiny, delicious frisson of perfect truth: the probability that I was right. The experiments, grants, and pro-jects had flowed from me in a stream of production that filled twelve pages of my resume. Now that seemed to have stopped. My research, which was about creativity and purpose, lacked either of those qualities. I could not write. I fell asleep over my notepad, so I tried dictation, wandering around the room with my little recorder. The results were jumbled and disconnected. Even my secretary shook her head in disappointment.

And then there was my poor dead body. The energy that had once surged through me was gone. I'd never thought of myself as pretty, or even cute. But through sheer force of person-ality and bright clothes, I'd been able to be seen as healthy and colorful. That was gone, too. My hair hung lank and darkening, my skin was strangely pale, and I didn't recognize my shape. The strong muscles developed from years of riding had disappeared during the long wait for my horse to be hauled from Iowa to Arizona. I rushed my sullen body through each day with effort, straining toward that moment when I could crawl into bed and have four hours of sleep before our baby woke.

So I had problems, we had problems, and we didn't even know what they were. We thought perhaps the stress of relocat-ing had robbed us of our capacity for happiness. We looked hope-fully toward summer, when we could return to the familiar sur-roundings of summer camp, our favorite place, in Western Michigan.

For fifteen years, we had volunteered as counselors at a camp on the shores of Lake Michigan, doing youth leadership training. It was a working vacation for the whole family. Our twelve-year-old son, Sam, worked in the camp store and even lit-tle three-year-old Gracie participated in beach cleanup. Chuck and I were occupied with activities from sunrise exercises to mid-night cabin-check. However demanding the tasks were, it was a time of renewal. Our sandy, shady cottage was a thread of conti-nuity across many changes of address. We were nicely isolated there, with no television, no phone, and nothing but the weekly *Oceana County Herald* to bring us news.

Once we arrived, we gave up wearing watches, and we lived by the ringing bells. The bells rang out the times for rising, exercise, quiet time, breakfast, leadership class, elective, lunch, competitions, free time, dinner, vespers, night's doings, lights out. Eighty years of this particular schedule gave it an authority to which we yielded complacently. It felt good to be part of this old rhythm, created for the adolescents of a bygone era.

Like Brigadoon, the place only came alive for a few weeks out of the year. So the Monopoly game our kids left out in August remained there till the next year, the Scotty dog behind bars without pardon and Boardwalk forever untenanted. The books in the camp library, the materials in the craft house, the costumes in the skit room remained the same year after year. Only the dunes changed, sneakily shifting shape from mound to ridge to bowl, while Lake Michigan whispered in the background.

Somehow, all of this contributed to a pleasant feeling of being outside of time. However, it took longer to enter the timelessness of the venerable old camp, because we were arriving more careworn and distracted than the year before. Each year, Chuck and I expected more from the camp experience, needing it to be the place where we felt at peace with ourselves and each other.

Chuck taught Outdoor Adventure and I taught Spirituality. Both were courses of study about which we were refreshingly ignorant. I liked to teach Spirituality, because the students who took the course were the most advanced group at the conference, the staff in training. They were college students from all over the United States and the world, who had been selected as leaders in their schools and communities. My class probably contained the twelve most eager and helpful nineteen-year-olds on the planet.

I also liked to teach the Spirituality course because I was on an intellectual vacation. I allowed myself to consider ideas to which I gave no thought during the rest of the year. My father, a nuclear engineer, had brought me up with science as my religion and I was a contented atheist. I believed I needed no deities to guide me, because I had excellent, loving parenting. The post-Sputnik schools for brainy kids I attended provided all the science I needed to compose a natural explanation for any event imaginable. Unlike people who were new to atheism, I had no need to bash religion, organized or otherwise. However, it had no place in my life, except at camp, where I was an observer and a facilitator of other people's spiritual lives. A theological voyeur, you might say. I liked to question students and other faculty about their spirituality, and I liked to try out techniques that various religions used to attain whatever they considered to be transcendent states. At the camp, there was an opportunity to stand on the pews and clap during the gospel services led by the St. Louis kids; to light the candles for a Shabbat service; and to sit still and observe the suspenseful serenity of a Zen tea ceremony. I found all of this quite pleasurable, and the feelings of community and exaltation seemed like nice rewards for participating in something I didn't understand. Like William James, the first psychologist to study other peoples' religious experiences, I believed, without regret, that religion was a "door forever closed to me."

A new twist to the Spirituality curriculum that year was a Native American sweat lodge ceremony. Mark, the director of the camp, had greeted me with the news upon my arrival: "We have Ten Bears, who can do a sweat lodge!" This he said with the kind of wide-eyed enthusiasm he usually reserved for resurfacing of the tennis court. I was instantly suspicious. I didn't like guest speakers foisted upon me. And my co-teacher Charlie and I already had a plan for the course. Mark's excitement prevailed, however, and I agreed to consider the addition of a sweat lodge experience.

Charlie was my friend as well as a co-teacher of Spirituality. Charlie had been an attorney who had transformed himself into a Franciscan friar and high school teacher. He was a perfect Franciscan, with velvety brown eyes, a melting heart, and a wicked sense of humor. Charlie and I discussed the sweat lodge and were in agreement: the kids could do it, but we certainly weren't going to do it. Charlie remarked that there were only three things he feared: heat, dark, and sweaty people, and this experience, unfortunately, had all three.

Seeing Ten Bears didn't allay my doubts. I caught a glimpse of him on the Craft House steps, surrounded by a small crowd of students that included the entire population of New Age and Outward Bound types. His indefinable ethnicity, cowboy hat and boots, and denim jacket embroidered with beads were somewhat exotic even in these surroundings. Summer programs like ours, which require people who will trade a quiet summer vacation for a musty cabin and the constant company of adolescents attract three types of people: teachers, camp alumni, and out-of-work impostors. Our camp community was easy work for a confi-

dence man (or woman) because of our code of cheerful acceptance and eagerness for new ideas. Motivational speakers, religious fanatics, and therapists at various levels of recovery occasionally oozed past our intellectual checkpoints and won room,
board, and an elective course. I was concerned that, although
Ten Bears was a friend of the director, he might be just another
one of these annoying distractions. Nevertheless, the date was
set. Charlie and I agreed to meet our students at the sweat lodge
site and to be available to them if they wanted to discuss the
experience.

I arrived late to the clearing in the woods where the sweat
lodge ceremony was to take place, bumping and crashing along
the terrible dirt road in my Ford Explorer. The students had been
there since morning, preparing for the ceremony. I had been
attending to some daily administrative tasks and arranging a
baby-sitter for our children. Chuck was sitting on a platform in
the treetops urging terrified second-year students over the "high
ropes challenge" course.

It was a cool afternoon with champagne-colored sunlight
and breezes alternately carrying scents of the lake below us and
the pines on the dunes above us. The sweat lodge site was a
wooded shelf surrounded on three sides by two-hundred-foot-
high forested dunes. On the west side, a band of pines, oaks, and
willows gave way to dune grass-covered hillocks, a wide white
beach, and the long, green vista of Lake Michigan. The sweat
lodge itself was a dome, about five feet high and twelve feet in
diameter. Covered with green and brown weathered canvas, it
looked as if it had grown from the earth. A small mound of dirt in
front of the thirty-inch arched doorway was covered with twigs,
ribbons, and what looked to me like the students' rings and
bracelets. Four birch poles surrounded the lodge, each with a differently colored streamer fluttering about it like a single stranded
Maypole. What looked like a bonfire burned near the lodge. In the
center, rocks the size of ostrich eggs hissed and crackled among
the orange flames.

Our students were standing in a circle around Ten Bears.
Despite their proximity to the fire, they seemed to shiver a little,
wrapped only in their beach towels. They were receiving some
kind of pre-sweat lodge instruction. I joined the group, fully
clothed, to hear what he was saying. He had changed from his

cowboy outfit to an Indian one, just a leather loincloth, beads of some kind, and a colorful blanket around his shoulders. Oh, boy, I thought, what *is* he?

He separated the women from the men, saying, "Come over here with me" to the women. Then he spoke. "Some of you are on your moon-time. Your moon-time is sacred. Because women already have this way of purifying themselves, they are very powerful in the sweat lodge during this time. If you haven't experienced this before, you may want support; just sit next to me." One young woman blushed and came to stand next to him. Sheesh, I thought, this isn't going to go over very well with some of our modest young Christians.

Gathering the young people together again, he pointed to the poles with their streamers. "These are the four great nations of people," he said. "Red, Yellow, Black, White." He paused and walked around to each. "These are also the four seasons of year, spring, summer, fall, winter." He paused again. "And the four seasons of life. And the four great directions: east, south, west, north. As you walk around the circle, and you stop at each place, and maybe say a prayer." He spoke in a conversational tone as he walked from pole to pole as he instructed us. Then he approached the opening to the sweat lodge. "Here is where we pass from this world into the spirit world. So, when you enter the sweat lodge, recognize that you are related to all things." He then said something I didn't catch. "Or you can say, in English, 'All my relations'." He then pointed to two young men. One was an African American named Ice with quiet eyes which could be loving or scary depending on his mood and the other was a young soldier I didn't know who had been in Kuwait. "These will be the Fire Keepers," said Ten Bears. "They will help you in and out of the lodge, keep the stones and water coming in, and they will take care of you when you leave the lodge."

Charlie and I went to sit on a log. "Are you going to do this?" he asked.

"I thought we weren't going to," I said. " I thought we were just going to help them process the experience afterward."

"But it might be good to go through it with them."

"Does the Church let you do this sort of thing?" I asked.

Charlie shook his monkish head and rolled his eyes. "This isn't the Middle Ages, Barb. Don't you think it would be interesting? I think I want to do it, but I think I'm going to hate it so much that I'd like you with me."

So I let Charlie talk me into it. I borrowed a beach towel and reluctantly disrobed behind my truck, which was sitting incongruously at the edge of the clearing. I joined Charlie at the end of the line of students entering the circle. As I watched my students, from places like Singapore, St. Louis, Ghana, and Grand Forks, I realized they, too, represented the many nations of people, and I was suddenly glad they would have a unique experience together that they would remember in their letters to one another.

We entered the lodge one by one, crouching and crawling in a clockwise direction, helped from hand to hand by those already seated. I craftily edged to the end of the line, and pulled Charlie along with me, so that we could be right next to the door. Last to arrive, first to leave had always been my motto, for all of the classes, meetings, and encounter groups I'd endured. It was desperately crowded, with our backs bent under the low struts of the lodge and our knees vying for space. There was little comfort to be had by sitting by the door.

A huge glowing rock, apparently named Grandfather, and twelve smaller sizzling rocks had been shoveled through the door-way and into the fire pit. Then the door-flap was shut. I lifted the canvas to create a tiny notch in the bottom for a little air. Ten Bears quietly said, "Cover that light." Annoyed that I'd been caught, I hastily let go. I knew then I had made a big mistake; this sweat lodge experience was going to be much worse than I had supposed. I was trapped in a tiny wood and canvas hut, on several inches of uncomfortable, itchy, extremely flammable straw. I concluded that, in all probability, my life, and the lives of my students were in the hands of a fanatic with no psychological training—or even CPR.

It was darker than the bowels of a cave in there, and the heat was quite simply unimaginable. The hot air burned my lips, mouth, and lungs. Perspiration leapt from my pores, in odd places like my wrists, my knees, my chin. How can he let it get this hot? I thought. Isn't this really dangerous? My hair lifted off my scalp in fear and then fell back in a wet mass. As my body temperature soared, my heart began to beat furiously. My God, I'm going to have a heart attack right here, I thought. I'm going to die, here in this place, now. I scrambled for air by laying my face down along where the canvas met the dirt floor. Ten Bears was telling some story about Iktome and the forty-nine warriors named Fear, Doubt, Jealousy, and so forth, but I wasn't listening very well. If this story was supposed to comfort me, it didn't. He was telling Indian stories and I was suffocating to death. How was I going to get my students and myself out of this situation?

Time was contracting and expanding as I tried the various strategies I knew to control panic. Ten Bears was saying something about this being the session of spring, of youth, and a time for prayers for children. To my amazement, some of the young people were speaking. One said a prayer for her niece, another for his little brother. How could they talk about kids at a time like this? This touched off a torrent of images of my own children, my sturdy Sam, my fairy-like Grace, and suddenly I was terrified. Where were they? Were they safe? What if I died here? As I was about to cry out that I must go, I must leave NOW, Ten Bears beat a drum and the first session ended.

"Raise the flap," he said.

"My children!" I gasped as I pushed my way out. Ten White called to a boy outside, "Go. Get on your bike, and go check on Barbara's children." The boy left immediately.

Several others were out now, and we were all being rubbed with towels and helped over to logs by the fire. Charlie was there. Hadn't he been next to me inside? I'd forgotten about him. He and I stared wordlessly at each other, like the driver and passenger who have just avoided a head-on collision at seventy miles per hour. I don't know how long I sat there, but suddenly the boy who had been sent down the road to check on my children was back, and standing in front of me.

"Sam and Grace are fine. They're playing by the flagpole." I realized this meant I might have to go back in for the second round. Ten Bears spoke from inside the lodge. "OK. Come back in now." Inexplicably, I crawled back in.

After that, I lost track of what happened. I know Ten Bears told more stories; but it was hard to listen to him because my heart was so loud and his voice was distorted by the heat and closeness. His voice seemed to become a voice in my own mind. We were in a womb, the womb of our Mother the Earth, and it was all right to entrust ourselves to our mother, he said. I was aware of young people opening up and self-disclosing, in that desperate way that teenagers have. One boy talked about his father's impossible expectations. Ten Bears listened without interrupting, seeming to let the young man's anger run out. Then he said, "Your father has high expectations of you because of your high potential. When you are aware of your potential, you won't be so disturbed by his expectations. You'll come to a time in your life when you realize his expectations were too low." The young man was now quiet. I heard the movement of someone next to him reaching for his hand.

"Someone here has a broken heart," said Ten Bears. Good bet, I thought, in a tent full of teenagers.

Then a young woman, in a soft 4-H accent said, "I guess that's me . . ." and went on to tell a familiar and heartrending tale of love, trust, and deceit.

I was struck, even in my state of confusion, by the way Ten Bears gracefully allowed each person a time to speak, and then helped him or her to be quiet before they lost their dignity. He would gently interject a sort of parable just as they approached tears, and then there would be quiet until another spoke. Charlie spoke about a friend dying of AIDS.

"We are taught that nothing lasts forever, except the Earth and the Sky," said Ten Bears. "Those we love are given to us for just a little while. Make sure you show them you love them every chance you get. Tomorrow may be too late."

Charlie whispered a prayer, and then, as if exhausted by the ordeal, he lay his head on my shoulder. I had just enough presence of mind to lightly touch his hair in reassurance. Amazing, I thought. Some kind of healing is happening in here.

When we got to the third round, the time of maturity, of the fall (When had they brought in that batch of rocks?), I said something about being forty and being tired. I said I thought it was time to get ready to be old. Ten Bears chuckled. Other things happened; I can't remember what. Time seemed to have collapsed. I was becoming, if not more relaxed, then at least more still, like a rabbit before it is clubbed. The next thing I knew we were all singing a song, very loudly. Ten Bears said something about animal spirits, about listening closely to see if we could hear our spirit animal guides. When we knew what animal spirits were trying to speak to us, we were to make that sound. Yeah, right, I thought. I could see that I was getting enough of myself back to be able to feel annoyance. The more suggestible people were already hooting, growling, and snorting all around me. Even more irritating than my lack of understanding of the point of this exercise was the fact that someone was cooing loudly in my ear, like a thunderous dove of some sort. "COO COO HOO!" hooted the voice. "COO COO HOO. COO COO HOO!" It went on and on. I turned to express my annoyance to the person to my right, but there was no one there; that was just the doorway. There was no one but me. I touched my lips with straw-covered fingers. I was the one making that sound. Puzzled and embarrassed, I covered my mouth, in the dark.

There was more singing and drumming. For the last round, twelve of the hottest rocks of all were brought in. How could it be this hot and all of us still be alive? The poles of the sweat lodge were now too hot to lean against. It didn't matter. We would be here forever. Drumming and singing, we all seemed to know a sonorous song about the sun (I felt its scorching rays from some other universe). Suddenly, it was over.

The door opened and we fell out, a multiple birth of hot, wet, stunned humans. Some yelled and ran down the dune, headed for Lake Michigan's cool waves. Others sat like Charlie and me on the logs, staring into space. I had no thoughts. A box of plums arrived from somewhere and we ate ravenously.

After a long while, I walked down to the beach and waded by myself into the lake. Then I toweled off, got dressed, got in the truck and went back to the cabin. "Hi Mom," said my twelve-year-old. "I heard you freaked out."

* * *

I would like to be able to say that first sweat lodge experience changed my life. It didn't. We went back to Arizona for our first full year of teaching (we had arrived the previous January). Things got a little better. Our moods lifted at the start of a new academic year, as is frequently the case with university folk. The children adjusted to their new schools. Chuck and I began to explore our new desert home. I volunteered as a counselor at beautiful Taliesin West, Frank Lloyd Wright's school of architecture in the foothills, and began to get to know some interesting people.

Oh, how I missed my women friends back in the Midwest; so smart and softly loving, they had seen me through pregnancy, childbirth, and professional crises. I also grieved for my other horse that I had left behind, my old Joe, who used to carry me in his slow, lazy, rocking-chair canter over the green hills. At work, I missed people who trusted me. Most of the time I coped; but sometimes, after a faculty meeting, the dry, dusty palm fronds outside my office window clattered together in a way that made me cry.

The sweat lodge experience made for good dinner party conversation with people I didn't know very well yet, and good letter material for my friends back in the Midwest. I could tell the story about it in a really funny way. However, as the year went by, I found myself thinking more and more about the experience and what it meant. I called Charlie and the young friends who had been with me in the sweat lodge to talk about it. Each person had had an intense experience of altered reality, and each had difficulty articulating what had happened. "There was so much love in there," said Charlie. "Did you feel it?" Is that what it was?, I wondered. Then why was I so scared?

I began to talk about the sweat lodge in my class for beginning counselors called "Introduction to the Helping Relationship." We discussed shamanic methods of psychological healing and the parallels with modern psychotherapy. In the middle of my lecture, I surprised myself by going back there, in my imagination, to the darkness and heat of the lodge. I tried to tell my students about what happened to me in there. The realization dawned that perhaps I didn't know. Was it an induced trance state? Was it suggestion during heightened arousal? Was it behavioral conditioning of some kind? Could it have some kind of healing capability? As I entertained these ideas aloud, my students sat staring at me in pleased befuddlement: "What has gotten into Dr. Kerr?"

Later, I tried to bring Ten Bears into focus in my mind. I could not remember how he looked. What I did remember was his exquisite timing; his delicate use of metaphor to round out the contribution of each person; and his modest self-discipline. At some point, I came to understand that I had witnessed a person using an ancient psychological technology that was more sophisticated than all of the psychotherapeutic skills taught to me in graduate school.

I wanted to know more. However, the books I read on Native American traditions were deeply unsatisfying. Most books on Native Americans presented them as vanquished and lost or vanquished and extremely angry. Native American art and culture were presented as charming or fascinating. What I had seen in the sweat lodge was not the science of a conquered or embittered spirit, nor was it merely "interesting." It was terrifying and power-ful. The New Age authors I also rapidly discarded; too often, in these books, a reference to Native American traditions was just an introduction for the author's own theory about UFO's, numerolo-gy, or astrology. The borrowing of traditions in these books seemed sloppy and self-serving. What I had seen was a rigorous discipline performed by a person with perfect self-control. To real-ly understand the sweat lodge, I thought, it would be necessary to do it again. When summer came, I made sure that I would be teaching the Spirituality course at camp, so that I could return to the little clearing in the woods with a new group of students.

This time I decided to do it right, with some preparation and some respect for the experience. So I left our cabin at three a.m. to walk several miles down the beach to the sweat lodge site. The glassy sand squeaked under my feet. Wisps of mist drifted low over the lake, but above the stars were shining brilliantly. Deep in August, I could see Orion, the winter constellation, appearing before dawn. I thought about how winter is really always there, waiting, and once again began to obsess about aging. How had this happened to me? How had an energetic and happy child become a tired forty-one year old? My grandmother had died of a stroke at fifty-two! I might be way past mid-life, I thought; I might already be in the winter of my life.

An unfocused hunger held me in its grip; hunger like after a long case of the flu, when you know you should eat, but you don't know what you want. If you could just find the right thing to eat, your appetite would kick back in. Then, you could get back to normal. This spiritual experimentation might be some kind of way of kicking up an appetite, I thought. Some feeling. But I didn't hold out much hope. If I just learned something new that would help me to be a better teacher and therapist, that would be enough, I thought.

I walked until I saw the tongue of sand that marked the path up through the wooded dunes to the clearing where the sweat lodge stood. As I came over the rise, I saw flames through the trees, and a few figures sitting by the fire, waiting for the rocks to heat up.

Ten Bears, a young man named Gerald who assisted him, Charlie, and my friend Sue, now a self-avowed sweat lodge groupie, sat and talked together. The young people were sprawled around in sleeping bags, most of them awake and listening to the conversation. Ten Bears was drinking a Diet Pepsi; his face was in shadow as he talked. Still in a cowboy hat and boots. Still unknowable.

When I arrived, my students greeted me cheerfully, and I sat on the log next to them. "We were talking about you," one said. "My mother saw you on TV being interviewed about your book." At first I thought I didn't want to discuss my book in this place, before dawn, in the woods. I had worked up a mind set that took me away from work, and didn't want to lose it. On the other hand, there was the irresistible pleasure of bragging. I wanted Ten Bears to know about my work so he would know that hey, I do things too, so don't mess with me. I was scared and I wanted him to know how smart I was.

"So you wrote a book," Ten Bears said.

"Yes," I said, as modestly as I could, "but it's not my best work." Now I remembered, with embarrassment, how I had written it in a happy, careless rush. I remembered the let-down after it was finished, particularly when people praised it. "I mean, it's OK, it's about talented girls, I liked writing it, but I didn't like promoting it."

"Oh. You like the hunt, but you don't much savor the kill."

What was that? I gave him a confused look, but I knew exactly what he was saying. Somehow he had seen the dissatisfaction that infused every cell of my body, but was hidden behind the face of precocious success. The conversation moved on. I sat on the log and tried to get a grip on my anxiety level, which had just been cranked up a notch.

Later, Ten Bears walked behind me and laid a hand on my shoulder. "How are you feeling?" he asked.

"Scared," I said with uncharacteristic honesty.

"Come in right after me. Sit next to me. When you're afraid, just touch me, you'll be fine." As I sat there formulating responses, I realized I would probably like to try that.

The students got quieter as dawn approached the clearing, like a company of young soldiers before a battle. Word had
spread to them from the veterans of the previous year of what
was about to happen to them. They wandered off, getting their
rosaries and high school rings for the little heap of precious arti-
cles we were to put on the small mound in front of the sweat
lodge. The mound formed the head of the turtle, whose body was
the dome of the lodge. Objects were laid upon the turtle's head to
be blessed. I looked at my hand. My wedding ring had been
embedded in my finger for years, and I didn't have anything else
to put there.

I wandered around the clearing nervously, now in my
beach towel and barefoot. I noticed that Ten Bears had gone into
the sweat lodge; he seemed to be talking to himself in there. I
moved closer, quietly. He was talking. He was praying in there, in
an even, conversational tone I had never heard anyone use in his
or her devotions. He finished and ducked back outside while I
hurried away.

The students had modestly removed their slept-in clothes
behind trees and were also, like me, wrapped in beach towels.
Then they organized themselves into a group to listen to Ten
Bears. This is where I had come in last year. He began the same
speech I had heard him give the year before. He told them that
the sweat lodge experience was not meant to challenge their religious beliefs or practices, but to strengthen them. He reminded
them that Native American people had many different ways of
doing the sweat lodge, and that his way was not the "right" way,
it was simply the sacred way he had been taught. It was a place
of respect and for being humble. It was as good a place as any for
Christians to say their prayers, he said, and for people of any
religion to think about their beliefs.

He then drew a medicine wheel with a stick in the dust by
the firelight. He pointed to each of the directions, and named
their qualities. This explanation was extraordinarily complex; the
wheel apparently had many levels of meaning, from the prosaic
measure of the months of the year to a hierarchy of states of consciousness. The wheel he was drawing was also a map of the
interior of the sweat lodge. It was mesmerizing. I couldn't follow it
very well with my analytical mind, but I felt as if my intuition was
smoothly gliding along with his words, yes, yes, that's right. "If

you need clarity, wisdom, illumination, sit here," he said, touching the stick down firmly at the eastern edge of the circle. "If you are thinking about growth, learning to trust, and the capacity to love, that is here on the Medicine Wheel." He hopped the stick to the southern edge, near the toes of the cluster of young people. The stick moved toward me, where I was standing alone, in the west. "Here is a place of experience. With introspection you may find strength." I stared at the pointer, and at my feet. Ten Bears moved on. The pointer moved to the north side of the circle, swinging toward the sweat lodge. "Here you will find cleansing, renewal, purity." He named the totems of each of the directions: eagle, coyote, bear, and buffalo, and talked about their gifts, like bear wisdom. Bear wisdom, I repeated softly. OK, that's what I need, and that's where I'm going to sit in the sweat lodge.

The sky was getting lighter behind the treetops. Ten Bears entered the sweat lodge. It was time for me to go in.

This time I had practiced the words. Mitakuwa Oyasin: all my relations. It meant that we are all related. I wanted to mean it.

Here inside sat my friend Sue, with many spirit-bead necklaces and an eagerness that almost made her wriggle with anticipation; a big Nebraska future farmer; a slight, emotional Parisian girl; a sweet-tempered, knife-scarred hip-hop dancer from St. Louis; then Charlie, who looked more at ease this year; a woman engineering student from Purdue; and a few others whose faces are no longer clear to me. Like last year's group, they nervously laughed and whispered to each other. I was too anxious to laugh, and too focused.

The ceremony began. The Grandfather rock was brought in. I knew its name now: Tunkashila. Its glow was magnificent, lighting the faces of the little group briefly as it fell into its place of honor in the fire pit. We smoked the medicine pipe, each person blowing the smoke toward the roof. Ten Bears told us a story of creation, of a Grandfather living in the Star Path who created Turtle Island, this place we live, and a Grandmother who lovingly laid her body down over the back of the turtle to nurture us as the Earth. Gerald shoveled in the first batch of twelve rocks, one by one. The scrape of his shovel outside brought a vivid auditory memory of my Dad shoveling coal into our furnace when I was little. I was able to feel the first surge of heat as a fiercely nurturing force. I began to feel the dissociation that came with the artificially induced delirium. I told myself to avoid trying to control all my reactions, but just to have them. Now came the story of the enemy warriors of fear, doubt, anxiety, and the brave warrior who planted himself before them, digging his spear into the ground and pinning his headdress there. This is what I have to do, I said to myself. Plant myself here. Dig in. The heat rose. Ten Bears poured a gourdful of water onto the rocks, and a stifling, pungent steam exploded. As I choked and teared up, panic found me. So afraid, I thought, so afraid, and I had wanted to see what was beyond the fear; now I wouldn't be able to. The fear felt like shards of glass tearing my chest, my stomach, my brain tissue. Very bad indeed.

Then I remembered what he had said. I should touch him—but how? Where? For an agonizing moment, I sat there with my left index finger poised over what I assumed in the dark was his knee. I made contact, a light finger-touch with a lot of hope, like a little moon landing, on his resting arm instead. And in that moment of contact, the fear simply lifted out of me, and softly evaporated. Not just the specific fear of heat and darkness, but a hundred other fears went out of me at once.

A delicious languor like that which follows the end of a long bout of pain filled me. I can remember sitting Buddha-like, feeling the sweat pouring like warm rain between my breasts, down my arms, off the tips of my fingers. The mixture of vapor and sage was not only breathable; it was invigorating, life-giving. And the young people around me—I imagined that I could see their faces—how fresh and beautiful they were in their youth! Charlie and Susan—what wonderful friends, how loving, how funny, how precious was their company! In this affectionate and wondering delirium, I passed the next rounds. I didn't and couldn't leave between rounds. I was fixed in place, marveling at the sensations I was experiencing. I don't remember the prayers that were made, the questions asked, or the stories told. I do remember the responses by Ten Bears. In the first round, he said, "You are the Mystery, and the Mystery is you." In the second round he said, "All things are sacred." Later I heard, "Respect and maintain the differences." These statements held little meaning for me at the time, or I had a confused understanding of them. There were stories, but I seemed to be absorbing them through my skin rather than hearing them with my ears.

At last something focused my attention. "Look up," he was saying. "See the stars." We did, and there they were. A sigh of amazement filled the close air as we gazed at the glimmering stars in the endless dome of the sky above our heads. My goodness, I thought, this is really very beautiful—those stars! "Feel your mother earth below you now." And then, pulsing and undulating like a living thing, the straw covered earth below us seemed to rise up. Some of us patted the ground gently; some of us gasped as if finding ourselves astride a great creature. "The lesson of this round is that nothing lasts forever, except the earth and the sky. So make each day a good day to die." Suddenly I was alert. Nothing lasts forever! I remember that! That means this will be over soon! It will be over, and I will have to go back! I'll go back to being tired, and getting older, and not being able to be satisfied with anything, just wanting and wanting, and being the kind of person who could never be beloved or precious to anybody, who thinks and thinks and tries to be good but can't feel, can't feel—there I was stewing away when Ten Bear's powerful arm reached over and took my head in a lock right over his chest. And gripped there, in that odd hold, I heard his heart thumping and, strangely, squeaking at the end of each beat. I was a bit uncomfortable, but at least somewhat distracted from my stridently self-pitying inner outpouring. What was he doing? I was a little wary. Still holding me close to his chest with one hand, he lightly traced a line down my side to the point of my hip with the other. Decorous, so far, I thought. And then, with what seemed like a great deal of force, he pressed his thumb HARD into the point of my right hip.

Now the imaginary stars above were not the only things shimmering in the darkness. In wordless astonishment, I felt and saw a golden light pouring in me, around me. He released his grip and eased me up gently. I stretched my limbs as far as they could reach, reveling in the sheer sensuousness of the moment. I saw the curves of my hips and breasts suffused with a delicious glow. I seemed to have been given a new body, beautiful in this light. And there was more. Something had come into me, some brimming and sweet life for which I had no name. Not just the absence of fear and annoyance, but the presence of promise and new life.

The drum beat, the rattle shook, sh, sh, sh and with a final boom, Ten Bears said, "Open it up!"

I lay smiling in the sweat lodge as long as I could without people getting worried about me. Then I entered the world again. A warm, fluffy towel awaited me. The box of plums again—ripe, cold, dew-covered, sweet! And everywhere the sounds of young peoples' delighted laughter as they snatched up granola bars, ate them rapidly and then ran down the dune to smash themselves into the waves of Lake Michigan. I giggled and shared anecdotes with them—"Could you BELIEVE the stars?!" but didn't venture to describe to anyone the full extent of what had happened to me.

This time change happened rapidly. The next few days, the last of the season at camp, seemed charged with a kind of holiness. Every moment seemed important, every interaction portentous and fulfilling. Nature played along, with sunsets almost melodramatic in their beauty (was there a volcano erupting somewhere, we all asked?). A magical fog rolled in as Charlie and I sat guard on the beach border at midnight. Once again we looked at each other in smiling consternation: "It looks different now, after the sweat lodge, doesn't it?" he whispered. As I went to sleep that night, a rosy moon lit a path across the lake clear to Wisconsin.

My husband had left for a funeral of an elderly aunt, and I ached for his company; I wanted to tell him what had happened. For the first time, I had a hard time explaining something to him. The only words I could think of to describe the experience on the phone were—"It was like my hard drive was erased." I even wept a little as I told him about it, because I felt a gulf opening up between us as I struggled to make sense to the person who had always understood, precisely, the meaning of my words. "I think you need to talk to Ten Bears," he said.

I realized that I missed Ten Bears. He had left, sometime during the day after the sweat lodge. I hadn't gotten to thank him, or to say good-bye. The urge to reconnect with him, to receive the words in the plain light of day that would explain what had happened, was getting stronger each day. I had somehow been exposed to what, a form of consciousness? A new worldview? It was as if I had been accidentally infected with a new set of schema, like a computer virus that sets to work slowly, changing an entire operating system. I had a feeling that somehow this accident was related to my dissatisfaction—that perhaps

I had somehow brought it on myself. But, no, I protested inwardly, it was Ten Bears who did this to me!

I wanted to know this person who had such a profound effect on me—I wanted to know him well.

I tried hard, as I had before, to fix an image of him in my mind, but couldn't retrieve more than a few details I didn't quite trust. His eyes had seemed dark by firelight but in the sweat lodge had taken on the greenish glow of an animal in its den. A large chest, powerful arms. There was, indeed, something bear-like about him, something in his looks that was powerful, composed, innocent. I seemed fastened to the idea of him. I asked questions about him to the director, the director's secretary, and to anyone who had spoken to him. I intended to do a thorough investigation.

He was indeed a white man, according to Mark, although one who had been trained in medicine ways throughout his childhood by an elderly Choctaw who had virtually adopted him as a spiritual son. This influence showed not only in his words, but in his nonverbal behavior. He had the sort of hesitancy and quietness I had seen in my Native American students, who would enter my office and stand there silently, hands at their sides, waiting for me to speak first. I was told that he had been practicing spirituality from the Plains Indian tradition for twenty-five years. I had heard of people like this, white people who had completely taken Native American spirituality as their own. I knew that Indians in academic circles were very skeptical about white people who "painted the white face red." However, both whites and Native Americans at our camp and in the surrounding area held Ten Bears in respect, so I knew he must be some kind of special case. People who had been through his sweat lodge ceremony sometimes referred to him as a medicine man, but I was told by Mark not to call him that, as he would refuse that title. "But what does he do?" I asked Mark. He named a company I'd heard of, and told me something that led me to believe that he was employed well, and was successful in his work. He was married, with a teenage daughter. He had been to camp as a boy. "Yeah, I remember him," said another former camper. "A great swimmer. Quiet." It was all confusing and incongruous. I simply had to know more about him, and the things he had done.

Mark gave me his name and address. I carried it around for a few days, behind my driver's license in my wallet. It seemed appropriate. In the event of death, take my eyes, kidneys, liver, etc., and call this guy. He knows something about me. At last, the last night of camp, I wrote him.

For one year, I wrote letters to describe my experiences following the sweat lodge and to beg and badger Ten Bears for explanations. He did not always answer my questions, but he gave me something more, much more than answers. Perhaps I was able to give something in return.

Ten White Bears speaks:

A long time ago, I was in New Mexico. I was with my friend, Thunderwolf. He was with me to learn the ways of the earth and the sky. He was learning how to be in the earth, not on it. He was learning how to be in time, not on time. He was learning the ways of my traditions that were taught to me by my teacher, who was taught by his teacher, and so on long into the past. They are the ways of being, not doing. Thunderwolf was with his friend Jason. The night before, when we were having dinner, Thunderwolf had challenged me to catch him. He asked with sarcasm in his voice. "Ten Bears, do you think you could track me?"

I asked Thunderwolf, "And what makes you think that I can't?"

Jason's mother, Sage, said, "You boys be careful, you don't know what you are asking. You could find yourselves in big trouble."

Thunderwolf announced in a loud and boisterous voice, "What? From and old man like Ten Bears! I don't think so." Jason nodded his head in agreement while they continued to laugh.

I said, "Tomorrow we will be at Tent Rocks. We will see then."

The next day, Sage, her son Jason, Thunderwolf and I went to Tent Rocks up on the Cochiti. It was a hot day. After we had wandered around looking at the place for a while, I said to Thunderwolf and Jason. "You go. I will give you time to run. Then I will find you." Jason's mother just shook her head and found shade under a pinyon tree. Thunderwolf and Jason went off shouting insults about old men.

Sage and I sat quietly for a while; then she spoke and asked me not to be too hard on them. I told her that I would teach them an important lesson about grace and agility. Then I left to catch them. It wasn't long. I had given them enough time to lose their attention. They were walking in a dry arroyo. I got close to them. No more than maybe ten feet. They could not see me. After I followed close to them for a while, I worked my way around to get ahead of them. Then I found a place under a tree to sit in the shade and wait. I crouched low. I was coyote. I was invisible. They couldn't see me.

It wasn't long before Thunderwolf and Jason came into sight. They were talking and kicking rocks. They laughed and spoke of losing me. I picked up a twig. They walked right past me. I stepped out from under the tree and followed them for a few steps. Then I snapped the twig. They both turned around and before they could think, I leapt and slapped Thunderwolf, hard, right in the middle of his chest. It took his breath away from him and he stumbled backwards, almost lost his feet. Jason held his hands and arms out in front of him in surrender. He didn't want the same treatment. The look of surprise on Thunderwolf's face was so funny that I thought I would bust my gut laughing. Without saying a word, I motioned to Jason to stay away from Thunderwolf or he would get the same treatment.

"Jesus!" Thunderwolf said, "What the hell did ya do that for?" He was attempting to rub away the sting in his chest.

"Coup," I said. Thunderwolf cussed at me and said, "Damn that hurts."

I told Thunderwolf that he needed to get his attention back.

Thunderwolf asked me where I had been. I told him, "Mostly right next to you, no more that ten paces, probably for the last twenty minutes." Well, Thunderwolf couldn't believe it. He kind of gasped and said, "No way." I just laughed at him and told him to follow the trail back and he would see. He was bent over at the hips and when he looked up, it was clear that realization had come into his consciousness. He was embarrassed at his situation and he began to laugh at himself between coughs. It was his way to recover a sense of humility.

Thunderwolf said, "Guess I won't make that mistake again." I told him he would because it was the way of his kind of people. "How did you do that?" he asked. I told him that I had shape shifted and become the coyote. Like the coyote, I had become invisible to him. Then I jumped out behind him and slapped him, good.

Thunderwolf was still bent over, so I asked him if it hurt. "Hell yes it hurts," he said. He had a stupid look on his face that made me laugh. He stood up and opened his shirt and there was this nice, very red handprint on his bare chest. He asked me, "How did you do that? How did you shape shift to a coyote? How did you do that? How did you become invisible?" I told him that I would teach him about shape shifting later. He needed to be put back together. So I walked up to him, put my hands near his chest and took the sting out of him. He was kind of amazed that it didn't sting anymore. Then he got thoughtful and asked me what I had taken out of him. I told him it was his arrogance. I told him that he had lost his attention. His mind had gotten in the way of his spirit and he was so self-assured that I wouldn't catch him he lost his attention. He started to smile again and we had a good laugh.

If you want to understand these ways you have to come apart. You have to understand being apart to realize wholeness. When I slapped Thunderwolf he came apart. It hurt. Then I helped him get it back together. It took him a while, but he finally got it.

Thunderwolf asked me to teach him to shape shift. I told him that a little way back was a cliff we could climb. There was a cave high on the second ledge. There is a mountain lion that visits there to sleep and stay cool. I told Thunderwolf we would climb up there and take a look. Jason went back to his mother.

So, Thunderwolf and I started to climb this cliff. The Tent Rocks are made of very fine dirt that will crumble away from you if you are not careful. I went up first and Thunderwolf followed me. Thunderwolf is a big man and he was having trouble. Just before getting the second ledge, there was this narrow chimney. It was tall and difficult to climb. You had to use all of your skills. When I got up through the chimney, sure enough, there were tracks of a mountain lion and you could see where she rested in the shallow cave. It was shady in there. Well, Thunderwolf was too big to get up the chimney. I stood there and watched him for a long time. He kept talking to himself and mumbling under his breath. Finally he said that he couldn't do it. He couldn't get up through that chimney.

I looked him straight in the eyes. I told Thunderwolf to become the mountain lion. Think like his sister the lion and climb with ease. I told him to think of becoming the mountain lion. Concentrate. Become the spirit of the mountain lion. He did and sure enough, he hopped up that cliff just like a mountain lion and nearly knocked me over. We stood there on the edge of the cliff and enjoyed the view. You could see for a long way.

Thunderwolf decided to climb down the cliff. He wanted to share his experience with Jason and Sage. I told him that I would stay up on the cliff for a while. I wanted to pray and talk with the Great Mystery. When Thunderwolf left, I just sat there staring out into that big beautiful New Mexico sky. I thought of all of the times Thunderwolf and I had been together. All of the things I had shared with him. I had given him all of my spirit and taught him all that I know. Then he would have all of the gifts of the Great Mystery that I could give him. I stood up, took off my shirt, raised my hands into the sky and prayed.

"Great Spirit, I stand before you humble. You have sent me your son to teach him what I know of the gifts of life, the gifts of your medicine. He has become my brother. He has been difficult. He has challenged me at every turn. He has questions that do not quit. He is hard to learn. His mind sometimes gets in his way. It has taken a lot of energy from my spirit to teach him. Guard him as he goes through life. Make him prosperous and a generous person. Give him the greatest strength of all. Let him be gentle. Our hoop is closed. I am old, Great Spirit, and I don't think I have the energy to do this again. I can take no more apprentices. These are the prayers of Ten Bears."

As I stared into the desert sky, a ray of light broke through the clouds and moved across the desert floor, up the cliff and shined on me. I heard the sound of a small rock gently falling from above and behind me. I turned to look up and locate the source of noise. Above me on the next ledge was the mountain lion, curiously standing with a swishing tail, watching me with intensity in her eyes. She fixed her eyes on me and we just stared at each other. I blinked. The mountain lion was gone. A voice came then, from the canyons around me, saying, "There will be one more, Ten Bears, one more."

Shelby, Michigan
August 14, 1992
Dear Ten Bears,

It is the last night of the conferences at Camp. One-thirty a.m., full moon, and a quiet lake. I am sorry to be leaving this friendly, holy place. Six weeks here is like being in what the aborigines call the Dreaming, an eternal, sacred present where the rhythms of daily life are themselves almost divine rituals. Tomorrow night at this time I will be in a taxicab with a bunch of tipsy psychologists in Washington, D.C., careening back to the convention hotel from the French restaurant. And all of this will be gone, vanished like the Dreaming when the rituals are broken.

I want to tell you the effect of my two experiences in the sweat lodge, because I must exorcise some disturbing thoughts, and (only secondarily) because it might prove interesting to you. I simply hate these sorts of letters from people who have boring enlightenments, but I hope you will read and be patient with me.

Here it is in a nutshell. I seem to have imprinted on you. Like a duck. You know, in those studies where they hatch the poor ducklings in front of a dog and they march around after the dog peeping piteously, thinking it is their mother. The image, no, the tactile impression of your hand on the point of my hip, of your forearm pressing my temple to your heart, is somehow stuck in my brain. And a vague image of your face in the darkness—how could I see?—puma eyes and innocent looking overbite. It's stuck in my head, and in my dreams, and in flashbacks when I am trying to read or put my little girl to bed. My feelings about this have ranged from the mundane, girlish ones to abject, sobbing fear of the power of images and thoughts that I did not intend to create or to nurture in myself. From what little you know of me, I am sure that you can tell that I try to be deliberate about the contents of my consciousness. So I know that I am responsible for these feelings, but I don't know why or how. I have two hypotheses I keep trying on—one rational one and one very irrational one.

The first is right out of my social psychology lecture notes. Two psychologists, named Berscheid and Walster, studied the process of interpersonal attraction, by trying to reproduce it in the laboratory. They learned that several elements are necessary to create attraction: proximity (the people must be in a situation which brings them into close contact); similarity (some similarity of style, values, or rare characteristics) and fear (there must be some moderate element of non-traumatic arousal, some situation that is scary and exciting). That pretty well sums up the effect oi me sitting locked to your chest, afraid of the dark and the heat. Throughout the time I was with you, I also sensed some important similarities. The similarity I see is between what I am and what I imagine you to have been before you gave yourself up to your religion: competitive, a little sociopathic, successful. Anyhow, the elements are there to explain my powerful attraction to you. So, once I had explained this to myself, I had hoped to be able to put this to rest.

My subjective, bizarre, intuitive explanation is quite different. I am bewitched. Possessed by a tricky spirit. *Being taught a lesson.* You said that I was hunter who loved the hunt but didn't enjoy the kill. Now I don't feel like a hunter. I feel like the prey: startled, despairing, caught in midflight.

I am not so vain or foolish to believe that any of your actions, or words, outside of a few pithy interpretations were aimed at me in any deliberate way. You seem to be completely free with yourself, spreading yourself around like sunshine, playing no favorites. I don't even presume that you remember what you said to me, or what you might have done to bring about these ideas in my head.

But I have a problem here. I have a life to get on with: a husband of twenty years, whom I love, every day; children to raise; students to teach; colleagues to contend with; my horse to train . . . and on and on. It's time for me to get back to Arizona and get real.

Yet my dreams are full of the sweat lodge, of the things I saw and felt there. I know that what happened there was the result of the artificial delirium brought on by the heat. Perhaps I'm having some kind of post-traumatic stress reaction. Sometimes in my dreams I am scrambling over black rocks, under the stars, in the night heat, away from everything familiar. I'm so afraid.

Is this really a lesson to me? Or a stupid accident of flesh and synapses?

Help me if you can. Don't be too mysterious if you can help it.

Writing is better because I would be too tongue-tied and embarrassed to say these things.

Sincerely, I think,

Barbara Kerr

I would never have written a letter like that if I hadn't been simply desperate to understand what had happened to me. I longed for the familiar worldview I seemed to have left behind at the door of the sweat lodge. So I began a process of trying to fit everything that had happened to me into my usual paradigm. To do this I used the method I had been taught as a scientist: break the phenomenon down into parts, observe the parts, analyze the parts, and then draw a conclusion. The letter showed Ten Bears that I knew how to explain everything in my own terms. The "imprinting" could be explained by the research on interpersonal attraction. The hallucinations in the sweat lodge were the result of delirium and post-hypnotic suggestion. Even the dreams and flashbacks afterwards were perhaps some kind of post-traumatic stress reaction. Demonstrating that I had these alternative explanations made me feel less foolish. However, these familiar terms were not very comforting, and an explanatory conclusion was not forthcoming. I was still anxious and distracted by my memories.

After a few weeks passed, I was still glad that I had written the letter. I just wished I hadn't sent it. I worried that I had invaded his privacy. I worried that it had been culturally insensitive to throw all the psychological jargon at him. Worst of all, when I re-read it a month later, it sounded—well—*seductive.* What had gotten into me? So I had to write again, to somehow undo any impression I might have left with him of improper intentions, and to show that I had come to my senses.

Scottsdale, Arizona
October 25, 1992

Dear Ten Bears,

Eight weeks have passed since I wrote that rather crazy letter. I'm so sorry! I have successfully re-entered real life, and have myself under control. Please forgive the adolescent crush and the fervid letter; I think I must be having my mid-life crisis.

I want to thank you for the sweat lodge experience. It has given me a different lens for seeing. I think I understand some connections that I didn't really see before—between me and nature, me and people, me and me. I hope that you will come back next year and share it again with our students, who I know will learn even more than I did.

I like to look at the prayer stick, which is in my window of my office. It reminds me that I wasn't always here. It reminds me I have so much to learn. I hope I will be able to continue to learn from you.

It's still summer here in Arizona, but night comes early. Silent, hot night. The desert seems in stasis. Not even a sense of thirst; just dead, still waiting. It is hard to believe that it will ever be cool again. I ride my horse at night, galloping up the mountains to the very top, where the ancient schist layers stand up vertically, like crumbling teeth. We drip with sweat. A coyote mother and her pups sometimes appear on a nearby outcropping. It's all new for me.

Please don't feel obligated to respond to my letters. I know you're not the letter writing type. I just wanted to let you know I'm OK now, and to say thanks.

Sincerely,

Barbara

There. That had restored my dignity a little. I had indeed recovered—not only from the momentary infatuation but also from the dreams of night places. I had not been entirely sincere about the "different lens". Although I had indeed seen another perspective on reality in the sweat lodge, I just didn't see its application to my everyday life. I felt ready to consign the sweat lodge to my mental closet of curiosities where I put other unclassifiable experiences. Then I could get on with my life.

Algonquin, Illinois
October 25, 1992

Dear Barbara,

Today is the day that the clocks turn back. By some magic, technology has added an extra hour to my life. I have decided to devote the entire 60 minutes to you and respond to your letter. I have, in a word, been very busy. My apologies for not writing sooner. Indeed, I have attempted to do this several times. Each time I have been interrupted and the flow of thought gets changed. Another difficulty is an attempt to translate oral thoughts and traditions into the written word.

Before the dawn I write. This is such a special time of life. I love to watch the sun rise, say prayers, and catch a new day. The transition of the night hunters to the day hunters is similar to the transition from this reality to the other reality—the Land of the Spirit Keepers. When I have the opportunity to lead a sweat lodge I give thanks for the gift to make the transition. It is in my prayers that the Great Spirit utilizes my being as conduit of healing, messages, and sacredness. I pray that all the Grandmothers and Grandfathers of the Four directions come to the lodge for the purpose of the people. I ask that the Guardian Spirits of the people of the lodge attend. And I ask the Great Spirit to provide protection.

The sweat lodge ceremony is a purification ceremony. When I am in the lodge alone, before the entering of others, I pray and ask to leave my body so that the Great Spirit will have no difficulty working through me. Some refer to this as an out of body experience. I prefer to describe it as lending my body to the Great Spirit while I rest in the Spirit land. Anyone can do this, all you have to do is recognize the power that is already given to you and ask.

If you are imprinted, it is with the Great Spirit. When my hand was on your head, on your hip, and our hearts close together, you were being hugged by Wakan Tanka. The Mystery moved something out of you and replaced it. What moved out only you can answer. What moved in I can guess is simply Love. Love from the Great Mystery brings balance. With balance, we can experience our power, which is a gift waiting for all of us.

I would offer this as opinion: you are bewitched, possessed by a spirit, being taught a lesson. The spirit that possesses you is the Great Spirit. I think the Great Spirit recognizes your desire and ability. To me you are a medicine woman in the making. You have spent a lifetime with the objective methods of healing. Maybe the Great Spirit wants you to know it is time to learn the subjective ways to heal. Your words.

Your dream: night, the black rocks, the Sweat Lodge, the Great Spirit. It is a gift, a message. My interpretation is that it is the Spirit World reminding you to remember. The black rocks, how wonderful, they may be, probably are Obsidian. Obsidian grounds a person to the earth and its energy. The rock teaches a person awareness of the earth's power and to find it within themselves. The thoughts of another people will come into your consciousness as you hold or wear the stone. Possession of the stone will allow you to clearly see the future. The stone will protect you from your confusion. Because Obsidian connects you to our Earth Mother it will connect you to your own femininity. It will bring balance to your life. Remember that balance (masculine and feminine) means experiencing the power of the Great Mystery. It is, in my opinion, love in its purest form. The sweat lodge is a purification process. The Spirit

World is simply reminding you of what you are through your dreamtime. The stars are a symbol of guidance.

If you have a rock shop near you, obtain some obsidian. Put it in your office, home, carry it with you. I'm excited for you.

Dawn has given to day. I hope this letter is not too mysterious. Get on with your life. People need you for what you are about to be.

The Great Spirit loves you. And by the way, so do I—

Ten Bears

He wrote back! Somehow this filled me with more glee than seemed appropriate. He was so respectful of the difference in our worldviews, and so accepting of my silly attraction. His interpretations of the events were strange to me. Imprinted with the Great Spirit? Me? How? It was Ten Bears who had touched me; it was his heart I had heard beating; it was his voice I strove to remember. And his words about my being a medicine woman in the making—oh fat chance! I thought, I'm a spiritual moron, and this guy ought to be able to see it. However, I liked his interpretations of my dreams; it made them seem less scary. I had no intention of buying any obsidian. Crystal shops were appearing all over Scottsdale, but I wasn't going to set foot in them. That would be going too far; I didn't put any faith in the healing properties of a chunk of discolored silicon.

However, I wanted to write to him to let him know that I wanted to keep learning from him. I needed to go somewhere outside where I could think. It was December, and the Arizona nights were cool and clear. Pinon and mesquite logs burning in open fireplaces filled the air with smoky incense. I decided I would take some time to write after the evening class I taught at Taliesin, the architectural school in the foothills.

Scottsdale, Arizona
December 9, 1992

Dear Ten Bears,

I am sitting in the ruins of a shelter built in the desert by one of the students here at Frank Lloyd Wright's communal school of architecture. This place is called Taliesin: shining brow. I'm watching the moon rise over Taliesin Mountain. It's nearly full. Behind me stretches sixty square miles of city. Before me stretches a vast desert wilderness—first, the

Pima peoples' land, then the Apache, then the Navajo, on and on; maybe for five hundred miles from here to another city. A coyote is howling just now—really. I work here at Taliesin, giving counseling and teaching in return for this: to be able to sit here, writing letters, in this beautiful and peaceful place. I've worked here for almost a year, but I've never seen the full moon or heard a coyote. I'm seeing a lot more lately.

It was nice that our letters crossed in the mail. Thank you for writing. You're a great teacher for me. Waonspiakiay is the word we use at Camp—how I love the sound of that word. Teacher.

I have some questions. How do I tell the promptings of the Great Spirit, as you call it, from my own desires? How does one keep from deceiving oneself with one's own words?

A rainbow just formed around the moon. Oh wonderful!

I hear one of the students approaching, feet crunching gravel.
It must be time to stop.

Barbara

I had written a simple letter, but it contained a critical message. I had called him my teacher. Few words held more significance for me, or conferred more honor. I didn't know if he would understand this. Now that I had conceptualized his role in my life as my teacher, I felt better. I would know how to behave: like a student. Students ask questions, do their homework most of the time, and treat the teacher with respect. This had once been a familiar role. I was glad to discover it again.

United Airlines, Sky
Dear Barbara

I love the dawn. It's such a special time. I remember so many of them, so important moments of renewal. Haleakala, South Point, Michigan, Lookout Mountain, South Atlantic, the Pacific, and the Mississippi River. All the dawns. I've always attempted to catch the morning star as it disappears. Tough challenge—it always sneaks away from me. For many it's the night that brings peace and tranquillity. For me, it's the dawn, it's the light that brings peace.

Today's is brought to me courtesy of United Airlines. I suspect we are about 30,000 feet—way above the clouds—beautiful dark blue above, golden clouds below. As I write, the morning star disappears.

I received your October letter a few days after I sent off my first to you. I suppose I should claim some disability to explain my slow response. The truth is, I'm not very good at being on time—I'm just in it.

Please don't be afraid. Your first letter is and was quite right with me. Remember, we all have our "first" experience—even in the sweat lodge.

Not long ago I had the opportunity to be in Columbia, Missouri to build a Sweat Lodge and Medicine Wheel. My friend Red Crow ran the lodge and I had the pleasure of being a participant. It was wonderful. Stumbling Deer, Thunder Wolf, Blue Otter, Mad Rain, and more were in the lodge. I said special prayers for you. I hope you received them. Red Crow is a special person. He can see my dreams. He told me all about you. Described you to a "t". He's teaching me how to do that in trade for some of the things I know about. He says you are doing quite well despite a few bumps. He also confirmed that you should get some obsidian.

The plane jumps around. I hope you can make out my handwriting. Years ago the teachers used to slap my hands when I picked up a pen with my left hand. Then they would scold and punish me for not making my "ooooo"s well enough. These hieroglyphics are the outcome. I should write them a letter. It would take them years to translate it and they would pray for me.

I hope your coyote friend is doing well. The Coyote people have a lot to teach us. They have a unique skill to appear—then disappear—then appear again. It's a good skill to learn. It's one of the first I learned when I was being taught shape shifting. It's a useful skill in today's world.

I hope your meeting at camp was successful. Please let me know the dates you would like to have Sweat Lodge ceremonies. There are many things we can do. Let's get together on the phone sometime and be creative if you wish. I would be glad to call.

It must be time to bring this letter to a close. We are about to land. Best wishes to all—I hope your family is doing well. Please write when the Spirit stirs within you.

Ten Bears

How strange that he wrote me on the same day I was writing him. Again. (From the friendly skies, too. Not very traditional, I thought.) We were apparently on the same schedule. My rational mind analyzed the coincidence. We were both psychologically sophisticated people. We both seemed to have a delicate sense of propriety. Therefore, it was nothing out of the ordinary that we could pinpoint precisely the right day to write.

It was nice that he had discussed me with his friend, the other medicine guy. I doubted that he had described me to a "t." Ten Bears had hardly even seen me in the light, so I was fairly sure Red Crow had given him an acceptably vague description of the kind of earnest white woman Ten Bears might meet at a youth camp.

Yes, indeed, I was having a few bumps. The dreams had started up again. I was being led over the black rocks toward something. In them, I would stumble, and then wake up. Then I had to get out of bed and go meet with my crabby colleagues and administer final exams to my students, still feeling bruised and footsore from my long dreamtime hikes. Where was I being led?

When classes ended for the term, I dealt with my dreams in all the familiar ways: exercise before sleep, thought-stopping techniques, and self-analysis. None of this worked. But I still wasn't going to buy any obsidian. I never read books people recommended or filled the prescriptions my doctor gave me for minor ailments. Why should I do something this silly?

On Christmas night, I had a new dream, an overpowering one, brought on by a fever picked up on our holiday travels. It was not as frightening as the others, but quite a bit more *provocative*. I decided I would write Ten Bears for an explanation.

Scottsdale, Arizona
December 27, 1992

Dear Ten Bears,

Again our letters crossed. Please don't apologize for late letters. I've heard from you twice, precisely when I wanted to. And I've written when I was moved to.

I am sick with the flu, or some other weird virus out of the rain forests. For five nights I have been lying in bed with my little girl who is also sick, our fevers mingling, and our fever dreams.

Now I am sitting in the sun by the cold pool, drinking tea with a fresh orange. I left the friends I loved and the work I loved for this December sunshine and this orange, so I must hope that the objects of such terrible sacrifice have strong medicine! Tonight my husband returns from his parents' place in Missouri. I don't want him to find me sullen and ill. In a few days we leave for Australia, where we will teach for two weeks at the University of Melbourne. All the more reason to heal, and heal quickly!

I wanted to tell you about a dream I had, one that came out of my fever. Why are fevers so miserable and yet so delicious? Well, here is what I saw: I saw a snake, actually two or three snakes. No, one snake with three heads. The snake was red and black and its eyes glittered like gems. It seemed be-jeweled, covered in diamond patterns with ruby and black gems, and some gold. It came forward, moving trance like, and then stopped. The image of you floated behind, smiling and holding the reins of the serpents, like a disembodied St. Nick. (This was on Christmas night, you see).

Now this relates to the questions I posed before, and points to the dilemma I have in understanding this Great Spirit business. How am I to know where this image came from? I hate to think that my subconscious would spew up a Freudian cliché like a *snake*, for Pete's sake, to indulge me in some phallic wish-fulfillment. It was so unlike that. It was like no symbol that ever emerged from my unconscious before. It wasn't like *me*. (My dreams are generally obvious, two-dimensional, and readily interpretable by psychoanalytic means).

The snake was glittering and beautiful, dangerous and ancient. I was not afraid of it, and of course, neither was your spirit who seemed to be in control of it.

Well, according to Gestalt psychotherapeutic theory, the one I rely on the most, you were not there at all. It was all me, the snakes, the jewels, even the image of you, which is the you in me, my projection of whatever I perceive you to be.

I don't know what to think. If it was you, if it really was your prayer, said in the sweat lodge, finding its way to me, wow, that would be cool.

When I write you I feel happy but just a little bit as if I were doing something wrong. My husband and son tease me about these letters, in a good-natured way. It was Chuck who suggested I write you, when he was at his wits' ends about how to comfort me when we returned from summer. I was so unhappy about being here, back from camp. He knew you had helped me before, and thought that your letters would bring me peace. They do, but in the moment I take them from the mailbox, I feel a wolfish sort of satisfaction as well. I suppose I just feel guilty about the pleasure which corresponding with you brings.

Would you like to do a sweat lodge for the Wakonse conference on Memorial Day weekend? The Wakonse conference is a camp for professors that Chuck and I and some friends from Missouri put together. We exchange ideas about teaching and talk about why we're professors. The sweat lodge has so much for these people. Intellectual and profoundly skeptical, they can be difficult and demanding. Yet they are the best teachers, who care the most about their students.

We definitely want you next August at Camp. We will discuss the spirituality curriculum at the planning meeting up in Michigan at the end of January.

Thank you again for writing. I'll write from Australia.

Love,

Barbara

I hoped he would respond to my letter and interpret my dream in the language of his spirituality. I knew he would have some interesting insights. I left for Australia, hoping there would be a letter waiting for me when I returned.

Chuck and I were at our best in Australia, teaching together, and more important, learning together. We eagerly drove out each day after our class, guidebooks in our laps, sharing bits of knowledge about each new place. We climbed all over Hanging Rock, where a group of schoolgirls had mysteriously disappeared almost a century ago. "Who could get lost here on this little mountain?" I asked, right before I disappeared down a deep crevice, twisting my ankle. Chuck helped me out of the crevice and half-carried me, both of us laughing, down the hill to our picnic table. Our friends had laid a table of Yarra Valley wine, sharp Tasmanian cheese, Pacific salmon, crusty bread, and pears. We dined in delight, my ankle raised up and my neck craned back so I could watch the koalas slowly munching in the gum tree above us. It was our first long trip without the children in twelve years, and we seemed to be remembering that we were old friends.

I had to stay on a few days longer than Chuck, and was sorry to see him leave. I still felt the urge to wander off to explore after class. It was the peak of summer in Australia, so one evening I took the train all the way out to Brighton Beach, on Mornington Bay near Melbourne. I walked along the beach as twilight deepened and then lay on a blanket on the sand. I searched for the Southern Cross, but stopped short in amazement. There was Orion, upside down. Suddenly I remembered my walk down the beach to the sweat lodge last summer, when I had gazed up at Orion in despair, thinking of winter in the midst of summer. I recalled how my heart had seemed to have grown old while still in the middle of my life. I watched the shimmering stars and listened to the waves lapping gently, just like the waves had that night in Michigan. Perhaps because I was literally pitched into summer while winter still reigned in North America, I realized my situation was now precisely the opposite. I began to feel the stirrings of possibility. Perhaps my heart could become young again, if only I traveled far enough from the familiar. Then, for the first time, I began to understand, in some inchoate way, the purpose of my dreams and flashbacks. They were like a deliberate provocation, a lure, driving me farther and farther away from the familiar.

I knew I must write Ten Bears about this, because I thought he would have something to say about this insight. But what should I say? That I was happy? Yes. That's what I would write.

Melbourne, Victoria
Friday, January 15

Dear Ten Bears,

I'm sitting on Brighton Beach in Victoria, Australia, watching the sun set over Mornington Bay. It has been a hot, muggy day, and many families are here, still bathing, as it gets dark. Like all beaches near urban areas, it's not pristine—but it makes up in cheerfulness what it lacks in cleanliness. I could almost believe I was at Camp, but the beach there now lies frozen beneath several feet of blue-green ice. I'll be back there next week—from the height of summer to the bottom of winter in a few days. The sky flames just a short distance over the horizon, and to my right, where the bay curves north, I can see Melbourne glimmering.

It has been a peaceful and hardworking trip; Chuck and I both enjoyed teaching the "Summer School" at the University. Although there have been new and exciting places, what I will remember are the simple things: the beautiful dusty green of the enormous mountain eucalyptus; the softness of the wallaby's coat and her innocent eyes as I petted her, the chalky smell of Aboriginal bark paintings. And of course, the weirdness of a place where south is cold and north is hot, January is summer and June is winter and where the constellations—which are appearing at this very moment—are as unfamiliar as those of another galaxy! Orion is upside down! I have been reading Aboriginal stories about the Sky Spirit, and the creatures through whom the Sky Spirit lives. The evening star has appeared, and now, as my ink gives out, the Southern Cross appears.

I'm so grateful for this life and I am happy to write you.

Love,

Barbara

There was a letter waiting for me when I arrived home. I read it rapidly as I prepared to leave for Michigan, where I had to attend a camp planning meeting immediately after my Australian trip.

Champaign, Illinois
January 10, 1993

Dear Barbara,

I hope by the time this letter gets to you that you have passed your cleansing time. That's what it seems to me every time I get ill. Fortunately, it does not happen too often. I hope the young lady has returned to health as well. Many blessings for the whole family. By now you have returned from Australia. What a neat place to go. On my list of lifetime objectives is to visit Alice Springs for the annual yacht club race down the dry Alice Springs riverbed. Lots of frolicking, exercise, and just plain fun. It's the kind of thing that piques my interest and stirs my soul. Other parts of Australia are also on the list. Especially the Outback, the Snowy River country, and the Great Barrier Reef. As soon as possible will be fine with me.

You had a very powerful dream. The fever cleared the way for this insight. Fever burns off all the junk. When I lived in Kansas we burned down the prairie to make the grass grow green. Although you may at first interpret this dream as a worn out, Freudian, phallic cliché, I would like to offer a slightly different point of view.

Snake Medicine is very rare and very good. For Traditional people, the snake represents transmutation. The ability to change. The power of the snake medicine is the power of creation. It embodies sexuality, psychic energy, reproduction, and ascension. The change from life to death,

death to life, is represented and taught to us by the life of the snake. The snake will shed its skin periodically and become new. It is the energy of wholeness, cosmic consciousness and the ability to experience willingly, without resistance.

The snake represents the knowledge that all things are equal in the whole of creation. It is the knowledge that things that appear bad or unfortunate can be ingested and transmuted if one maintains the proper state of mind. The snake represents the integration of the balance of life. It is a complete understanding of the male and female in all of creation. A balance. When these two aspects are in balance, two becomes one, the power of the Great Mystery is experienced, recognized, and realized. Snake Medicine teaches you on a personal level that you are one with the Great Mystery. Remember, you are the Mystery and the Mystery is you.

One Snake with three heads. This represents the oneness of the Spiritual, Emotional, and Physical planes that cannot be broken. By accepting all these aspects of life as one you can transmute, cross-over, and synergize ambition, physical health, dreams, resolutions, passion, understanding, wisdom, wholeness and a host of other attributes. Realizing that you have this ability is a connection to the Great Spirit.

You have chosen a powerful ally. The snake is there to help you change (transmute) some thought, action, desire, behavior, or hidden ability so that wholeness may be achieved. We speak of not only personal wholeness, but also of family, community, and universal wholeness. It all becomes one. It will bring you to a balance that is very calm, serene, and beautiful. Others will notice you are balanced. Be on the alert for those who wish you not to be that way. Think of your dream, the snake ally, when they attempt to get you off balance.

Remember, you have recognized, then realized that you are one with the Great Spirit. It will be impossible to change that now. No matter who or what tries. Not even if you try with your own self indulgence. Believe me, I know from my own experience.

Do you recall the colors of the directions of the Medicine Wheel? Red is in the East, Yellow is in the South, Black is in the West and White is in the North. Your black and red snake represents the black and red road. This is sometimes referred to as the Red Road. Black Elk is the one to first bring it to the attention of the New World. It is the spiritual road of the people. It is a very fortunate symbol for you. It is the sacred and the secular all mixed up together. It is the balance so many seek.

Snakes have eyes like jewels; they always glisten. They have a skin that looks like a fine beaded belt. This snake in your dream is a real snake. It appears to have three heads only because you know how to see the truth and recognize the balance.

You asked in your letter if I was there. Think about this. The Dreamer is the Dreamed. I was there. My gift is to be there when I am needed. I am not always there physically, but I am always there spiritually. Often times when I think about people or dream about them, they let me know that they have thought of me or dreamed of me also. I am Ten Bears, Keeper of Dreams. It is all natural to me. If I brought you the snake medicine it is because you asked for it and the Great Spirit sent it to you.

You are a very wonderful and exciting person.

I am not sure at this time if I can commit to doing a Sweat Lodge at your conference. I have been invited to Dance in late May or early June. The time has not been firmed up at this point. It is a celestial determination. The Dance is a ceremony that requires the dancers to be sponsored. You dance for someone chosen by the sponsor. I will know more as we get closer to June. If my commitment changes I will let you know.

Not much else is happening here. It's winter. Like a bear, I would prefer to sleep through it all. We made it through the Holiday Season. Now is the time to wear off the extra stores laid in to endure the winter.

There is no word in Traditional American language for good-bye. Isn't that nice.

Wakan Tanka nici un. Ake' Oh. (The Great Spirit is always with you and so am I).

Love to all,

Ten Bears

It was a wonderful letter. I began to analyze it as I had all the others he wrote, to make the translation from spiritual to secular language. What was he really trying to tell me? Then I stopped. Perhaps he meant exactly what he said; that I was on a road, a Red Road, seeking new knowledge of the spirit. In some way, maybe I had asked for the snake medicine, and the Great Spirit—um, that is,—my unconscious mind, had sent it. Then I realized it did injustice to his words to constantly re-evaluate them in my own terms. Like changing gold coins into old paper currency. Perhaps he had been seeing something in me that I just couldn't see—when I used my own lens.

I thought about his letter, and our entire correspondence, on the plane trip through snowy skies up to Michigan. I began to wonder just how far I wanted to range from the familiar.

I had been corresponding with Ten Bears for five months now, and I really didn't know what I wanted from this exchange. An escape from routine? The thrill of writing a stranger? Spiritual insights? All of these motives seemed to be betrayals of one kind or another. If I was using these letters as an escape from routine, then I was betraying my family and students, who believed and expected my attentions to them to be in earnest, not a mere performance of duty and habit. The letters distracted me. I thought about them when I should have been thinking of these others. If it was the thrill of writing a man who seemed alien and fascinating, then it was a betrayal of a much more specific sort. Despite the occasional edginess in my relationship with Chuck, I considered myself to be married for life. These letters seemed to threaten that promise. I felt this even more acutely after our trip together. It was much worse than betraying a vow to be faithful to him as a wife; I was betraying our shared worldview. If I let this spiritual fishing expedition go too far, I would be giving up a life-long commitment to objectivity, rationality, and individual responsibility for one's actions. On the other hand, objectivity and rationality hadn't really helped me to cope with my dreams and flashbacks, and the strange letters from Ten Bears had. As a result of all these conflicts, my thoughts about this relationship with Ten Bears were now an equal mixture of apprehension and pleasure.

I was ready to reconsider the letter-writing and perhaps put it aside. My letters had been answered with helpful dream interpretations, lore, and friendly observations. I had learned to respect and value Ten Bears' thoughts on these matters. I had even opened up a few doors in my own mind. Perhaps now I could manage pretty well on my own. Besides, with our letters crossing each time, it was hardly a logical exchange. I would write another newsy, natural letter like the one I wrote in Australia—perhaps in the spring—and that would be the end of it until the next summer's camp.

This was my plan until the snowy January night I arrived in Michigan for a camp planning meeting, fresh from the Australian summer. In my new stockman's coat and hat, I stomped into the winterized dorm around midnight. A door opened. Mark stood there in his pajamas. He announced, "Ten Bears is here. We invited him up here to do some building inspections. He's two doors down. He asked you to stop by when you arrived."

Confusion sent my adrenaline soaring. I didn't know he would be attending this meeting. I was not ready to meet this man outside of the sweat lodge clearing. Letters were fine, but real life was different. I hesitated, walked a few steps, hesitated again, and finally knocked on the door of his room.

Two voices answered, the loud and hale voice of Jeff, the manager of facilities, and Ten Bears' softer voice. They invited me in. They were sitting up in their bunks in the dark and laughing as I inadvertently showered the room with snow.

"Sit down," Ten Bears directed, pointing to the edge of his bunk. I sat. I chattered about my twenty-four hour trip here from Melbourne. They made girl-on-the-floor jokes straight out of college dorm life. I wanted to get out of there, and I wanted to stay. I got up, saying cheerful good-byes, and stepped out into the hall in my socks. "Dream well," Ten Bears called after me.

And dream I did, although I really didn't sleep much. I was desperately jet-lagged, my biorhythms wracked, and my magnetic poles in a seeming state of reversal. So that whole night, as the snow blew against my window and the sounds of my friends' snores mixed with the noises of the fitful heater, I lay in a hot, half-sleep. I must be ovulating, I thought—all these waves of warmth and weird feelings of excitation. Voices whispered in my ear, and my mind spoke back in clear, rounded tones in English, French, Greek, and bits of the language we called Camp Lakota, a Blackfoot language transmuted by seventy years of White ignorance into our own ceremonial dialect. Over and over I heard, "Waonspiyakiay. Now you be the teacher," and, "Gala sophia. Enseignez." It was probably the sort of word salad my mind tossed up every night in the few moments before sleep. I usually ignored it and went on into unconsciousness. But that night I couldn't. "One degree of difference," said a woman's voice—mine? And the words appeared, in flat print, like a banner across my consciousness. I just looked and listened. I remained in that state until the cold dawn, when I showered and dressed before everyone else woke

How different I looked! Not tired (How could I not be tired?). Anything but tired. I hadn't looked into a mirror for more than a few seconds for almost a year, not even after seeing my body change in the sweat lodge. The last time I had paid attention, I had a resigned looking dark blonde pageboy. Now it was blonde blonde, streaked throughout, and long, brushing my shoulders. I pushed it over on top, and it fell into a side part, as if it had been waiting for years to be transformed, with the flick of the fingers, from the dumb Prince Valiant look to something— well, something not very professorial. And I had a tan! For the first time in my life, the combined Arizona and Australian summers had warmed my pale skin to a smooth, rosy gold. The lumpy maternity underwear I had inexplicably worn into my child's third year I had finally replaced. I had black jeans that fit and a soft black tee shirt. I had an absolutely gorgeous black, red, and white Navajo blanket coat, which I'd been given for Christmas, the night of my snake dream. I felt *great*—except that I didn't have my lace-up roper boots. Where were they? I remembered that I'd left them in Jeff and Ten Bears' room. So I spent the next hour in the kitchen drinking coffee in my socks and waiting till it would be appropriate to slip in and grab my boots.

Thinking the two men had left the room for breakfast, I listened cautiously for a moment at the door, and then sneaked in. Ten Bears was sitting quietly on his neatly made bed, his pipe on his lap. He looked at me, unsurprised, and asked, "Did you dream?"

"Oh boy did I dream. Word dreams. Linguistic stuff. I'll tell you about it later. Got to get to the meeting!"

I flew out, boots in hand, to breakfast and then to my planning meeting. Ten Bears was in a separate meeting, so I was able to concentrate on the agenda: last year's evaluations, this year's themes, and this year's resources. At the breaks, friends who hadn't seen me since summer approached me and commented on how different I looked, using their own peculiar locutions. "Healthy," said our Dutch Calvinist. "Glamorous," said our Southern Baptist.

The meeting was lively, funny, and productive, like most meetings at our camp. Years of mutual affection and respect made this little planning group the very embodiment of the ideals of the organization: servant leadership and balanced living.

However, my eyes kept drifting to the window as the camp truck drove back and forth, with Jeff and Ten Bears doing some kind of survey of the buildings. I still felt alarmed and off-balance. I tried to calm myself. I had nothing to fear from Ten Bears, I reminded myself repeatedly. If we're here together, so be it. I'll see what I can learn from him.

So, when I stepped out of the conference center after the meeting and saw Jeff and Ten Bears were signaling me to hop in the pickup, I did so without hesitation. We rode around the camp, plowing through snowdrifts to finish their inspection of some wiring in several buildings. It was the zaniest inspection tour I had ever seen; they kept circling the camp and revisiting places they had just checked. They argued and kvetched at each constantly. I was almost alarmed, but when they burst out laughing, I saw how much fun this was for them. I got into the spirit of things. Jeff surreptitiously tied my bootlaces together, causing me to shriek when I nearly tumbled out of the truck. Ten Bears offered me a ginseng capsule, which I accepted with delighted suspicion. A few minutes later we were all watching the winter sun set over the ice-locked lake, parked in the pickup at the crest of the road over the dune. "How do you like the ginseng?" Ten Bears asked.

"Oh very nice," I said. "Like LSD without the hallucinations."

Jeff suddenly bailed out of the truck with many noisy farewells, as if on cue, and disappeared along the snowy path toward the dorms. And there we were, the professor and the medicine man, watching the sky flame out and the cold blue shadows rise, at a complete loss for words. Actually, I was at a complete loss for words, and he seemed comfortably silent. At last he spoke. "So, tell me about your word dreams. What do you have to say to me?"

I objected that it was all nonsense, no interesting images, just words. "I like languages," I told him, "so sometimes my unconscious dishes up lots of bits and pieces. Like gala sophia, which might be the Greek words for milk and wisdom, milk-wisdom or something of that sort. And many words for teach, and teacher, and the command, 'You be the teacher,' which I certainly am, I'm a teacher, but not your teacher, it's the other way around," I said.

We talked about this. He asked me several times to repeat the Greek phrase, its pronunciation, and its translation. It meant nothing to me, but it seemed very important to him. I told him I'd like to learn to be like him. "You don't seem to worry about things. You seem to do exactly what you want to do, and yet you have time for everybody."

He looked out at the ice floes on the lake. "I know that the Great Spirit will provide me with everything I need," he said, "but I must create what I want."

Suddenly I remembered the banner of letters across my mind. It had been very clear, but un-meaningful. It was like e-mail for somebody else on my computer screen: ONE DEGREE OF DIFFERENCE.

"Oh," I said, "Perhaps I'm should tell you about this, this phrase, 'one degree of difference,' I don't know what it means."

"Why are you touching your throat?" he asked.

I *was* touching my throat, seemingly taking my aerobic pulse. "Well, I'm warm now . . ."

He reached for my finger and placed it on his throat.

"About one degree warmer than me, the difference between a man and a woman at certain times. Thank you. That is exactly the message I've been waiting for," he said. I hastily removed my finger. I felt as if I'd been shocked by some galvanic source within him. "And what does it mean to you, this message, one degree of difference?" he asked.

Holding my finger gingerly in front of me, I pulled myself together. "It means to me that we are not so very different, you and me. That men and women are much more alike than they are different in abilities, personality characteristics, and attitudes. People are entertained by the differences and want to believe that they're important, but they're not. So when you say, 'respect and maintain the differences,' I wonder if you know how minimal those are . . ." I was suddenly aware that I was lecturing, and that he was nodding attentively and smiling.

Nearly faint with embarrassment now, I was ready when he shifted the pickup into reverse and took us back to the dorm for the supper.

I realized I was letting these feelings of embarrassment, attachment, and fascination interfere with learning. Here was this splendid opportunity to learn from a person who had an extraordinarily different worldview, and who had demonstrated therapeutic skills that seemed more advanced than mine. I was letting the stupid fact of his being male and my being female get in the way of getting what I really wanted—all I had ever wanted in life—real, new knowledge. As I made the decision to really go ahead and find out what Ten Bears had to teach me, I felt rising in me that wonderful, sumptuous delight I used to feel on the first day of class in college. To be given information I didn't already have; to have it structured by a mind very different from my own; to observe the surrender of self that occurs whenever the teacher is completely at one with the teaching: these are the experiences that had always given my life meaning.

So that night, as a group of us sat in my dorm room, comfortably contorted over the four bunks, I listened as Ten Bears and my friends told stories. He talked about shape shifting as casually and as naturally as other people talk about their golf game. Shape shifting, he said, was the ability to become another creature in shape, size, and skill. He liked being a bear, he said, although it was also useful, when climbing rocks, to be a mountain lion. Wow, I thought, he has major powers of self-hypnosis. He told a story about a dream he had a long time ago. A friend of his was going to be married. He dreamed of a wedding basket for her and how he was to find it and bring it for the ceremony. He found exactly that basket on a trip through Northern Arizona. He told us about the medicine woman who made the ceremonial basket. She had scoffed at him and wondered why it took him so long to find her. Many people told of experiences like this, of revelations in dreams and synchronicities that pointed the way to the next stage in their lives. I was skeptical, as usual; surely it is the dreamer who gives the meaning to the dream, rather than the other way around, I said to myself.

Our conversation turned to everyday conflicts at work and how people found ways of solving them. Ten Bears seemed to favor paradoxical strategies and metaphors for resolving conflicts: "Give them the seeds of good. Ask them what kinds of seeds they are planting today."

I ventured to describe my problems with my colleagues; they were men, they were older than me; they thought I was a threat, blah, blah. My friends offered advice. Vanette said, "Maybe you should just ask them to get their true feelings toward you out in the open."

Mark suggested, "Maybe a retreat of the whole faculty would help."

Jeff guffawed and advised, "Tell their wives how they've been treating you and they'll turn around fast!"

Ten Bears listened quietly to their suggestions and then turned to me and smiled. "If you weren't such a crybaby, maybe this wouldn't be happening to you."

Ouch, I said to myself. But I smiled with pleasure, because it was true. And I vowed, right then, no more tears. Stop grieving for what you left behind and what you hoped would be. Just be where you are.

The conversation continued until late in the night and gradually people drifted out to their rooms. Ten Bears sat across from me. I tried, not very successfully, to get him to tell me about himself—things I could relate to, like where did he grow up, where did he go to college and what was he doing during the Viet Nam years? To these questions he gave one-word answers, or none at all. All I learned, using my best interrogatory skills, was that he had an out-of-body experience while riding his tricycle when he was four. I rolled my eyes, but realized it was probably true. Meanwhile, he learned a lot about me, important things that I hadn't known I wanted to tell somebody. His ability to turn and guide the conversation was so ridiculously good that it was like being in a dream where you keep turning a corner to find out you're walking down the same street you just left. So eventually I just wound down and sat there watching him. Then we were both quiet.

I suppose I was staring at him. "What do you see?" he asked.

"It's what I'm afraid I'm seeing . . ." I said.

He waited.

"The genuine article," I said slowly. I stared some more. "I'm afraid that you're the genuine article. That you're not a phony or a fanatic."

And in those moments that I looked into his face, I realized that I was seeing not only the face of a man, but the face behind the face, Ten Bears, and further still, through the portals of Ten Bears' eyes, for a fleeting moment: —All. All.

It was like falling face forward into the vast, benign indifference of the stars. I was seeing the whole universe—great, entire, interconnected. And I was there too, looking back at myself. I was too stunned to do much except to keep staring. He let me look for a while in the friendly and generous way a seasoned traveler shares his map. Then he stood up, held my hands in his briefly, and left.

That, I suppose, was the moment I lost my reason.

I don't remember much about the rest of the weekend—or for that matter, the next few months. I was in crisis. My construction of reality had been swept away, and it had happened not in a sweat lodge delirium, or under the influence of exotic mind-altering drugs, but in the friendly, warmly lit dorm room in the course of a simple conversation. Ten Bears had not pushed me. I had gone there myself. But, I didn't know where I was. I groped desperately in the following months for the hand of the only person whom I felt could pull me out of the deconstructed mess of my worldview.

From January until May I taught my classes, attended meetings, and gave lectures in several states. I cooked meals and cleaned up afterwards. Chuck and I went to movies on Friday nights, and discussed them over pie and coffee afterwards. I washed my little girl's hair and tucked her in with stories. But I was actually, as they said in my favorite eighteenth century novels, "quite mad." These are the letters of that time.

Scottsdale, Arizona
January 31, 1993
Dear Ten Bears,

I had a sturdy little sorrel mare once. In the middle of the Nebraska winter, she came into season. I could not breed her then; the foal would have been born eleven months later, in the dark and cold of a January night. It would have frozen and died. So I penned her up by day and locked her in the barn at night. All day she wore a trail in the snow along the fence line, sniffing the wind, whinnying, and trotting. At night, she kicked the walls of her stall, over and over, bang, and cried out. I felt sorry for her, but what could I do?

The image of that mare came to me as the plane flew me toward Camp. What rotten luck. Every three or four years, I have a few days of immense fertility. My body, normally quietly cycling along with the moon, suddenly bursts into a fever, my mind comes alive, and my conscious-ness *readies itself for something new.* The last time this happened, my husband and I created our splendid Grace, and I began a book, which I think will be my most important one. This period for me is preceded by weeks of dreams. It is accompanied by intense desire, physical and spir-itual. I want, I want, something, something more. The difference between my mare and me is that she was not ashamed of her condition. "Poor lit-tle horse," I said, looking out the window into the dark land below.

I was not ready to see you, even to speak on the phone! Even under normal conditions, I would show off and stick to you like glue. You have intelligence and power, and I like to be near it. In my state of hyper-fertili-ty I was afraid of being overwhelmed. If I behaved foolishly, please for-give me.

At the spiritual level, I was not ready to see you. All those stories you tell, about dreams coming true and wedding baskets, and shape shifting. I'm not ready! Something is being born in me, but it is so tentative, so skeptical, and so young. You set this in motion, in the sweat lodge. I am willing to believe there is more to life than was previously dreamt in my philosophy (or studied in graduate school), but really, aren't some of the people you talk about just crazies? You don't care though. You don't care if they're phonies or not, as long as they allow you a little more understanding of the medicine/magic. How can you stand to learn the truth from crazy people? I doubt my own dreams, not to mention those of others. Why did I hear voices saying, "You be the teacher." I have noth-ing to teach you.

The only gateway I have ever found to my own spirit was through your eyes.

Here is what happened on the 747, on the flight home. I think I was try-ing to do a little Gestalt therapy with myself, by having a dialogue with myself.

What do you want out of this relationship with John?

I don't know. It's good to be with him! I want to be around him! It was fun!

What was all that nonsense coming out of your unconscious? The "one-degree of difference"; the "milk-wisdom," all that crap?

I don't know. It felt partly real, partly unreal. As if I had started out pre-tending to have knowledge, and found out there was actually something there for him. Like a message left on my personal Ether Net, for him.

Uh-huh. So does John love Barbara?

In the usual sense? No. He has a life. He has a good wife.

Does Barbara love John?

Well no. I have a life. I have a good husband. And John is not my type!

Then why can't you sleep? Why do your energies become totally focused when he looks at you, even when he is behind you?

Because I love Ten Bears!

And then seemingly from the frozen air outside the plane came a *third voice*, saying:

BUT TEN BEARS HAS NO BODY TO LOVE

Here is where I began to cry. I laid my head against the Plexiglas window and sobbed. The flight attendants avoided me politely as I choked in my misery. My neighbors across the row held up their papers to give me privacy. *No body*. How I grieved! How stupid of me, to fall in love with a disembodied spirit, with the Wakan I can only see as Ten Bears. And all I have is this body, this poor, heated body. I can't hear anyone's dreams. I can't see visions. I can't shape shift. I have nothing sacred. Nothing sacred to give Ten Bears. Then, again, the third voice:

TEN BEARS HAS NOBODY TO LOVE

Yeah, right. Nobody but the cast of thousands. The men and women who have been with him in the sweat lodge, in ceremonies, in conversations. He has many people to teach him, and many others who follow him around as greedily as I do: "Teach me, teach me, Ten Bears."

TEN BEARS HAS NOBODY TO LOVE

Well, it won't be *me*. I have nothing he wants. So forget it. I change my mind. Barbara does not love Ten Bears.

At this I curled up and prepared to sleep off this crazy weekend. A pillow, a blanket, my boots off. Resignation, sadness, fatigue. Barbara does not love Ten Bears. As I dropped off to sleep, this is what I heard:

BUT LITTLE HORSE LOVES TEN BEARS

Yes; yes, she does. And then I slept, a soft and dreamless sleep, and peace came.

Here is what happened to my mare. Spring came, and she came into season a couple of times. But I was too busy; other things came up. I had no time to take her up to the stallion in the stable up the hill. Finally in July, she seemed to have her last lackluster estrus of the year. I bred her at last. The foal, born the next summer, was the last of the year's crop. He was small and scrawny, and his mother was indifferent to him.

She refused to give him her milk. It took years for me to bring him up to weight, and years to heal his spirit of the neglect he had suffered. I never want to make this mistake again. One spring night, when I am ready, I might let the little horse go free.

How will I ever have the courage to mail this letter? I will put it aside for a few days, until I am more rational.

I'm lying on the dusty floor of my office at the university, writing on a pad on the rug. Surely here I can be rational. Should I mail this letter? It sounds so weird, and so brazen. I don't even know what this letter means, because most of it emerged from a source other than my rational mind.

I suppose it's about my conviction that you and I have work to do together, some kind of medicine to make. But it all comes out in the stupid language of desire, which seems to be the only language men and women have to describe the creation of something unified from two people.

If I was wrong to write this, if this is not what you want to hear, please tell me, you don't have to be delicate. I would rather be silent forever on these topics than to risk the gentle and cheerful relationship we have only just entered into.

Again, my teacher, my friend, I ask for your guidance and help.

Love, Barbara

PS Am I also this Little Horse person?

Now that letter, and the experiences it recounted came out of absolutely nowhere I'd ever been before in my mind. I suppose that psychodynamic theorists would say that what had just happened to me was the process of "splitting." That is, I was having feelings and desires which my superego, or conscience found unacceptable. I had begun to participate in a belief system that was incompatible with my previously held beliefs. Under the weight of that crisis, my unconscious created another self, Little Horse, who could have those feelings and desires. Little Horse could speak freely of the spirit world. I knew all of this theory at the time.

However, as the awareness of that spirit-self grew stronger each day, I realized quickly that it was in no way a substitute personality or a fragmented set of cognitions, thrown off of my true self like some rogue satellite. It was me. I had always been Little Horse. I knew it before I had words, a two-year-old galloping around the living room and pressing against the screen door to get out to the green, green grass. But the learning of words had continually forced the wisdom of that little horse into the background, as my intellect took over and I began the process of separation: "This is real; that is imaginary."

Yes, I knew the theories. But I had no use for them. By this time, I was way beyond the reach of psychodynamic interpretations, or any of the other ways I had been taught to understand my mental experience. I had given up on the familiar because the familiar had failed me. I now saw my former self, and the belief system that governed that self, as frozen and limited. However, I did not really have a new belief system yet; just the knowledge that I was a horse. I wondered what that meant.

If Ten Bears was what I thought he was, he would know what the whole experience meant and would help me to understand. If I were wrong, then perhaps he would be put off by the weirdness of my letter. And I would never hear from him again. And I might go crazy. It didn't matter. I had to send the letter.

Champaign, Illinois
February 13, 1993

Dear Barbara,

You do write some interesting letters. It is good for you. It is good for me. I like reading them; I enjoy the communication, so please keep writing.

Your vision was a good one. We can learn a lot from our brothers and sisters in the four-legged clan. We can even learn to talk with them. Our ancestors did it all the time. I'll bet you already do, especially with the horses. You ask them a question and they answer, giving you their perspective of the world and wisdom.

I like to spend time with the four leggeds. They have taught me about how to live in the embrace of the Mother Earth. Just watching a deer, coyote, mountain lion, bear, or a horse can teach us so much. For instance, you know how a horse walks down a steep slope. They sort of prance and have a wide hip movement. It makes the trip down hill sure footed for them.

You can do the same yourself. Imagine you are a horse next time you walk down a steep slope. (That's the first step to learning shape shifting). Do the same sort of prance and let your hips make the same movement. You will get to the bottom of the hill in a much safer way. That's just one of the many lessons a horse has taught me.

Bears teach you how to be strong, patient, and loving. They are also very protective of their clan and know healing medicine. Bears will make their own poultice when they have an open wound. They also teach us how to rest and be balanced.

Coyotes are mystical. They can teach you how to disappear, and then reappear in a different place. They are also good teachers of survival under impossible conditions. They have been hunted as varmints for years and yet they are learning to adapt to city life.

Some of my most wonderful teachings have come from those that know how to fly. Owls will teach you about change and death, pretty much the same thing in my mind. Hawks will show you the way to go when you think you are lost. This is true spiritually, physically, and emotionally. Eagles will teach you about mystical things and broaden your worldview. Ravens teach us about magic, hummingbirds about love, and blue jays about thunder beings.

So my friend, your dreams, your visions, your story of the horse, they all mean something. It all is good. I think you were given a name from the Spirit World. They call you Little Horse. I think that is because you are small in stature but have a sense like a horse. You know intuitively about things and those around you, just like a horse. You are also strong, with intellect, and know what to do and how to do it. You are independent, just like a horse. You like your freedom and you like to run with the wind. Just like a horse. This is good. There is always something for us to learn from knowing the horse.

Whenever I have been with a horse, I have realized that they know a lot more about the world around me than I do. So I listen and learn. Horses are very sensitive. Insensitive people think they are dumb, and hard to train. Horses are smart and have a keen sense of the moment. If you appreciate their sensitivity and respect them you can have a very wonderful relationship with a horse. They will protect you and love you just like a mother. If you don't respect them, they will make life tough for you.

And so, I have listened and learned from you.

Actually, I think that every event, everything that is said, and everything we see, is a message from the Spirit World. To me all lessons are shared lessons. If a teacher thinks they cannot learn from the taught, then they only fool themselves into believing they are teaching. If the ones being taught thinks that it is a one-way relationship, then they will not learn. They will only be able to regurgitate someone else's life patterns. Sounds boring to me.

So Little Horse thanks for sharing your dreams, your visions, and your thoughts. Thanks for sharing a part of your life with me. Thanks for allowing me to share my life with you.

Remember when you told me about the dream you had at Camp. You said that in the dream you heard the words "Gala Sophia." (I'm not sure I spelled that correctly). You said that you were told to tell me those words. After you explained the meaning of those Greek words, they made a lot of sense to me. In fact, you brought to me a message that I have been told before. The difference is that this time it made a difference. I have changed my life appropriately. I got the message this time. I have made adjustments and my life in general is just a whole lot better. Thanks!

Your vision on the airplane as you returned to Arizona must be testing your skeptical intellect. The Spirit world was telling you about me. You are exactly right. Ten Bears has no body to love. Ten Bears has nobody to love.

I am a lot of things to a lot of people. Most of the accolades and criticisms I don't think I deserve. What I am and work most to be is a Warrior. One of the first things that I learned when I chose the path of a Warrior is that: "A Warrior loves no one, a Warrior loves everyone." Those, of course, are very powerful words and have led to long conversations way into the night.

What they mean is, that as a Warrior, one chooses to love unconditionally, with the same intensity, and the same energy. Warriors will not differentiate between lovers, sisters, brothers, mothers, fathers, or friends. We love the trees, the grass, the Father Sky, the Mother Earth, the four clans, all of creation. The same. Even our so-called enemies, we love and respect. A Warrior will only choose a worthy opponent. We find no value in conflict. Especially a conflict that is easy to win. Warriors find peace in balance. Warriors work towards loving as the Great Spirit does. Warriors love all, the same.

It is an easy thing to say. It is not necessarily an easy thing to do. The rewards are great though. Learning to love without conditions or expectation of something in return frees the Spirit. It frees the Spirit from anxiety and fear. Iktome's most powerful warriors.

A Warrior also learns that we own nothing. We only are given the chance to take care of "it" for a while. We can't own the land, we can't own the Mother Earth, and we can't own the Father Sky. What we can do is make use of the opportunity to take care of the gifts that are provided us. The Great Spirit provides us with all the gifts.

If we can't give away a possession, then the possession possesses us. If we are possessed by our possessions then we find ourselves needing to protect them. If we need to protect them, then our ability to do so will always be in question. This gives us the opportunity to feel guilty and fearful. And alas, the trap works. Many people spend a lifetime feeling inadequate, guilty, and anxious because they fear they will lose their lover, land, children or their life. They become intimidated and out of balance. They begin to believe they are separate from the Great Spirit. A Warrior knows all things are gifts to be appreciated, taken care of for as long as we can, then given away to those who can do a better job. Native American people call this behavior the "give away." Our ancestors took this very seriously. If as a Warrior, I was blessed and was given a buffalo, I would give it all away to the people I live with so that they may prosper. Another Warrior would provide the gifts of sustenance to me. Can you imagine living in a society like that in our present day?

This goes for everything. Remember, when we watched the sunset together, I said to you that the Great Spirit provides me everything I need. I truly meant it. Every moment of life is a gift to me, and everything in that moment is profoundly sacred to me.

So my friend Little Horse, every moment I am with you, every moment I think about you, every word you say, and every thought you have is sacred to me. I believe we are all part of the Great Mystery and we cannot be separated no matter how hard we try. The great Mystery is sacred and so are we. Your words are sacred. Your dreams are sacred. Your thoughts are sacred. Your visions are sacred. Your life and everything about you is sacred.

A long time ago, in a land far from me now, I buried my heart in the Spirit land. It was a significant moment in my life. It was important to me then and is still as important to me now. I prayed to the Great Spirit. I was given a song:

> It was late December,
> Full moon,
> And the Pipe told its tale.
> I buried my heart in the Spirit land,
> And the white earth turned to spring.

This song I sing often to remind myself of the Mystery. As you know, a council of women gave my heart back to me. It was given back in a healed way, in a way that allows me to love unconditionally.

You are a very special person. And yes, there are things that you and I have been brought together to do. We will do them for as long as the Great Spirit has us do them. And when the time comes for us to move along, and we have learned all we can from each other, then I will cherish the memories. And when we get back together in the future, it will be as if we were never apart. It is the way of the Warrior.

Love (unconditionally)

Ten Bears

His letter had given me both hope and annoyance. Hope, because he knew horses. He knew me! He understood what I was trying to say. I had thrown myself in his path, a little mare blocking his way, saying, "Listen to this! Let's see what you think about this!" And he had responded with grace and unconditional love. I felt the power and purity of his caring. For about two seconds. Then some frightened and quibbling part of me wanted to possess that love.

This of course he had deftly anticipated with his little sermon on unconditional love and nonpossessiveness. Hell, I knew that stuff. I'd read Carl Rogers, too, even met him in an elevator. Who believed in *that* anymore? I stamped my foot in impatience. W.H. Auden, in his poem, "September 1, 1939," lamented that most of us want "not Universal Love, but to be loved alone." I could relate to that. Wasn't it irresponsible of him to throw around words like "love" in boldface, no less, around a woman in my condition? Didn't he realize the havoc this could wreak?

Spiritual novice that I was, I didn't understand then that the greatest gift of the letter was the song he related to me. I just skipped over it. Only later, much later, did I realize that he was telling me that he, too, had once been in crisis and confusion. His heart, too, had once grown old and seen a premature winter. And his heart too had once been buried beneath the snow. And he had found spring. I'm sure that some part of my spirit heard the message. But I wasn't ready. I wanted to do some kicking.

Indianapolis, Indiana
February 28, 1993
Dear Ten Bears,

I'm in Indiana, snowed in at a Holiday Inn, removed by the weather from the lecture circuit. This could be a long letter! Thank you for your wonderful letter. It is great to write you and to read your responses. When you write to me, you are pure spirit. Here in these letters, we can be completely free with one another. Being with you in the flesh is too hard; there is too much interference. I sense the strict school teachers in the tense way you hold yourself around women; Westminster College in the upturned tones at the ends of your sentences; and the Viet Nam years are there, where they always show up in sensitive men, in your silences. I know these are not you, not Ten Bears, but only the residue of your past. But I do respond to this stuff, and it calls up behaviors from my past, types, veterans—of the war, or the anti-war. Someday soon, I hope, I'll be able to be wholly with your true self.

So I'm Little Horse. I didn't tell anyone. Last week I received a couple of birthday presents from friends. One was a picture of the cave painting of a horse from Lascaux. One was the children's book, *The Girl Who Loved Wild Horses*. These were nice coincidences.

I was such a lazy and wild child. I wouldn't let anyone cut or brush my hair, so it was always a tangle. I galloped and galloped through the weedy lot near my house so my dresses were always torn and dirty. Living in the city, completely separated from horses, I fretted. When I was made to go to school, I imagined a bit in my mouth—Spit it out! All of this disappeared when I was an adolescent. Then these images reappeared when I was in graduate school. I would look up from my statistics book to hear the sound of galloping hooves. As I walked, head down in the icy rain from the Psychology building to our brown apartment, the thundering beat shook my bones. It was a warning to get out of that place, I guess. And I did. Back in Missouri, I found two horses, and I have lived with horses for eighteen years now. I know them in the dark by their smell. Joe smelled like antique leather bound books. Sandy smelled like new fallen snow. Ragtime, my wounded one, smells like an electrical fire about to happen. I love my horses, though not as pets. They have both saved my life and nearly killed me several times.

You seem to know a lot about horses. It was exciting to read what you know—that they are intuitive, and loyal and love their freedom. Did you know this: You can love and respect a horse for many years, and one day she will kick you, hard, or bite you on the butt while you are cinching up the saddle. It's not meant to be mean-spirited, and it's not a sign of any underlying vice. It's meant to remind you: Don't get too comfortable with yourself and your way of doing things. I think that's why I was sent your way: to love you, to be loyal, to work with you, and also, to kick you a little. I hope you like it.

In your letter, you talked a lot about unconditional love, the same for all. I wonder why. Maybe you're not sure if I understand the idea. I do. I was brought up that way. Even if I was a strange and unpretty girl, I always knew I was cherished and beloved. I tried to practice unconditional love in my own unsophisticated way in college, in the commune I tried for a while. Unfortunately, some people thought that the love I was giving freely was something they were taking by stealth. Things sure got complicated.

Now I have a different idea of what unconditional love is, and I don't believe in trying to have equal love for all. Unconditional, universal love that is a warm and caring feeling expressed toward all doesn't mean much to me. Leave it to the New Agers in Sedona. For me, there is no love without acts of love, no love without action. Also I believe unconditional love must be tied to particulars if it is to have any meaning.

I don't trust the idea of universal love, the same toward all, although I do not deny its possibility. I would not like the consequences to my family if I practiced this kind of love. Did you ever notice how lousily the great saints treated their wives? Buddha abandoned his wife the night she gave birth to his first son; Gandhi let his wife be a servant and indulged in funny perversions with his disciples; Martin Luther King used women. It worries me that in practicing universal love, love towards all, that these holy people forgot about the thousands of daily courtesies and considerations which are the truest substance of love, and which are the duties of the hearth. Did Joan of Arc remember to put something special in the children's lunch boxes? Did she remember to phone her husband to tell him where she would be camping with the French Army? Maybe the Warrior's path is not for me.

Well, you must make allowances for me if I choose to love you a little more than I love humanity in general. Forgive me if the sight of a letter from you gladdens my heart more than the bill from the vet. I, too, am a lot of things to a lot of people. But I am *your* little horse, at least for a while. Little Horse loves Ten Bears, and I don't expect you to do anything about it except keep on your Warrior path, even though I don't understand it exactly.

This letter took hours, a whole blizzard's worth of time. I watched the snow, and even got to go out in it. My first snow in two years. Beautiful! It even made Indianapolis look good. Now I'm going home.

Love,

Little Horse

I liked the letter I'd written a lot. It didn't sound as crazy as the last one, at least to my ears. And I had made a lot of good points, I thought. I wanted Ten Bears to know I was no intellectual lightweight who would accept all those vague humanistic statements about unconditional, universal love. I was also reminding him, and myself, that I had specific relationships and duties. If any philosophy or spirituality would lead to my slighting these, then I wasn't signing on. However, my defenses felt very fragile. I felt even more vulnerable when he didn't answer my letter. I didn't like the way I was thinking about the experience in January all the time, and it seemed like the first time since adolescence that I was losing self-control in a relationship. This frightened me. My independence was precious to me. As a feminist I knew the terrible danger of deferring to a man's opinions too readily and of becoming dependent upon a man's attentions. I knew that in that direction lays confluence, the tendency of women to submerge their identities in that of a man. My husband had been the only man I had ever met who respected my desire to remain a separate being, and who positively encouraged my autonomy. I doubted there were many like him. Surely not Ten Bears.

Mountain Preserve, Arizona
March 25, 1993

Dear Ten Bears,

I'm sitting on a small peak in the Mountain Preserve, with some nondescript name like Peak 1108. Although I've given my horse the opportunity to graze on the little tender grasses growing around this black rock, he's decided to hover over me, turning stiff-necked this way and that to scan the washes below for something to be alarmed about. My exhausted black collie keeps coming back to pant and slobber. Thousands of acres of open land, and these two animals have to crowd onto my rock. They are beautiful, though, as they gently nose one another. The wind up here lifts their coats out, feathering their tails.

The wildflowers are growing like mad after all the rain we've had. On my particular rock are a big brittlebush bursting with yellow daisy-like blooms to my back and a tiny, furry leafed plant with rows of purple buds up the six stems to my right. And of course, the ever-present baby barrel cacti make sitting here a little chancy. To my left, a large creosote bush covered in yellow buds. A little world, within this four-foot long chunk of black schist. This rock is some of the oldest on earth. Intensely compressed layers, turned vertical by some amazing force. Now Ragtime is giving some earthshaking whinnies, having spied other horses in the valley.

You know, horses and bears usually don't have much to do with each other. Bears are not interested in horses. Horses are too big to serve as prey for an animal that prefers berries and fish. Horses inhabit a very different environment, preferring the open prairies and lowlands while bears like the rocky heights (That is why Ragtime keeps tugging on the lead. He wants to get down off this mountain). Horses insist on being afraid of bears when bears really can do them no harm.

All of this worries me. Today I'm worried. I'm going to put this away for a while . . .

I'm worried, I think, because I have gone so far down the road of listening to my "intuition" since beginning these letters. Sometimes I feel as if I am abandoning my intellect and my skepticism. My intellect and my skepticism are all that have saved me from the fate of ninety-nine per cent of the women in this world: drudgery, dependence, and disappointment. I'm not talking about intelligence. There are plenty of intelligent women who are trapped by circumstances of their own device. I'm talking about confidence in one's intellect and skepticism about knowledge that seems to come from sources other than observation and rational analysis. Somehow, it seems that when a woman gives way to notions of spirituality or religion, she promptly gives up control of her life. Are there any religions, which do not have at their heart the maintenance of the status quo, the maintenance of imagined differences between men and women that inevitably work toward the detriment of women? I really get nervous when I hear you say, "Respect and maintain the differences."

Because I have always believed in my intellect, I have never accepted work which was below my abilities; as an adult, I have never been economically dependent for so much as a week; and also since adulthood, I have never been disappointed in my relationships because rational relationships seldom involve overly high expectations. Now these are no small rewards for a life without religion, spirituality, or reliance on "intuition."

It is true that since the sweat lodge, I have seen that there is more to know about the world than I had previously thought. What you call the Mystery, I guess. I saw a "psychological high-tech" that went way beyond the skills I had been taught as a psychologist. I saw a healing power not explainable (yet!) by any principles that have been well-defined. I found a capacity in myself to have images, dreams, and intuitions, which are remarkable in their symbolic and metaphoric accuracy. I want more of this; I want it very much. But what will be the cost?

Besides these concerns, I have had some disturbing debates with a young faculty colleague here who teaches Native American studies. She was brought up in an upper middle class family, but has a Yacqui grandmother. She does ethnographic research on white people who adopt Native American spirituality. She believes that white people should explore their own ethnic heritage and their own religious roots, and should not "appropriate" Native American religions. She speaks of white people who participate in sweat lodges with contempt and sometimes withering pity. I ask her, "How can you study people you dislike so much?"

I *know* she knows that I am one of the white people that she is talking about, and she has an uncanny ability to make me feel foolish, insensitive, and defensive with her words. And yet . . . she seems to like me, even seeks out my company at meetings occasionally. And I admire her bright courage and her brilliance; her presentations are eloquent and original, combining science and poetry in daring ways. I like her. I am afraid if she knew what I write in these letters, that she would hate me.

If only I could convince her—and myself—that all of this is the true fulfillment of my German heritage of curiosity and investigation, wonder and exploration.

Sometimes I believe her attraction to me is actually an attraction to you, as manifested in me. If you get my drift. There I go, off on a mystical tangent.

Tomorrow April is here. My least favorite month. In academe, it means rushing to finish up the year. Tempers and resources are short. I spend hours with students who were not accepted into our counselor training program, explaining and comforting. Our family, with two professors, will also suffer because of stresses at work. We will snap at each other and at the children.

Meanwhile the air is full of the sweet perfume of the orange blossoms. The mockingbirds are awake and trilling at 3 am. Hummingbirds are everywhere. The night air will be warm, the desert floor cool. How I would like to be out sleeping under the stars, instead of sitting up late at the word processor!

It is dawn and I will have to end. I would like to see you again.

Love,

Little Horse

PS: In "trail" competitions at horse shows, one of the events involves confronting a horse suddenly with an animal or machine to see if it spooks. Typically, a goat or llama or snow blower is brought out. The majority of the entries blow up. The horses buck, run, and rear. One or two remain. At the national finals, in Trail class, occasionally they bring out a bear. These superbly trained horses, for the most part, go nuts. Sometimes, though, there is one who stands there, perfectly still, quivering all over, sweating, tail switching, but standing there, still. I want to be the one who stands still.

I had written two letters in a row detailing my concerns about the suspect nature of unconditional love, the deleterious effect of religion on family life, the relationship of religion to the oppression of women, the difficulty of bears and horses getting along, and the political incorrectness of my exploration of Native American spirituality, and he hadn't even responded! A whole month, and he had no reply to my excellent arguments. It was like attempting to confront one of those martial arts masters: you can kick and lash out, but just when you expect to make contact, he's not there.

I was frantic. Didn't I tell him I was willing to learn? Why wouldn't he teach me? Here I was, apparently contemplating some kind of crazy dive into spirituality, mainly because of this strange relationship with Ten Bears, and he wasn't even going to help me with my concerns. Didn't he understand I needed answers to these questions before I made any changes in my beliefs? Of course, maybe he was offended by some of the things I had said. But I doubted it. More likely, he was using the same technique he had used when I had interrogated him endlessly in January, trying to hook him with my questions into my own cognitive scheme: silence.

My crisis increased, my misery grew. I went to the Arizona State University Pow Wow with my little girl and bought some obsidian from an Apache teenager selling earrings, dream catchers, and crystals. "It helps clarify your inner state," I said. "Whatever," he replied.

Champaign, Illinois
April 4, 1993
Shonkawakan Ketala
(Little Horse)

Such a fitting day to write. The sky is blue, the wind is calm, and it looks as if winter will leave soon and give way to spring. I hope so; the bear in me is ready for the summertime. It is truly my favorite time of year.

Preparation for the Dance begins in earnest today. While saying my prayers this morning Shonkawakan Ketala, you came to my mind in my visions. Iron Knife suggested that I write to you about the Dance. He said that it would be good. He said that it would help me to organize my thoughts in preparation for the time. He said that it would be good for you. He said you have a way to see beyond and the Spirit People know this. He said they are teaching you and you were struggling with the lessons. He said you would understand.

My good friend Stumbling Deer has invited me to Dance. We will do this in late May. It will be a time when the stars are easy to see, the grass is cool, and the sky is blue. It will be a time when it is good to give away.

We will begin the Dance before dawn with a Sweat Lodge ceremony to purify us. We want to be clean inside and out so that we can hear the Great Spirit speak to us. We want to be clean in our hearts so that we will have clear visions, clear instructions, and clear spirits. We will come out of the sweat lodge at dawn and face the sun, our father, and Dance for two days.

A long time ago I knew that I would be asked to Dance. Many years. I have been asked before by Stumbling Deer and the Spirit World directed me away. Now, this spring, it appears that the Spirit World has made all the arrangements and cleared the way for me. Iron Knife says it is time. So be it.

There is already a strange sense of detachment to all this. I will be dancing for the people. I thought that I would need to muster my courage and endurance. All seems so distant, unnecessary and petty. Fear is such an illusion. I have not forgotten its ability to capture and exasperate and steal life from a person. Long ago I knew this enemy too well. I am saddened for the people that are held in darkness by Iktome's greatest warrior. Fear is such a weak enemy, lance the ground and he runs like dust on the wind. Fear is afraid of himself. He has no substance. He can only make believe, and by doing so make you believe.

I will seek nothing for myself. I will seek health for my sick friends. I will seek healing for our Mother Earth. I will seek peace in the lands, minds, and hearts of the Four Great Nations. I will ask the Great Spirit to show the people how to help themselves, to be strong, to love, and have good hearts and minds in the ways they have chosen to believe.

I will dance to the Sun as I have been told to do by Iron Knife and all the Spirit People. I will give myself so that others may heal. I will cry for a Vision for the People.

Shonkawakan Ketala, keep these words unspoken. They are sacred. They are words from deep inside a Warrior. They are words of a prayer commitment asked for by the Great Spirit before the ceremony. It is the way we keep ourselves focused on the purpose of the Dance. Iron Knife asked me to share these words with someone I trust. It is a part of the tradition. I asked, "who?" Iron Knife said, "Shonkawakan Ketala."

I hear the cry of the hawk. I must go and speak with her.

Ten Bears

I was so relieved to hear from Ten Bears. I was so happy to say the beautiful name, the words for Little Horse: Shonkawakan Ketala. Once again, he had given me a great gift that I didn't quite recognize with my conscious mind. He had shared with me his plans for the Dance. Only later, as I came to understand the great secrecy and the private nature of that dance, performed as a sacrificial offering, away from the eyes of tourists and anthropologists, did I know what he had given me. But my heart and my spirit understood.

By now I burned day and night with a secret, feverish desire to be with Ten Bears and to be learning what he had to teach me. I was deeply ashamed. My attraction to him felt so obscure and wrenching, while his love for me was so pure, open, and sunny. And although what I experienced was certainly some cousin of romantic desire, it was far stranger. For one thing, I still had no image of Ten Bears that I could entertain; I simply could not visualize him. I still did not even know what color his eyes were. At night sometimes I heard a voice, saying "Shonkawakan Ketala," Little Horse. Was it his voice? I didn't know. He said the spirit people were teaching me and that I was struggling with the lessons. I *was* struggling and I needed his help. He was my gateway to the spirit world, a world that had become more real to me than the one in which I breathed. I didn't just want to be with him; I wanted to become within him, merging cell for cell, so that I could go There, like he did. What had started as a need to learn from him, to be close to the power he radiated, now felt like a compulsive need to smash myself into him as I would a door that held my life on the other side. Having no words to explain these feelings, I listened to my favorite Wagnerian opera scenes over and over, especially Brunhilde's Immolation Scene, which captured for me the feeling of obsession and oncoming doom. Love, fire, death, Oneness. I knew that the increasing recklessness of this feeling could destroy everything I had lived for, and I did not know how to be released.

When my best friend, Roseann, visited in March to celebrate her fortieth birthday, I knew it was time to unburden myself. With another dear old friend, Pipp, we sat around my fireplace late one night sipping Bailey's. I brought out the letters, told them my story of the sweat lodge experiences, and finally admitted to my crazed mixture of spiritual and romantic obsession. "Something's wrong," I whispered. "You have to help me. I don't want to destroy my life."

"He's a *guy*," said Roseann. "Never forget that."

"But he doesn't *act* like a guy. He doesn't have needs like other guys, to prove something, to grab what he wants . . ."

"I believe what you say about him—I think he's probably a real medicine man, and he does magic with you. But he's still a guy, Barb, and you need to be careful."

"I don't know how to be careful! And it's not just the infatuation thing; it's the spiritual thing. Forgive me, Pipp (she's a very spiritual person), but you know that's not how I am! If I let this go too far, I'm afraid I'll let go of my beliefs and become like a Moonie or something. Boy, do I understand the Jim Jones thing and the groupie women in cults. They might as well sign me up, because if I believe all this stuff about the Great Spirit, then I guess I could believe anything."

"So for you, any kind of spirituality is about losing control," said Pipp.

"Well, yes. It's like I've gotten on this train and I don't know if I'm going to be able to get off!" We were silent for a few seconds, and then, in the distance (and believe me, from where I live, it would have to be a very *long* distance), we all heard a low, long train whistle. At first we thought it was the whistle of wind in the chimney, and we all three leapt forward toward the fireplace, cocking our heads. "Did you hear that?" we asked each other. Then, like three teenagers over an Ouija board, we collapsed in shrieks and laughter, waking up our men and putting an end to the evening's conversation.

I tried hard to be a good mom and wife, spending a lot of time with my family. Chuck knew something was wrong. He looked at me in a puzzled way a lot of the time, and asked about my absent-mindedness. I was so sad that I could not tell him about my crisis. I suppose I was afraid that he alone would have the rational arguments necessary to explain away all that had happened to me and to make sense of it. If he did, I thought, the gateway I had discovered would close forever.

I tried to teach my classes well. However, I kept getting confused in my schedule for my Advanced Counseling Techniques class. Somehow, my lectures were out of sequence, and I ended up several lectures short. It would be six months before I realized that I had left out the entire series of lectures on transference. Transference: the irrational attraction of the patient to the therapist, or the projection of feelings that one has toward a lover, husband, or father onto the therapist. Transference is critical to the success of psychotherapy because it is the vehicle of change. My students didn't get those lectures, or those readings that semester. I had lost my notes, and my self-understanding as well.

The April planning meeting for Camp was coming. Ten Bears would be there. How could I survive it without making a fool of myself? I was sure that Ten Bears had no idea how out of control I was. I was afraid he would refuse to be my teacher if he saw the signs of my abject and helpless attraction. I thought that he would be as embarrassed by my behavior as I was.

The weekend arrived, a sunny, chilly Michigan spring. I remember cold sand blowing on the dunes and lilacs growing by the sun-warmed road. This time I arrived on a Friday afternoon and immediately joined a group who hiked the dunes. I climbed a dune and stood at its bright, gusty crest, enjoying, behind the privacy of my sunglasses and billowing coat, the scene of sand, lake, and scampering people. Ten Bears appeared on a sand dune across from the one I had just scaled. He waved to me, and then disappeared over the top. A few seconds later, I saw movement in the woods just to the side of the dunes. There, lumbering through the trees, in and out of shadows, was a brown bear. Then it was gone. My first thought was: Are there brown bears in Michigan? My second thought was: When did he plant that suggestion in my unconscious? My third thought was: It's him! I didn't see Ten Bears again until we all were walking back along the beach. He walked out of an opening between the dunes and joined us, greeting me with a friendly squeeze. "What have you been doing?" I asked. He grinned. "Just showing off."

Later that night, I was utterly confused about how to behave. Should I carefully wait for Ten Bears to speak to me? Should I ask to see him? For what? After the meeting I thought it might be best to take a walk, so I bundled myself up and trudged up the main camp road, among the darkened and boarded up cabins. Why did I not know how to approach Ten Bears? There was simply no small talk left in me. Suddenly I heard leaves crunching, footsteps behind me, and remembered that I was a woman alone at night. Terrified as I remembered stories of recent trespasses by drunks from nearby towns, I started to run. I saw nothing behind me, but the footsteps became louder and faster. I arrived breathless into the pool of yellow light from the lodge where we were staying and snapped around to face my pursuers. There was nothing there except a dust devil, a whirling little cyclone of leaves that had apparently followed me all the way down the road. Feeling foolish and still frightened, I burst into the lodge, ran down the hall, and pushed into Ten Bears' room. The lights were out, but I could see both Jeff and Ten Bears turn toward me from their bunks where they had been lying chatting before sleep.

"I knew we were missing someone!" Jeff joked. "You couldn't stay away!" A truer statement was never made.

"A whirlwind chased me here." I said. Jeff laughed uproariously, and Ten Bears reached out to me.

"Come here," he said, patting the bunk. I sank down to sit beside him, dropping my coat and hat in a heap as I went to him.

He reached over and hugged me, saying, "Hey, you really did get scared!" and to Jeff, "She's trembling all over."

"Ooh," said Jeff, "Can I comfort her, too?" The three of us talked in the darkness, catching up on events since January. While Jeff loudly told a story, Ten Bears whispered, almost sub-vocally in my ear, "Did you see me today?"

"Yes," I hastily whispered back, "I saw a bear." We kept on talking, about Jeff's attempts to preserve the camp's facilities from the ravages of wind, sand, and teenagers. I began to relax.

Ten Bears watched me in the darkness, keeping a hand lightly pressed against my shoulder. "You're OK, now," he said in few minutes, so I stood up and said my good-byes. "Dream well, and give me what you brought me tomorrow."

Back in my room I puzzled over his last statement. What had I brought? I had my usual duffel bag I brought to camp, and I never completely unpacked it. I had thrown some of our Valencia oranges in my bag to share at breakfast, and I took those out as I looked through the contents of the bottom. There were some scraps of soft leather from the moccasins I had made at camp the year before; some embroidery floss; interesting seeds, shells, feathers, and cedar needles my little girl had gathered and left for me to clean up in the last sweep of the cabin last summer.

Looking at these little bits of camp, I suddenly knew what I had brought. What Ten Bears called a medicine bundle. I had read about these. People gave warriors who were going to dance the Great Dance medicine bundles as offerings. A song came into my head, which sounded like one in the sweat lodge, and I knew exactly what to do. I picked a few things and lay them on a scrap of leather. Each had a clear meaning for his dance: protection, endurance, vision. I knew—and of course, I don't know by what mechanism—that I was to ask him to dance "with understanding of a woman's spirit" or something like that. I had a strong compulsion then to touch my hip, remembering where his thumb had pressed me into this new reality. I lifted my clothing away to see that spot. A red spot, my own personal stigmata, appeared there. Again, I knew what to do; I knew that a tiny piece of my flesh was needed, and I lifted a sliver of myself, and placed it in the bundle. I wrapped it carefully. It was done; I went to sleep.

The next morning I could converse quite naturally with everybody. I concentrated, and did the work of planning our conference. We had a joyous day of creating a schedule, selecting classes and speakers, and entertaining ourselves with stories of past disasters and triumphs. After the meeting was over, we adjourned to the large stone amphitheater we call the Council Circle to sweep out the leaves, which had gathered there over the winter. As I swept, I knew something important was about to happen to me, as surely as a woman knows she is to give birth.

I have seldom spoken of the transformation that took place that April afternoon, because of all the things that happened to me that year, it is what I am most reluctant to describe. Several things make it difficult. First, there is the ridiculous company one finds on the other side of conversion. The born-again dreck of Tammy Faye Baker; the "we-know-something you don't know" smugness of those old Anglican windbags C.S. Lewis and T.S. Eliot; the skinny, vegetarian narcissism of the Rajneesh followers; the argumentativeness of New Agers who want to teach Indians how to do a proper medicine wheel—this is what I wanted to avoid. However, I remembered a conversation in J.D. Salinger's *Franny and Zooey* in which Franny complained angrily about the hypocrites of the world. "That's none of your business," Zooey admonished. It's none of my business what others do with their enlightenments. It's my business just to try to explain what happened to me.

Second, there is the humiliation of writing about an experience that involves the loss of rational and emotional control. Approaching conversion to a worldview that did not just tolerate, but was founded upon the interconnectedness of all things, all beings, and that used words like "Great Spirit" comfortably, I felt much as I had approaching childbirth. I avoided childbirth for nine years for many reasons, but one of the major ones was the indignity of it—the screaming, the sprawled legs, the ubiquitous fluids. I had even thought of adopting an older child just to evade the punishment decreed for women in Genesis, the little design flaw that ensured that some fetal brain cases would be too large for some pelvic thresholds. But as time went on, I began to long for the experience of motherhood, even if I had to go through childbirth to get there. It took a long time for us to have our first son, Sam, and the delivery was nothing like I had feared it would be. Chuck and I read Jane Austen to each other, and watched old movies until the time of delivery came. Nine years later, Grace was just as easy. Both of my babies slid out of me soundlessly, perfectly, in a few sweet moments of rapt anticipation.

I knew before it happened that somehow this transformation would not be so clean, nor so deliberate. Here is how it happened.

It was late afternoon, and the dead leaves we were sweeping formed an enormous, musky pile in the middle of the camp's Council Circle. The air had turned lightly warm. Needing to give Ten Bears his medicine bundle, I asked him to walk with me; he agreed, and went to get his medicine Pipe. We then walked down the road until we came to the bridge leading over the creek and out of the camp. To our right, hidden by the budding branches was a shelter, a gazebo overlooking the creek. In there we went, and sat for a while watching the pale spring sun on the water. He filled the Pipe in his ritual way and prayed to the four directions. We smoked it together. Then he looked at me expectantly.

"I brought you this," I said, "It's a medicine bundle; it's filled with things you need for the Dance—I knew how to make it, but I don't know how I knew."

"Thank you, Shonkawakan Ketala. I'll wear it here, next to my heart," he said.

"And I have this prayer—it's so difficult—it's so very awkward to pray—I never have, you see." I almost choked on the words as I hastily said, "Great Spirit. This man is going to dance in your honor. I pray for him, and I give him this medicine bundle, and I ask that he be allowed to dance with the understanding of the spirit of a woman." I stopped for a moment and looked up at him. "I have this feeling that this is why we were brought together—so you could help me become this, so I could then help you, to prepare you for this experience. But I'm not worthy to do it. I don't even know what I'm doing. This has all been so strange, probably just because—." Here I stopped again, in dreadful embarrassment.

"Why? Tell me. You know." The sun had set and the air was cold and still.

"Because I have this weird desire for you, this love that makes no sense. And I am so mortified by my own feelings. I have tried to get rid of these feelings and I just can't do it. It is so wrong, when I love my husband and family and my work so much, to feel so *compelled* to be with you all the time."

Here I actually fell out of my seat to the ground (*fully aware of the melodramatic nature of my actions and absolutely unable to stop!*). I sobbed so hard it felt like the ground was shaking under me, and I stayed there in a miserable heap. Ten Bears lightly moved over a space, so that I was no longer at his feet. I looked up; he smiled at me pleasantly.

"Well, good! What a nice thing, to feel desire and love! What a good thing, to be given these wonderful feelings!"

"But it's not *nice*, it's terrible, I'm debilitated by it. Help me please. Please make it go away."

"Don't you think that the Great Spirit understands? Little Horse, you were so intellectually fortified against the Great Spirit that perhaps there was no other way to get to you except through your body. Is that so shameful? The Spirit World calls you now. The Great Spirit is not calling you to me but to yourself."

"I don't want to fight anymore," I said. Kneeling there, my head down, my hands empty, I let it happen. The process, which had begun in the sweat lodge, was complete, and I surrendered control, for the first time in my life, of the sturdy little ego that had insisted on its own aloneness. In the darkness behind my closed eyelids, I felt myself lift up, and connect. I was plugged into a pulsing web of life: the strong earth, the evening stars just appearing, everybody, and everything. Not just for a visit, like in the sweat lodge, but to live there. My eyes snapped open. I stared at Ten Bears in wonder, and he laughed aloud. Serious again, he took my cold hands in his, and lifted me up to the bench, saying, "Well, you are a very desirable woman. But you are safe with me, because there is no need to act on those feelings. You'll go back to your family and one day when you don't need this desire anymore to remind you of what you've learned, you'll know. Then you can just ask for it to be taken away from you. It's a very good thing. It led you to the Great Spirit. Now you know the way."

And that was it. We walked back to the lodge where dinner was served. I was somewhat unsteady on my feet. I ate a lot. I even volunteered to say the grace.

The next day, Ten Bears drove me to the airport. He played a tape of Navajo flute music for me; I played my opera tape for him. We were sitting quietly in the car together as he

drove down the highway, listening to the music. We had not spoken a word for a long time. I was getting uncomfortable and
beginning to fidget. As if anticipating me he spoke softly. His
voice had changed to a lower register, as often would happen
when he spoke from the spirit world.

"You must seek your Vision. The Great Mystery gave it to
you. Many of the legends and stories speak of the time when you
are born. They say the Great Mystery blows the breath of life into
you and it is at that time when you are give a vision of your life.
You can follow your vision or not. It is up to you to decide.

"As we grow up we tend to forget our vision in this culture. Sometimes we are taught that what we see and feel is not
true. Children are scolded for being intuitive and they are told
that their spirit friends do not exist. They are taught to ignore the
spirit world. This is too bad, but it happens. Because of this we
must seek our vision. There are many ceremonies to do this.
Some of the ceremonies include the family and the community,
some are very quiet, individual, and personal. Some of the people
seek their vision only once in their life. Others seek it many
times. How you do it does not matter if you do it in a sacred way.

"I will go on a vision quest four times in my life. I have
done this ceremony twice. The first time I was with a medicine
man and we went into the sweat lodge together. We prayed and
sang a lot. We got the rocks really hot to purify or minds, bodies,
and spirits. After the sweat lodge ceremony I went into the mountain to a place that I had prepared with tobacco ties and a blanket. I was there for four days and four nights fasting with only a
bottle of water. I prayed for my vision and I was lucky, it came to
me. When I came off the mountain, my spirit teacher sat with me
and we discussed my vision. We talked for a long time and he
helped me understand the gift of the Great Mystery. He gave me
my name and told me to seek my vision four times in my life. He
also said that I should never speak of my first vision again. It is
between the Great Mystery and me. Other visions, he said would
tell you how to live your life and you can share them.

"I will tell you of the second time I went on a vision quest
and how I met the council of women."

*It was on one of my many trips to New Mexico in 1990. I
would go every summer to visit friends and renew myself with the*

earth. Often times I would go into the mountains or high mesas by myself and live quietly for several days. Not seeing anybody. Just being with the Mother Earth and Father Sky. I usually only took a knife and a blanket with me. Sometimes I would take a little water.

You know there are many ruins of the ancient people in New Mexico. I was walking around on the third day of my quest and I saw some old ruins. I think they were from the Anasazi People. Well, I was looking around, being very careful not to disturbed anything. I was being very careful with every footstep. I was being so careful that I was not paying attention. As I looked over the wall of a ruined kiva, this hand reaches up and grabs me by my shirt just at the chest and pulls me over the wall. I landed flat on my back and it nearly knocked the breath out of me. I am kind of fussing and trying to get up but this person is holding me down. She says to me, "Slow down. It's me, Yellow Eagle. Geez, you are hard to catch."

I had known Yellow Eagle for many years and asked her what she was doing. She nearly scared the life out of me. She just laughed. She told me that she had been following me for two days but that I was too cunning to catch. She decided the only way was to hide until she could throw me down. I told her she did a good job of that as I got up and dusted myself off. She could read my mind, as I was about to ask her why she was following me, she interrupted before I could speak and said that she had been sent to get me by the council of women. She told me to follow her and be quiet. I got my things and we walked together for a long time. We eventually came into a small pinion forest near a river. The forest opened into a small clearing and there were six women sitting in a circle. They were sitting in a medicine circle around a small fire.

Yellow Eagle sat down in the east and instructed me to sit next to her on her right. Mad Raven sat to her left and Blue Otter sat in the south. Next to Blue Otter was Hawk Woman and Clear Rock sat in the west. Two Horse sat to the left of Clear Rock and Medicine Swan sat in the north. I knew all of the women except for Medicine Swan. After we had all sat quietly for a while a man called Dancing Corn came up behind me and sat down outside the circle. Everybody, except me, was dressed in the traditional way.

The women started talking with each other as only women can do. They were buzzing like bees. It was as if they could hear everything each was saying while talking to themselves. Then all together they got quiet.

Yellow Eagle put her hand on my leg and said, "We have brought you here to teach you about the woman in you. When you know the woman in yourself, then you will understand the world of women. Each of us has a gift for you and you must listen carefully."

And so each of the women spoke of the gift they would give to me. Yellow Eagle spoke of the spirit in women, of their strength, and their desire to keep all things sacred. She said that the woman in a person is the keeper of the sacred. We must honor this and never forget it. It is the creative way.

Mad Raven spoke of the mystery and magic. She said, "Always remember that the magic is in the mystery. The mystery is not in the magic. Magic is only what you don't understand." She spoke that the magic of life is to bury your personal history. "Now" is all that you have. What you are doing in the now and what you are about to do is what counts. You are only limited by the limits you choose. Reviewing and talking about your personal history limits you to past events. The lessons have been learned. Leave them alone and seek new ones. Each moment is a lesson to be enjoyed.

"Tell stories, they allow you to become a third party to history. This is why oral traditions are so spiritual. Stories can be told to teach the lessons of life and they can be passed on from generation to generation. Tell stories on yourself, especially the funny ones. Remember, those that have lived an event that creates a lesson are not bound or weighted down by having to say, 'I did this, or I did that.' The attention of a story should be on the lesson and not on the aggrandizement of the person. To tell a story in the first person only inflates the ego. And you know the ego is an illusion that separates you from the Great Mystery. Bury your personal history for others to dig up later much like the anthropologist that digs up bones."

Mad Raven spoke, "the magic is not just the illusion. The magic is in the message of the illusion. The illusion is the way for the message, which is the magic."

Blue Otter spoke of patience. She said that patience was the only virtue of the feminine. She said that there were lots of strengths of the feminine, but that patience is the only virtue. To be quiet under stress and difficulty was the mark of true skill. She sat quietly for a long time waiting for me. I asked her if she would speak more. She said, "See, you need to learn patience. It will help you quiet yourself and give you the opportunity to see the world as it really is. Men are the interlopers; you want everything to happen quickly and efficiently. Women are the creators and with patience they allow every thing to emerge with the wisdom of the Great Mystery. Creation takes patience. It is the feminine that creates."

Blue Hawk Woman was sitting to the left of Blue Otter. She scowled all the time and was mostly despising. She just glared at me as if she was disgusted with all men. She said that she was the messenger and that it was time for all men to understand their womanhood. The sooner. The better. She said the world has been out of balance for a long time. She reminded everyone in the circle that it was time for men and women to find balance through respect of each other.

The Hawk woman stared at me for a long time. Then she said, "You men better change. Change now. There is not much time left in this age. Once, women ruled the world, then men. The new world is almost here. If you don't change now you won't be ready for the fifth world. If you are not ready you will have a very difficult time living through the transition when it comes. The fifth world is for those that understand the male/female self as one. This balance will rule the universe. Not male, not female, but both. Both the male and female of a person will be understood as oneness. Oneness is the key to survival in the fifth world. People will be united in their self, inseparable, indistinguishable as separate beings. A ball is a conceived as wholeness. It is not considered as this half of the ball and that half of the ball. So it will be with the sacred people in the fifth world. They will be one and be thought of as one. Not separate. One with themselves. One with the universe. One with the Great Mystery."

All of this time Dancing Corn was behind me teasing and taunting these women. He would laugh and dance around the circle and distract me from what the women were saying. He called Blue Hawk a bawdy broad. She giggled in a wicked way and formed in her hands a blue ball of fiery light. She threw the ball at

Dancing Corn who was standing behind me. I ducked as the ball of light flew past my right shoulder and hit Dancing Corn who yelped in pain. All of the women laughed with glee at his pain.

I asked Dancing Corn why he taunted these women. He spoke very seriously, "I am here to make sure you don't lose your masculinity. With all of these women around you, and with all of their power, it is too easy to become seduced by them. You will want to be like them. If that happens you will become a contrary. Balance is what matters. Balance is the path of a warrior. You must keep your male heart as well as your female heart. Neither is more important than the other. What you are challenged to understand is that what matters is that neither of these hearts matter. Being together is what is important. Creating this togetherness is what you know as impeccability. One without the other and you are lost in imbalance. You are separate. Being equal and together in your heart is the power that exhibits itself as impeccability and grace."

"You humans are too focused. If I weren't here all you would want to do is be a woman. You can't do that. You were born a man. Respect that. The Great Spirit sent me to remind you that you are a holy man. To remind you of your physical masculinity so you don't go too far the other way and become a contrary. That's the challenge of being in the human form. You have to work at being focused and nonfocused at the same time. When you accomplish this you experience a vision of the universe with a unique point of understanding. You see your world and the spirit world simultaneously. You have to work at it, but like everything else, after a few times it gets easier and easier to look and see at the same time."

I noticed he always danced around the circle and would not enter it. I asked him if he was afraid. He chuckled and said, "Afraid? No I am just smart."

Clear Rock sat in the west of the medicine circle. She spoke, "We are your council. We are a gift of your will, your willingness and desire to understand." She spoke of power being the balance of the masculine and the feminine. "With this power all of prosperity is at your will. To be one or more of the other is to be out of balance. In becoming one, we are one with the universe and the Great Mystery."

She spoke softly, "I am in this circle to help you with your intuition. It is your most powerful ally. When you sit in medicine circles, sit in the west. My spirit will be just behind you and next to your left shoulder."

Blue Hawk interrupted and said, "Yeah, behind very good man is a woman!"

Dancing Corn bellowed, "Yeah, in front of every good woman is a man."

"Exactly the point we are making with you," Clear Rock claimed. "Soft and hard, up and down, right and left, male and female, they are all ways of balance. One cannot exist without the other. It is simultaneous, all happening in the present."

I asked her if there was a council of men for women. She said, "Yes. In the fifth world decisions will be made in the feminine and the action will be effected by the masculine."

She then shape shifted into a mountain lion and stared quietly into my eyes, then she changed to a clear and bright multifaceted crystal. Then she disappeared and reappeared.

"This is the medicine of the west. It is our gift to you. You can visit this council any time you wish. Make a medicine wheel and sit in the northeast. You are known to us as Medicine Horse of the White Hand Clan. It is a sacred name and only to be used by you in this council. When you desire our council, speak your name and we will come to you. Ask any question you wish and we will give you the answer from the spirit world. If you want to shape shift, sit in the west, I will be behind you and guide you. With our council you will be balanced. This balance has the strength to create and accomplish anything. Do not abuse it and remember to always be impeccable." Clear Rock fell silent after these words.

She stared into my eyes. I could not lose her gaze. She said, "Look down." The two of us were sitting, cross-legged, knee-to-knee, in the sky.

When we returned to the circle, Two Horse began to speak. "I am the keeper of your dreams. I will bring wisdom to you at night when you are asleep. You have had the gift of intuition since your birth. I am heavyset because in your development it was important for us to hold you back. The world you live in would not and could not accept you in your early age. I have been keeping your intuition for you. When we enter the fifth world you will be accepted and you can tell your story. Not before then. You will know the right time. We will tell you. Your story is for the fifth world. Remember, creation takes patience."

Sitting in the north was Medicine Swan. She was different from the other women. She was dressed in a white buckskin dress that was finely beaded with white sea shells. She had a glow of white light around her that pulsed with her heartbeat. Her long curly hair hung to her waist with two eagle feathers hanging to the left of head. She had beautiful sea blue eyes. She was the essence of purity and grace. Medicine Swan did not speak through her mouth. She spoke from her heart.

From her heart she said, "A long time ago, when your wife was ill we had you bury your heart. You took a heart-shaped locket of gold and put it into the earth. This was important at the time so that you could be strong for your family. What you didn't know is that you buried your heart in the center of this circle of seven women. Now we will give it back to you."

Medicine Swan put her left hand on my chest, over the heart. She held out her right hand and in it was the heart-shaped locket I had buried many years before. Her thoughts began again as she put the locket in my hand, "You will no longer be 'in love.' You will be 'love.' Your love will be unconditional, without bias, prejudice, or fear. Your unconditional love is what we call grace and it comes from the Great Mystery. It is your task to show the people of the fifth world what can be done. You can do this by telling stories or writing, but most of all by your own actions. The warriors of fear, bias, prejudice, hate, sickness, dis-ease, and illness are all illusions. They know better than to approach you. They cannot defeat a balanced person. They are cowards and will pick on somebody that is out of balance. With your heart back, in a balanced way, it will show and people will recognize it. Remember, you are the mystery and the mystery is you."

She sent thoughts to me and let me know that she was the essence of my spirit that lived on the other side. She was my equal in the spirit world.

Medicine Swan returned to her position in the north of the medicine wheel. Dancing Corn sat down beside me to the right. As we all stared at the fire it grew brighter. All of the women turned into ravens and flew into the sky. I looked to my right and Dancing Corn was gone.

The next thing I remember is sitting by a fire in the early dawn. Seven ravens were flying overhead as the sun rose on the high desert. I drank some water to refresh my body. In my hand *was the heart shaped locket that I had buried a long time ago in Missouri. This was my second vision that was given to me by the council of women.*

It was a fascinating story, but hard to understand. I doubted that I would ever have such a complicated vision. We were quiet the rest of the way to the airport. He dropped me off at the curb, and I went into the departure lounge. I sat there a while, a book open in my lap, looking off into space. For the first time, I saw a very clear image in my mind of my teacher and friend. "Ten Bears," I said softly. "Come back." A few minutes later, the security alarm started beeping as if an army of terrorists was stampeding through. I looked up to see Ten Bears at the security checkpoint, removing his silver belt buckle, his bracelet, and his watch, even the silver ankle bands on his boots. He walked up to me, smiling broadly. He caught me up in a great-hearted embrace, and then strode out again, sweeping up his silver in one hand on the way out. I laughed out loud several times on the flight home, waking the guy in the seat next to me.

Champaign, Illinois
April 12, 1993

Shonkawakan Ketala

Shonkawakan Ketala, you are from a long time ago. You are from a time before anything moved, you are from a time before the breath of life, you are from a time before the wind. Shonkawakan Ketala, you are Wakan Mayheduya, deep Spirit. You are a Woman who knows.

Ten Bears

This letter was clipped to the front of yet another letter. I read the first one, my breath shallow and an ache rising from deep within me. Of what? Recognition? Longing? I took a moment to get my breath, and then went on to the next letter.

Champaign, Illinois
April 26, 1993

Shonkawakan Ketala,

How wonderful it is to be with you. Thank you for sharing a part of your life with me. After I am with you I feel full of life. The fire of life grows larger in your presence.

A five-hour drive gives me lots of time for singing, laughing at myself, and thinking. I sometimes pray too. On the trip home I was saying prayers for you and the Mystery suggested that it is now time to put on paper a dream given to me in 1992. The Great Spirit said that I should put it in a letter to you. The Great Spirit also said that you could share it with anyone you wished because it is an important dream. The Great Spirit said that you would understand and know when to tell the story about to unfold.

In late summer I was camping in Mesa Verde with my friends Thunder Wolf, Lone Fox, and Sage. We had spent the day visiting the ruins of the Anasazi People. It was a beautiful day as I remember. Blue sky, warm starry night.

The dreamtime came late that evening. Many spirits were in the area. Thunder Wolf and Lone Fox were preparing for their Vision Quest. A Great Horned Owl had swooped very close to us after dinner. At one point it touched Thunder Wolf with its wings. It flew straight at me and suddenly changed its flight path, going straight up, just before it would have collided with me. It spent the night very close by, singing its night song, till dawn.

And so, I fell into a deep sleep. I first saw in my dreams the Sun. The Father Sun. It was as if I had been soaring in space and decided to visit my Grand Father. I could see into the heart of the Sun. Deep inside, close to the center, occurred an explosion of energy of enormous, unimaginable magnitude. So large was the burst of energy that its power moved to the surface of the Sun before the explosion ended its initial burst. The shock wave sent out a radiant bright light, ever expanding, all over the universe.

Born in the heart of the Grandfather Sun was a cleansing storm that would reach the earth and take all living creatures by surprise. The Great Spirit created the storm. The Storm was the Great Spirit.

I then found myself looking West into the mountains from far away on the plains. The western sky was darkening, as the Storm clouds grew larger. The clouds were black, deep indigo, and absorbed all light. The Father Sun was rising in the east and the morning dew was still on the tall, golden prairie grass. As the storm grew in its size and intensity, it soon became apparent that the clouds were not clouds. What first appeared as clouds became an enormous flock of Thunderbirds that reached from the southern horizon to the northern horizon. The storm circled the earth. Thunderbirds so thick that their blackness would not let the smallest ray of light from the sun show through.

The wind grew in its strength from the flapping of the Thunderbirds' wings. The wind became so strong that all living creatures lay down to protect themselves. Clashing of wings created rolling thunder. Lightning crashed to the ground from the eyes of the Thunderbirds. They had come to cleanse the Mother Earth of all evil things. Fear would be replaced with courage. Hate would be destroyed. Light from the heart of the Great Spirit would fill the world with Chont Kin Yah Wakan (Spirit Love).

As the Thunderbirds flew overhead, intent on their task, I could only see they were being driven, like a herd of buffalo. Two horsemen, one in the south and one in the north. Both on white stallions, both dressed in white buckskins, finely beaded, leggings and war shirts. Each with long black hair and two eagle feathers blew as they whooped and yelped. A man from the south, a woman from the north. They rode on the wind, encouraging the Thunderbirds to exercise all their power to destroy forever all that had been, was, or could be evil.

After they had driven the Thunderbirds around the Mother Earth four times, these horse Warriors came down to the prairie in front of me. Their horses were spirited and pranced with Spirit energy, waiting the directions of their riders. Both held their white horses before me, he in the south, she in the north, as I stood in the east, facing west.

Both then gracefully dismounted, and walked their horses towards me. The horses panting and prancing behind them. Gently holding reins, stepping softly, eyes glowing with love from the Great Spirit. They held hands and began to speak. As they spoke the clouds of Thunderbirds began to give way to a crystal blue sky.

They said the time had come for all good things to live and prosper on the Mother Earth. They said that the Great Spirit had taken all evil thoughts and things from the Mother Earth. That she was pure again as she was meant to be in the beginning time. They spoke about the four great nations of people, and that from now on their children would live in harmony and peace. They said that the Great Spirit would live in the hearts of all living things. They spoke that once again all of the Creator's loved ones would speak the same language, just as they had on the first day of Creation. They spoke that all the water of the creeks, rivers, and lakes had been purified. They said that the ocean had been cleansed and that all our brothers and sisters that lived in the waters were once again strong. They said that the sky was again blue and that the air we breathe was the breath of the Great Spirit.

They said that all things were sacred and that the great hoop of life had been repaired. The hoop had been closed and was no longer broken. These are the words they spoke. It is time for all the Creator's loved ones to hear. It is time for all the loved ones to live their traditional ways in peace. It is time to respect the Mother Earth so she can give her gifts freely.

This man and this woman faced each other and embraced. As they did so they disappeared into a mist and returned to the Spirit World where they will watch over us and guide us. From the Spirit World they spoke and encouraged everyone to sing, dance and live life in the old ways as they were first taught by the Great Spirit on the first day of the creation time.

The trees stood up first. Then the grass. The four-leggeds, the crawlers, the two-leggeds, and the flyers took to the sky. Joy filled every corner of the Mother Earth. And the Buffalo again grazed on the prairie.

Chont Kin Yah Wakan

Ten Bears

I hardly knew what to do with Ten Bear's visions. Just like the incomprehensible vision he had told me on the way to the airport, his two letters to me in April revealed a complexity of symbols and names that to me were still obscure. There were some strange references to me in there, too. His vision of me being from "a long time ago." It stopped my heart to read that; I reread it over and over. Not me, I thought. Not me, I'm from now. A woman who knows? Knows what? That I was wrong about everything?

And his vision from his Mesa Verde dream. I didn't even read it very carefully—it was so very *strange* and apocalyptic. How could I handle a vision of the apocalypse sweeping the earth clean when I was just trying to figure out what was left of me after having my reality swept clean?

Ten Bears was preparing for the Dance. He was in an ecstatic state, which explained why he was writing these strange letters. I wondered how *he* was managing to work, to be with his wife and daughter, to do his ironing.

I could not write him back immediately after his first letter. I was trying to get on with life; I was hoping every day for the desire to be taken away from me; I wanted to see what would be left of my new spirituality if that strange attraction were stripped away. He had said that all I had to do was ask—when I didn't need it anymore. I wasn't asking, I was *begging* the Great Spirit to remove these feelings. For a month after that meeting, I continued to suffer. I didn't understand that the transformation was not complete; there was more to do.

Scottsdale, Arizona
May 1, 1993
Dear Ten Bears,

Your dream was so big that my mind wasn't large enough to encompass it. It was scary and good; I kept being reminded of the kind of feeling you get in the morning right before you set about a great task: Work to do. Important work. I know that literally the Great Spirit is not going to come out of the Sun and take care of us, removing the mercury and PCPs from the streams and kicking the hate-mongers off talk-radio. We're going to have to do that. Perhaps a vision of interconnectedness, a real belief in the impossibility of separating ourselves from the earth and each other, if given to enough people, might change hope to action. I think your vision is happening right now.

I just heard recently that time is nature's way of making sure that everything doesn't happen all at once.

I've been dreaming a lot about fire. I don't know if it's connected to your vision, or a simple reflection of my state of mind. You know how it is with me now. When you said you would always be with me, you weren't kidding. I can barely chew my food or drive the car; your presence is so constant and overwhelming. Yet I am like a child in a dark room; I know you are there, I reach out and call to you, but I cannot get to you. My spirit, like my mind, is not large enough, or disciplined enough. This little spirit horse is wearing iron shoes.

Don't misunderstand me, I'm not complaining. I am so happy to have had the gift of your real physical presence this last weekend (Well, that's a conundrum. Your "real" presence. I'm not sure you have one. I can't remember from one moment to the next what you look like, because your projection—is that it?—of your soul is so powerful. Ten Bears had no body to love.). It was good. That's all I can say. But very frightening. I feel like a bundle delivered to your door, or should I say, to the door of the Great Spirit. I feel puzzled, even shocked at my behavior. I felt the same kind of self-astonishment after my religious experience that most women have when they wake up with a stranger. What was I doing? I'm not changed, but I can never be the same.

I went to the doctor yesterday because I've had no voice. I have some growths or something on my vocal chords. Voice rest has been prescribed. Silence, in other words. At a time like this, I guess I need it. Did you notice (how could you not?) how I chatter on? More than anything, I wanted to focus on you last weekend, on your preparation for the Dance. There was more I was supposed to ask you, but when I scared myself, it all became about *me*.

You probably don't even know that I have this gift for a special kind of listening. More than the "I hear you saying" crap you get from most therapists. It's just a few linguistic tricks, but they work. On the rare occasions in which I've managed to use this ability, it was like I had slipped as neatly and quietly into that person's worldview as an otter into a night pool. Well, not exactly, but you get the idea. I wish I could give you this. I wish I could give you something.

Love,

Little Horse

It is almost embarrassing to reread this last letter. After the celebratory feeling following my conversion experience had come doubts and guilt. What happens now, I wondered? Do I put on beads and a leather dress and wander off into the desert? Do I become a sweat lodge junkie? If I go off the deep end, will Ten Bears be there to catch me?

I had transformed, but I had no words to describe the experience. Perhaps that is why I lost my voice for several weeks. Where were the words to describe the vertiginous feeling of being everywhere at once? If being at one with the Great Spirit was so great, why did I feel kind of sick, like when you get a new prescription for your glasses? I would be driving into the foothills at sunset and see the sun shining through the clouds, and suddenly see a huge bear, so golden and real that I would shiver and slam on the brakes. Sitting under a lightning blasted pine in Northern Arizona, I looked up to see an eagle—a real one— perched up at the top. Which was fine, until she spoke to me, in my mind: "It's lonely up here, but I can see everything." How do people live normal lives with visions appearing out of nowhere and animals talking to them? I wondered.

I escaped to the desert as often as possible, to try to learn to use my new consciousness in a quiet, safe place. When I was learning to drive, my Dad used to take me out to an enormous parking lot in Forest Park. His words were, "So you won't hurt yourself or anyone else." That's what it felt like, taking my consciousness for a spin on Taliesin Mountain.

Scottsdale, Arizona
May 6, 1993

Ten Bears, My friend,

Taliesin Mountain. I'm under a Palo Verde tree looking out over the green desert below. My arms and hair are speckled with mayflies, medium sized gnats that are swarming today. It's May, it's their right, but they certainly do make noisy, distracting companions. It's only 8:30 in the morning but all the other animals are already taking cover from the desert heat. I'll take cover soon in the little conference room, where I'll have counseling sessions with the apprentices. Mostly I'm here today to be quiet and listen.

My voice will be fine. Some green pills and a week or so of freedom from public speaking (after my lecture in Dearborn tomorrow)! And I think I get the lesson in all of this. I've been talking and talking for years now as if I knew the truth. People have been paying a lot of money to hear me talk. I wasn't using my voice very wisely. I didn't know the truth, only a piece of it.

A mystery is unfolding for me and I have to be quiet to watch. I just want to quiet the noise in my head. Today is the first day I have been able to sit still for a long time. I'm no longer disabled by this new way of being. You know, for a while, I kept applying psychiatric labels to myself: "Obsessional thinking;" "Hysterical conversion disorder;" (that was for the little red mark that keeps appearing on my hip); and "Sociopathic behavior." Actually, I think I'm just fine, and that you and your teachings are becoming firmly and quietly a part of my consciousness.

What a tiny hummingbird! I thought it was a bee but it was a perfect, tiny bird. My love today is a hummingbird. Drink deep. Fly fast, wings beating in stillness. Always there.

Shonkawakan Ketala

It was the time of year when I usually traveled a lot. Classes were out (my goodness, how did I ever grade my finals?), and I had many professional meetings between May Day and the Memorial Day weekend. It was so disconcerting to attend meetings as a new person. A completely different group of people was attractive to me. They were the ones I had previously politely avoided, because in talking about talents they might veer off into "transpersonal" skills, or some other highly speculative topic. They were people who before my conversion had seemed a little too flaky or a little too intense. I realized I might be more like them than like my colleagues back home. With the crumbled sage in my pocket, my tendency to go into a sort of fusion with nature when I set foot out of doors, and my generally heightened sense of the moment, I probably seemed a little strange to my old friends. However, I also noticed that when I shared my sweat lodge experiences with people, the most surprising things happened. Even my most skeptical friends seemed lately to have had experiences that can only be described as mystical. My friend the anesthesiologist had seen a vision of Our Lady of Guadalupe at a particularly devastating moment in her life. Another psychologist I met was writing a book about what she had learned from a near-death experience. And one of the most rigorous researchers I knew—who had spent his life measuring people's cognitive response times using computers—had been having dreams of wolves. I listened, and I learned from all of them.

I heard nothing from Ten Bears in May. I knew he was preparing for the Dance. Yet I felt a deep sense of loss. How were his preparations going? What was he doing?

I thought about his vision, and read his words. How would a dance help bring world peace, I wondered? What is the connection between this Great Dance and the restoration of balance to the world? Did the dance change the dancers in some way that they then profoundly affected those around them, in a sort of ripple effect? Were the dancers somehow tapping into that vast energy source that had jolted me awake during my transformation? By now I understood that neither Ten Bears nor anyone else could answer these questions with words. I did not write or phone him to interrogate him. There were other ways for me to understand the Dance.

I reached out over and over with my spirit, asking for some insight. As the time for the Dance approached, I became more and more agitated. I knew from what I had read that Ten Bears' breasts would be pierced with bones or sharpened sticks. I knew that his flesh then might be attached by long leather strings to a center pole. He would dance for at least twenty-four hours, and the pierced and tethered flesh would be likely to tear. Throughout the dance, he would stare at the sun, and blow on a bone whistle as he danced. How will he do that? I wondered. How will he stand the pain? How will he dance so long? The whole process seemed both gruesome and exalted.

I thought it had nothing to do with me—that it was his thing. And that is precisely why I could not connect with my friend, his visions, or the Dance.

About a week before the Great Dance I was rereading his vision when the light began to dawn. I think it finally hit me that this was not a weekend pow-wow with a little self-mutilation thrown in. *It was a serious attempt to change the course of human and natural events.* Ten Bears and the other dancers were harnessing the power of their own sense of connection to create a new consciousness on the part of others. He really meant what he said. I realized that Ten Bears was dancing for the *world*, that is, *me* and everyone and everything I loved. And paradoxically, when I realized the enormity, the sanctity of what he was going to attempt, I saw Ten Bears for what he was. Suddenly I knew he was not some mysterious being with supernatural powers. He was *just a guy*, a man who had accepted the gift of oneness with the Mystery, and wanted to give something in return. He was a person like me, who had decided to do this very courageous and painful thing because he believed with all his being that it might help make the future better. People had done crazier things to show that their hearts were bursting with love for the world. I thanked the Great Spirit for this insight, and went to sleep.

I woke up in the middle of the night in my hotel room in Iowa City with a vivid command in my mind:

TELL HIM THE MILK WISDOM

There it was again! What did it mean? What was the milk wisdom? What did it have to do with me?

Then came a sweet image into my mind of my little girl nursing, over two years ago. Was this it? Was this something I had to teach him that he didn't know? I thought about it. I had somehow been told that Ten Bears was to dance with an understanding of a woman's spirit; that he needed to be balanced to participate in the dance. Perhaps I was supposed to share something about the feminine spirit, that way of living. But why me? I was probably the least feminine woman he knew. I found myself reaching deeply into myself, asking myself, what is the essence of this illusive construct, femininity, and where is it in me?

Femininity was not to be found in my childhood memories, because I had rejected all things girlish when I was very young. I saw even then the connection between girlish behavior and powerlessness. Femininity was not part of my physical self-concept. I had had to work *hard* to attract men, with a spell of words, not with the simple gestures and glances prettier women were able to get by with. It was not in my communication style, because I had never learned the self-effacing lilt at the ends of my sentences so critical to feminine speech. I had associated femininity with weakness and dependence until I was almost thirty years old. It was then, the year that I gave birth to my first child, that I discovered one aspect of being a woman which required a powerful, loving strength: breast feeding.

It was my experience of nursing, more than anything else, that had taught me what it was to be feminine. Unlike seduction, or sex, or even the brief, gutsy work of childbirth, nursing was one long, intense exercise of one's female capacities. It was connection without capture or captivity. Perhaps men didn't know about this. Maybe Ten Bears needed to know about that special connection, and this was something I could give him, as he went into his Dance.

I remembered that Ten Bears had once said that women, in having a "moon cycle" already had a means of purifying themselves, which men were imitating, or re-enacting when they entered the sweat lodge. As a woman's womb purifies itself each month, so the sweat lodge washes the inhabitants clean. Perhaps, I thought, women also have an equivalent of this Great Dance that Ten Bears was about to do. He had said that the dance was a way of sacrifice, and that the pain that he would endure when his breasts were pierced would be a joyous pain.

Breastfeeding, I thought, is a joyous pain, and a woman's sacrifice to the future of our kind.

So I rose up, went to my notepad and began writing. I wrote about what it was to be a nursing mother. I wrote till dawn, and then hurried the letter down to the front desk so that it would go out with the morning mail. For the first time in many months, I felt at peace.

A few days later, while Ten Bears danced the Great Dance somewhere on the prairie, I went to camp to do my work with fellow professors at the Wakonse Conference. During a quiet moment, I stood alone in the great bowl of Vesper Dune under the roiling clouds, and wished Ten Bears well in his Dance. I hoped that the rain now beginning to wet my face would refresh him, too. In my mind's eye, I saw him dancing, and I said words of encouragement to him.

I thought about all that Ten Bears and I had done and said that year. I realized that the desire I had felt for him had not been a burden but a beautiful gift. My desire for him had renewed my body, which now felt sensuous, vigorous and strong. It had un-locked my intuitive skills and freed up a whole new intelligence within me. And it had been the vehicle that had transported me into my new spiritual life. Yet for weeks, I had been praying to the Great Spirit to take it away as if it were a *disease*.

Not only had I been saying the wrong things, I had been praying the wrong way. Being inexperienced at prayer, and having only a Judeo-Christian model, I had thought that prayer was supplication. I realized that when I prayed in this begging way, I was creating a false separation between the Mystery and myself. There was no need abase myself, to beg and plead. There was no superior entity separate from me to plead with. I was part of the Great Mystery, and the power to return my desire to the Great Spirit had always been mine.

So I raised my hands up to the Great Spirit and said, "It's all right now. Thank you. Take it back." A few seconds later, the strange desire, the mysterious fire that had burned the lining of my mind for so long, was gone.

Iowa City, Iowa
May 25, 1993
Dear Ten Bears,

I wrote this for you to take to the Dance. This is the milk wisdom.

GALA SOPHIA

First there was seawater, salt and life bearing, gently washing through the cells of those early moving things, our ancestors. Then the seawater was blood, enclosed now, encased in bodies that moved on land and saw with eyes. And, then just a short time ago, maybe eighty million years ago, there was milk, at first seeping through marsupial pouches and then swelling through teats, coursing through breasts.

Until the very last few moments in the woman's body, it is just blood, blood like a man's. Blood enters the woman's breast and trickles through passageways and tiny vessels. Along each passage, at each turn, something is removed or added. The red-blue fades as iron is removed—the baby doesn't need that much iron, it would stop her up. A yellow tone appears as the rich globes of lipids—butter really—are added, to fatten her up. Then microscopic pebbles of calcium, powder of limestone, the rock that makes bones, are added until red turns white. And in the mix is medicine, because the history of every illness ever suffered by this body is contained in the antibodies that now push forward into the liquid stream. The rubella you had at seven; the strep throat you had at nine; the cold last January—it is all there, now in a draught that will protect the baby from all of those diseases. In every drop of milk, there is good medicine. So blood becomes milk and pours forth.

You wake and the first thing you are aware of is that you are torn. "I had a baby," you say. But she has slept all the time the last few days. And you have slept, feeling the exquisite pleasure of sleeping on your stomach after months of sleeping on your back, your side. Now you are suddenly aware of your breasts. Your breasts! You tilt your head down to gaze at them. They are enormous! And they are tight, taut, even the aureoles bursting tight, with the nipples just peeking out of the puffy mounds that have formed around them. You lift yourself up little more, and feel the wet sheet, the stickiness below your breast. A smell, unmistakable: sweet, light, and grassy. Your milk has come in!

Your baby wakes and cries her first milk-cry. Loud now, and bleating. It's time. You lift her and hobble back to your bed. You make a nest of pillows. You support your right arm. You hold her tiny body to yours. Her head is so small and your breast is so large! How will she manage? Her head is rooting, pushing against your breast, her first search. It is all very awkward. You try gently pushing the nipple into her mouth, but her tiny wet mouth misses. Her mouth is already working a little, and she cries in frustration. You try again, this time squeezing your whole aureole and nipple, elongating, tilting. And she's got it. Oww. And it *hurts*. It hurts. She does not "suckle". She bites. This is how babies feed. Her jaw—amazing its strength!—presses her hard gums together, pushing the nipple of your breast to the roof of her mouth.

Over and over, she clamps, bites, and the pain is remarkable to you. You look at her sweet face and soft hair. Relax, you say to yourself. Relax, and the milk will come. You take a deep breath (biting, biting, clamping, biting) and you whisper, "Here is your milk, take my milk." And then, whoosh, a feeling both water and electric as the milk flushes through. And this, too, hurts. An invisible tendril reaches clear down to your womb. It cramps (ouch) and shrinks. Your womb is knitting up; in a few days it will change from an empty sack to a tiny, hard, pear-size organ again. Your milk, your prolactin, tells it to shrink. You are riding along with the pain, enclosed by it. You can take it. You look at her, working furiously, nursing hard. To change breasts, you must break the fierce suction of her mouth with your finger. Now support the other arm. Guide her mouth, press your nipple—there! Bite! Oh! You laugh, the pain is so bad.

She makes soft sounds, a sigh after each gulp of milk. She is ecstatic, her eyelids twitching, little arms and legs tense with the pleasure of her own survival. Then, as suddenly as she began, she stops. She is asleep, tiny mouth open, rapid breaths so light they couldn't move the down off a dandelion seedling.

In just a few hours, it's time again. She cries, you wake. You're wet and sticky again, and huge. Your nipples feel sunburned, touchy. You lift her, position her, place her—oh, the pain is worse now, the nipple was already tender from the last feeding. Now it sears. My baby, you say. My baby. Have some milk, sweetie. The milk flows, you hurt, you sing softly, love sounds.

She is even surer of herself now. How quickly she learns! She finds your other breast, and begins again. She nurses and nurses. She does not want to stop; but the pain is quite bad, so you take her away, finger to her lips, gently. She cries a tearing, enraged cry. Oops. Maybe a little more. Back to the breast, and she drinks for a long while before she sleeps. You have been nursing thirty minutes. Your breasts are flaccid and empty.

Two hours later, she wants milk again. Your breasts are full again! They drip as you raise up, and you are seized by a thirst so bitter and intense that you must let her cry while you gulp down one glass, two glasses of water. Then you lift her, press, squeeze, position—and she bites down while you jump in pain. You laugh softly and re-position. "I think we can do this, Baby," you say. "Could you just go a little softer?" She doesn't hear you—she must have her milk. This time it's forty-five minutes. Your nipples throb long after you have laid her in her cradle.

This happens time after time until you lose track of time. You and she exist in a bubble of ecstasy and pain, gentleness and hurt and love. Day and night mean little, but when you look out the window, over your baby's bobbing head at night, you see a light in a neighbor's window. You imagine that it is another mother in the night, nursing her baby. You feel a connection to her. The two of you give life, and suffer, and surrender.

Your breasts are a little cracked by now, and one night one of your breasts mixes blood with milk. You rock in pain, hoping that healing will come soon. A voice says to you, this milk can heal you, too. You squeeze a little of the white warm liquid and rub it into your sore nipple. Immediately, it feels cooler, less inflamed. You do this each time, through the night. The anti-inflammatories and the antibiotics in the milk begin to work for you, too.

For weeks you have walked about your room bare breasted, unable to wear anything against your sore nipples. Now you are seized with the urge to go outside, just like this into the sun. And so you leave the soft, animal smelling cocoon of your bed, and you find the sun. In an open window, or in an enclosed yard, you find a place to expose your bare breasts to the healing light. You do this every day.

One day you wake up to another transformation. Your breasts are no longer swollen; they are exactly the right size, holding just enough milk for each feeding. More important, the aureoles are polished and the nipples are leathery and pliable. Now the baby doesn't need to bite and bite to start the flow. Instead, the milk rushes forward at the touch of her pink lips, and stops precisely as she pulls away.

You and your baby are now perfect together. The pain is gone. You delight in the rush of milk, her sighing gulps. You giggle together, and nuzzle; you both enjoy these quiet, joyous moments. Where is the poetry to glorify this miracle? you wonder. Why are there no songs to celebrate this precious union of perfect love? Your baby fills out; her ruddy, wrinkled skin becomes pearly, sleek, and smooth. For the four months, your milk surges, the baby drinks, the baby grows.

One day you will have to give her food that has not been processed through you. That is the way of things. Before you give her the first spoonful of pabulum, you say, "Every cell of her I made." Now she will take in the world.

And another day, you know that it is the end. She doesn't toddle to you anymore, urgently demanding, with new syllables, her milk. At night she likes the comfort, but she dawdles between sips. On that day that you give her your breast for the last time, you feel nostalgic and puzzled: how did this moment arrive? She doesn't care about last things, though. She has her life ahead of her. So, for the last time—her eyes wandering to the blowing curtains, her lips stopping to smile—for the last time, water becomes blood, your blood becomes milk, your milk becomes her, and she becomes the future.

Dance well, my friend, dance with this milk wisdom.

Love,

Barbara

Not long after the Dance, I received in the mail a beautifully wrapped box; in it was a horse effigy dancing stick, brown stained wood with a horsehair mane and tail. Chuck, Sam, and Grace gathered round as I unwrapped it, admiring it. Above our mantle, we have a large picture of a horse effigy dancing stick that we have had since 1977. "It looks like that," said Grace, pointing to the picture. Soon after that came this letter, with Ten Bears' account of the Great Dance, and the vision he was given.

Champaign, Illinois
June 15, 1993

Shonkawakan Ketala,

It has been a couple of weeks since the Dance. I am still recovering from the effort. What an honor to be asked to participate. I want to thank you for your support and all the wonderful things you have done for me. Your letter arrived just before I left for the Dance. I took it with me, and opened it at a stopping place in the woods. I leaned against a tree and read your vision. In the cool shade, I read and understood the gift of your wisdom. Serenity embraced me. With quiet reflection and subdued excitement I send you this account of the Dance. As you know, you were there in Spirit.

You haven't met Stumbling Deer. He is a good friend of mine. Years ago he sought a vision at Bear Butte. In his vision the Spirits told him to lead the people in the Dance. He was told to create the Ceremony so the Ancient Ways could be celebrated in a time when many changes are happening worldwide. The Ancient Ways are medicine ways. They heal . . . They are sacred. They are good.

I remember long ago in the Mesa Verde country when I sought the second Vision of my life. In that vision a council of Medicine Women told me of the Dance. They said I should pierce my chest for the people. They said to pray for the healing of differences among people and to heal the Earth Mother. They said I would face my Father the Sun and many people of many different traditions will do similar ceremonies all over the world to create world peace. It was then Stumbling Deer called.

He invited me to join his Vision and Dance. He said he would be honored if I would dance. I recalled my vision of many months earlier with the Medicine Women and agreed to consider dancing. I prayed and fasted for many days. My prayers were answered by the Council of Women. They said this was the dance they told me about long ago. They said it was time. They advised me to prepare for the endurance by keeping my spirit and heart clear. They instructed me to lose my winter fat. They encouraged me to stay pure in thought, intention and behavior. To be gentle. They said in unison, "dance." So I agreed to Dance.

The days before the Dance are filled with preparation work. Trees for the dance circle need to be blessed in the traditional ways and made ready for the Medicine Circle. Each dancer makes prayer ties. Drummers practice the sacred songs. Gifts for the give away had to be made or acquired. Food for the feast at the end of the ceremony is prepared. A Sweat Lodge needed to be built.

The Ceremony begins on the evening before the dancing starts with a Sweat Lodge ceremony for the dancers and their sponsors. Stumbling Deer called us to the lodge. I sat in the South. South on the Medicine Wheel represents the summer time and youth. Sweet grass is the sacred herb, Wolf is the totem, healing and guardianship are the guides, red is the color, and water is the element.

Coincidence makes sense to me. In your letter to me you spoke of water being the first blood of life. You revealed to me your knowledge about being a woman. So there I was in the Sweat Lodge, in the South, the element is Water, the first blood of life. It just happened.

The Creator stone was brought into the Sweat Lodge at Stumbling Deer's request. It glowed crimson and prepared us for purification by the first blood of life. As other stones were brought into the lodge, the heat began to rise. My mind drifted to the many lodges I had led in the past. I was reminded of the courage needed to trust the lodge leader and the Spirit people. If I did, all would be well. The lodge is the womb of the Mother Earth and she will protect us. Some began to sing their songs. Some sighed at the heat. Some began to cry.

Stumbling Deer called for the door to close and darkness embraced the lodge. He told of his Vision and prayed the dancers had the courage and endurance to complete the ceremony. Stumbling Deer prayed for the sponsors and gave thanks for their willingness to support the dancers. Water was poured on the stones and the steam went to its task of purifying the lodge and the people in it. Songs were sung and more water was poured on the stones. Stumbling Deer called for the door to be opened and the first round of four ended. The cool night air rushed into the lodge bringing relief.

The second round began. More hot rocks were brought in to the lodge. Songs were sung and water put on the stones to again raise the purifying steam. The lodge leader, dancers, and sponsors speak more prayers. I closed my eyes, held my head against my knees, to endure the heat.

I opened my eyes and a soft blue light illuminated the darkness of the lodge. The purification process was working. I could see my friends, new and old. The Spirit was treating them well. Stumbling Deer called for each of the dancers to speak prayers for others to hear. I prayed for peace and healing of the Mother Earth and thanked the Spirits for their lessons and gifts of courage. The door was opened and the second round ended.

More rocks were brought in for the third round. My friend Red Crow asked to join us and we welcomed his good medicine into the lodge. Stumbling Deer asked for his Medicine Pipe, lit it, and passed it around. Stumbling Deer poured water on the stones, the purifying heat returned. We sang more songs. The hotter it got the louder we sang. The heat and steam stole my voice and I could not sing anymore. I hid my face in my arms and prayed. When I thought I could endure no more, Stumbling Deer called for the door to open.

Rocks were brought in for the fourth and final round. Again the steam heated the lodge. We sang good heart songs and prayed for a good dance. As quickly as it began, the fourth round of the Sweat Lodge ended. The Dance would begin at dawn. My strength and courage were back. I was pure in body, mind and soul, ready to dance.

Sleeping after the Sweat Lodge was all but impossible. The wind blew through the camp and treetops. The rustling of the leaves sounded like gentle rain. A whippoorwill called to our spirits all the night long. She stopped only when the Night Hawk whistled its distinctive song. Four Coyotes came to the camp and played outside our lodge, curiously sniffing and nudging the side of the tent. I called out to them and they left with what sounded like glee. The Trickster is always a good sign to keep you on your toes and wits about you.

Somehow the dreamtime prevailed but allowed me little rest. My dreams were filled with images of friends and relatives who had passed on to the Spirit World. All the while in the background of my mind I could hear someone calling my name. "Moh toto Nahqui, Moh toto Nahqui." The words were spoken over and over, beckoning me to come.

Just before dawn I awoke to make last preparations to dance. I painted my face with a white line across my nose and cheeks. I put on my breechcloth and stepped into my skirt, made especially for this dance. I put on my right wrist a spirit bracelet made especially for me to protect me from bad medicine. A headdress made of sage and red cloth. Around my neck I wore the medicine bundle that Shonkawakan Ketala had made for me. I was ready to dance except for one last step. The Eagle pierced my chest. At once I felt full of light and energy, a part of everything, embraced by a Great Mystery.

At dawn the dancers and sponsors gathered at the North of the Medicine Circle. Stumbling Deer shared his Pipe with us and he gave us whistles to blow whenever we needed energy or courage to continue dancing. He gave us feathers for our hair. One red, one black, one yellow, one white. They represent the colors of the four directions and the colors of the four great nations of people.

When the drummers were ready, Stumbling Deer lead us to the East side of the circle. There we all faced toward the rising Father Sun. He asked us to blow our whistles as he sang melodic songs from his Vision. When he was done we moved to our places on the Medicine Wheel.

The sun was breaking when the dancing began. The sky was cloudy and some stars could still be seen. It was cool. It made the skin shiver. I was in the western part of the Medicine Wheel and would face directly into the sun as it lighted the day.

The dancing started slowly. All of us, especially me, wanted to pace our-selves. I knew it would be a long journey. I had not slept well for two days, and now I would dance until the next dawn. I began to question my wisdom. What was I doing? Why had I pledged to do this? What could I gain? Do I have the endurance? Am I too old for this? What will I see? I redirected my self-centered thoughts to focus on the pledge, the center tree, and the center of the universe, the dance. Too soon I would have the answers to my questions.

The sun rose high above the trees and warmed the dance circle. It became hot and sweat poured from my body. I was becoming very tired. Stumbling Deer called for a break. The drumming stopped. My sponsor Blue Otter offered me water. Such a sweet taste. I gave thanks for the thought of it. It brought my strength back to me. Renewed, the dancing began again.

As the day went on thunderclouds came across the sky from the west. The Thunder Beings came to guide us, encourage us, and bless our cer-emony. At first they came gently. Then the wind picked up and it started to rain off and on.

As the Dance continued, I began to notice slight changes in my aware-ness. I would look at the center pole, stare at the buffalo skull, and see faces of ancient people, of departed friends and family. They spoke to me of the future, preparing me for changes in my life and the transitions of those close to me, loved ones, into the Spirit World. It was emotional, I was getting tired and dancing was wearing on me. Thoughts of quitting entered my mind. I would shake them off and they would come back. Thunder rolled in the distance. A big storm was coming.

Then rain came in earnest, a torrential down pour. Straight down, right out of the sky. The first blood of life came to cleanse us. It was actually quite fun, dancing with the Thunder Spirits. It revived us. I looked straight up into the sky and opened my mouth to drink the nourishment of the Mother Earth. It tasted so very good, this Thunder water. It gave me strength, purified me, and renewed my strength and commitment.

When the rain let up just a bit, I looked at the fork in the center tree just above the buffalo skull. I saw a rider on a painted black stallion, my long time friend and spirit guide, Iron Knife. The vision flashed in and out of my mind. He was dressed in breechcloth with buckskin leggings, shield and lance. Two eagle feathers hung from his long hair. He shouted, "Moh toto Nahqui, you have returned. Your family waits for you. Hurry! It has been a long time and we wish to have you at our lodge fire soon."

It was getting late in the afternoon and the rain continued relentlessly, the thunder rolled. I stared into the tree. A bright flash of lightning, quick thunder, and I became aware of a Spiritual presence behind me. I knew, without looking it was you, Shonkawakan Ketala. I thanked you for joining me. You said you had come with the rain, the first blood of life, to help renew us and cleanse us. You said the Great Spirit was watching over us and not to worry about the thunder and lightning. You said to ride with Iron Knife and all would be well. Then, as you appeared, you disappeared.

I continued to dance to the pole and back in the traditional way. Lightning flashed just above the Medicine Circle, thunder rolled, and the eagle fell from my chest. All the exhaustion, pain, and hunger from dancing disappeared. Then came the enlightenment. It came gently on the wind as the rain stopped.

Thunder clouds, lightning flashing behind them defining their enormity and shape. That's what I first remember. There were two of us were riding through the tall buffalo grass, hard across the prairie with the wind song. We rode up to the top of a small knoll. Below us we could see in the valley below, the encampment. The Father Sun broke through the rain clouds to light the prairie. Dark clouds on the horizon assured more rain to cleanse the Mother Earth and renew life. The camp was full of joy, laughter, and harmony. The People were celebrating. As we rode closer, horses on loose rein knowing the way, we talked reverently about the old times. We talked of the time when the Earth Mother was strong. Of the time when Eagles flew free in the sky. When the Bull Buffalo roamed across the land as he wished. Of when the wolf howled at night and the fish ran the streams full. Iron Knife took me to the lodge of the holy man Buffalo Thunder.

His lodge was a large with a wide blue band painted around the bottom with stars painted into the background making it appear as a night sky. Iron Knife announced our presence and we were invited to enter the lodge. I was asked to sit across the lodge fire from Buffalo Thunder facing the West. Next to Buffalo Thunder, on his left sat Willow Heart, his wife, friend and confidant. On my left sat a woman named Medicine Swan, behind us was my friend Iron Knife.

Without saying a word Buffalo Thunder quietly loaded his Pipe. When the fire in the bowl was burning he passed it to me, requesting I hold it while he talked. For a long while we sat in silence, reflecting, lost to our thoughts, in the warm comfort of the lodge.

Buffalo Thunder spoke softly, with a gentle tone. "Moh toto Nahqui, it is good that you have come to our lodge. We are grateful. We have missed you and we are happy you are willing to return. It has been many long summers. You bring harmony to our lodge."

"You have many questions," he knowingly read my mind. "Sit quietly and I will do my best to answer them."

"Shonkawakan Ketala will do well. She has chosen to learn the Medicine Way with hard lessons. It is because she has been taught in a way that has no Spirit. It is not a bad way. It just does not teach about Spirit. People taught this way will always get lost. The Creator waits for them. They eventually seek balance and understanding of ways of the Great Mystery. The Great Mystery has much patience and will wait with an open heart for their return." Buffalo Thunder sat quietly as if contemplating his next words.

He chuckled quietly beneath his breath. "Long ago the Council of Women took your heart from you so we could change it, balance it, make it honest and pure. They had a difficult time giving it back to you. Do you remember?"

I recalled the time I was in New Mexico. As I often do, I went into the canyons by myself for several days, packing only a blanket and knife. I was looking over the edge of a Kiva ruin, when suddenly I was grabbed by two hands, pulled over the wall, and thrown to the Kiva floor. I looked up, and towering above me, with hands firmly attached to her hips, was my friend Yellow Eagle.

"They," he continued to laugh respectfully as Willow Heart poked him teasingly, "had a challenge to catch you. You learned well how to make yourself invisible. To be the Coyote, but in the end you were no match for the Spirit world. The Eagle Woman was sent to trap you. Do you remember?" I nodded my head shameful for being caught so easily. He said, "Good," and belly laughed at my shame.

It took some time for Buffalo Thunder to compose himself. He apparently found great humor in the way Yellow Eagle captured me. As quickly as a cloud covers the sun, his mood became serious. He spoke.

"Then you were trapped, but today you are here because you chose to seek our counsel by offering yourself in the Dance. Even now the mark of the Eagle is on your chest."

He reached to his right and picked up a small bundle of paint. He asked that I come closer to him. On the left side of my bare chest, over where the piercing had occurred he went to work with paint. He spoke no words as he worked. When he finished, without comment he motioned me to return to my place on the Medicine Wheel of his lodge.

"On your chest I have painted a Medicine symbol. It is sacred. This symbol represents the balance of the Spirit World. The Spirit World includes everything. The world you call the dreamtime and the world you call reality are one. The center circle has been divided into four equal parts. Red in the east, yellow in the south, black in the west and white in the north. It represents a balance and harmony of the four great nations of people. Around the Circle of Nations is a blue circle that represents the Mother Earth. This is so because, from afar, she is blue. Around the blue circle are the feathers of Eagle. This represents the Father Sky. Together all the symbols are the Great Mystery. The Circle of Life." He fell silent so that we could reflect on the meaning of his words.

"You should continue to live your Vision," he went on to speak. "We have taught you well and you have learned the ways that are as old as the sky and earth. Soon the world will change and there is not much time left to teach all the people. Many of all nations and different traditions, like you, have been sent to open the eyes of the lost ones. World peace, harmony, respect for the Earth Mother and the Father Sky will soon become a part of everybodyís hearts and minds."

"The Sacred Hoop will be closed. It will be closed in many ways and in many traditions. It is important to know healing will happen and the Sacred Hoop will again guide the life of all people." Buffalo Thunder continued to stare across time and space. I tried to speak but could not. He went on in his gentle way, "We have taught you all things are Sacred. We have taught everything is of the Great Mystery and cannot be separated. We have taught you to respect and maintain the differences. And we have taught you to make everyday a good day to die."

"Go and share what you have learned," he gently directed. "These lessons are the only ones that apply to all people. Others have been taught as well. They are working to spread the word. They are all over the Mother Earth and speak in every language, in every nation. Be gentle, it will give you strength. Be patient, it will give you wisdom."

"Bad Medicine is the notion that you are separate from the Creator. The Great Mystery will intervene soon and destroy Bad Medicine and all his warriors. The Great Mystery will do this by purifying the hearts and spirits of all people. All will see that Bad Medicine is weak and has no power. Before his destruction, Bad Medicine will leave behind a trail of sadness. It is for you and others to follow the trail. Help the wounded. Respect the dead. They will live in the lodge of the Great Mystery. Say good prayers for them. They have chosen to live in the Spirit Lodge rather than continue with the ways of Bad Medicine." Buffalo Thunder again fell silent, staring into space as if to retrieve ancient wisdom and the words to speak.

"Moh toto Nahqui," he went on. "You will live a long time. You have chosen to do a lot of hard work. Your life will be prosperous. The Owl of death has threatened you four times and you have survived. The Owl will visit you no more. When it is time for you to walk to the Spirit Lodge, the Great Mystery will come to you in you dreams. It will be as you have wished. You will return to the lodge of Buffalo Thunder."

"Soon it will be time for you to go," Buffalo Thunder said. "We are happy you have chosen to visit us. You have lived with us before. You have always lived with us in your heart. You have never forgotten. We will always be with you. When you wish to return say so in your prayers. Remember to be a gentle person and you will always be protected." He looked into the fire and it grew brighter. "This is the fire of life." Then he blew flames of the fire into my chest. The light around us turned a soft blue. "This is the light of wisdom and truth," he spoke as he blew the light into my forehead.

Buffalo Thunder asked me to smoke the Pipe he handed me earlier. The coal was still hot and the sweet aroma of the knic kinick filled the lodge. As I smoked and prayed, Buffalo Thunder held his arms towards the Sky in the Traditional way. Small stars of blue light fell upon the people in his lodge like snow the size of goose down feathers. Willow Heart, Medicine Swan, Iron Knife, and Buffalo Thunder all embraced me. They laughed and smiled joyously as the stars fell upon us with a loving embrace. Harmony was the way in that lodge. Willow Heart gave me a dance stick for Shonkawakan Ketala. She said it would help her to have courage with her present challenge. She encouraged me to know that Shonkawakan Ketala will soon walk softly. ""Shonkawakan Ketala will overcome her fear of the Spirit World and become balanced, a Medicine Woman will be in the future," she said. "The Medicine People are watching over her and her family."

Buffalo Thunder asked me to look into the Fire of Life and close my eyes.

In the Dance circle, dawn was breaking, the last distant flashes of lightning and the low roll of thunder bid farewell to us with blessings to all. I stood face to the sky in quiet reflection before my Father the Sun. In my hand I held the dance stick given to me by Willow Heart.

All the Sky Spirits were pleased. Dawn brought new energy to the Medicine Circle, the Dancers, the Drummers. All seemed momentarily frozen in time. One last beat of the drum and the Dance ended as it had begun.

The mood of the people was at once, relief, reflection, and excitement. All shared a feast and for the fourth and last time, Stumbling Deer passed his Medicine Pipe. The Circle was complete. The Hoop closed. The Earth renewal ceremony was done. New life began.

With Love to all,

Ten Bears

I have often considered the two visions—my simple story of breastfeeding, his vast vision of a changing world consciousness—and tried to understand how they related to one another. What strange balance was achieved by these events? What was fulfilled? He taught me to know the Great Spirit; I taught him to know a woman's spirit. I wrote about the experience of nourishing; Ten Bears used that experience in his dance; he wrote about the dance; I was nourished. My transformation was completed. I had accepted my connection to the Great Mystery.

I had begun the journey in a state of dissatisfaction and unease. I had had a comfortable life and consistent successes; but when I attained the goals that I had been taught were important and enviable, they did not seem worth celebrating. A person under extreme stress becomes physically accident-prone. I think a person under conditions of extreme worldly success becomes spiritually accident-prone. Some walk up the steps to a church, perhaps to admire a pretty rosette window within, and end up finding peace and new life. Some meet a holy man while touring in India, and their lives are changed forever. I fell into a Sweat Lodge. So dissatisfaction in the ordinary world leads to the accidental incursion into the spirit world—what Ten Bears calls an "intentional accident."

An intentional accident may seem to be an obvious contradiction in terms. However, this is Ten Bears' way of explaining his belief that there are no real accidents, no real coincidences as far as the spirit world is concerned. These accidents are happening all the time; to profit from them it is simply necessary to become intentionally aware of their presence.

People are always giving the advice to "open yourself up to new paradigms," but nobody ever seems to get specific about how to do that. I believe that spiritual accidents happen to people who take the risk to explore a culture and religion different from their own. They can also happen when one is pressing one's physical limits through exercise, dance, and endurance. And now that I have read the works of so many mystical physicists and mathematicians, I believe that these accidents can also happen when one is pushing the boundaries of one's intellectual abilities. All of these experiences break the usual pattern of habits. They also tend to heighten arousal and excite the senses. They prepare the spirit for rebirth and change. For people like me, the Sweat Lodge has all of these conditions: it is an experience of a new culture and religion, a test of one's physical endurance, and a challenge to one's intellect. However, the sweat lodge isn't the only way to metamorphosis. "It's like a school bus," says Ten Bears, "it gets you there. There are other vehicles in other traditions."

There are some people who go from one emotionally charged experience to another, constantly searching for connection to their spirit. From sweat lodge to encounter group to channeling they go, intent on enlightenment. Although it's not my place to judge others' search, I think they're missing the point. You can't catch the Great Spirit by going on a hunt. That is further separating oneself. The Mystery surrounds us. We don't capture it. We take our place in it. We can do our work and go on with our lives. If we find ourselves feeling empty and dissatisfied, then we can push our boundaries with new cultural, physical, or intellectual experiences. Then we can look around to see what accidents are being provided to take us to our next way of being.

After my first exposure to the Great Spirit in the sweat lodge, I was not willing to change my original paradigm for understanding the world. I merely wanted fit this new experience into my familiar worldview. All through the autumn that I was trying, in my letters to Ten Bears, to explain away what had happened, the Spirit World seemed to be deliberately provoking me. My dreams grew more intense and my visions more disturbing. I conceived an inexplicable attachment to Ten Bears, and struggled to fit that relationship into some category I understood—without success. I wish someone had been able to convince me to stop trying so hard to return to the familiar. It just isn't possible to turn back, after the Spirit World has shown itself. When one tries to turn back, by intellectualizing about the spiritual experience, the Spirits will gleefully send dreams and visions; they will bubble up from the unconscious at more and more inconvenient times. If one struggles to translate every dream and coincidence into the most ordinary or mundane terms, then in my experience, the spirit world becomes even more insistent. One sinks into the unconscious in the middle of one's daily routine. Events in one's personal life take a bizarre turn as coincidence piles one upon the other. Old friends surface with surprising tales of similar spiritual experiences. Gifts appear with an image from a dream. Strangers bring messages. Ten Bears had said, "You have recognized that you are one with the Great Spirit. Nothing, not even your own self-indulgence, can change that."

The familiar failed me; so at last, I rejected the familiar.

At the beginning of winter, I decided to call Ten Bears my teacher, and to go where he might guide me. My intention to leave the familiar behind jettisoned me almost immediately into crisis. One January night at camp, Ten Bears showed me, in a single moment, the Great Mystery. The effect of this lesson was too much for me to handle by myself. A new self emerged to help me, my spiritself, Little Horse, who now guided my internal life. In the ordinary world, I found it very difficult to go on with my life. I worried about the effect of this new way of seeing the world on my feelings about my family and my intellectual independence. I raised a spirited resistance to accepting a new worldview. However, there was no one to resist. Ten Bears had never attempted to persuade me to accept his spirituality. He had respected my differences and simply set his ideas out for me to take or leave. Yet, when the familiar failed me, and my crisis deepened, I behaved as if I was being dragged unwillingly into a spiritual life.

How like my own horses I was! Training a horse is always such a pain. Most of them feel like they have to raise objections every inch of the way, from the first touch of the halter on a little one's nose to the final moments of starting and shying before entering the show ring. The best way of training a horse is to never be the one who forces the issue or gives the pain. You just set things up so the horse punishes herself if she struggles. The curb strap tightens; the pressure on her flank increases; everything is miserably uncomfortable until she moves forward, bends, extends—then ah! it's ease and freedom. Once out in the ring, under the spotlights, as horse and rider work in perfectly graceful, gliding movements together, the whole foregoing struggle seems to have been so pointless. Anyone observing the joyousness of a well-trained horse in action can see how her heart has yearned for this gently guided union. In just this way I had struggled, in my argumentative letters. And in just this way, one spring evening, I had finally given way to the ecstasy of oneness I had wanted all along.

I learned, as I suppose a lot of little horses have learned before me, that transformation isn't something you have to fight for: you just have to stop fighting against it. This is how transformation came to me. Like any metamorphosis, it took some time. There was a whole new language to learn and skills to try out. I had a great big new consciousness, more supple and capable than my old one, but at first I didn't know how to use it. Or rather, I didn't know how to be it. What was to happen next was the opportunity to learn to be in my new consciousness. This is the stage of practice and realization.

For me, the practice and realization stage involved prayer, work and loving relationships. When the practice of one's new spirituality is integrated into everyday life, realization occurs, and the ordinary world and the world of the spirit come together. Here is how that happened for me.

My conversion from an atheistic worldview opened me up to many spiritualities and I was eager for epiphanies of all sorts. I had learned the language of dreams. I had transcended the narrow, mournful cynicism that had robbed me of my capacity to feel. Whereas before I had put all my eggs in one basket—that of my intellect—I had found, at forty-two years old, that I also had a spirit and a body that I could count upon for wisdom.

There were new teachers. I found one my own backyard: my horse trainer, Nancy, who sees teaching people to ride as her "ministry on this earth." For her, riding is a vehicle through which people learn the suppression of pride and force in favor of humility and patience and the sacredness of our responsibilities to those in our care. Before the sweat lodge, I could only see

Nancy as the person who taught my horse go on the bit and take the proper lead at a canter; now I see her as the person who carries on my spiritual instruction through the rigorous, sometimes frightening discipline of learning to ride with grace.

There was my friend Sandy, who showed me new ways to access the wisdom of the collective unconscious. And there was my friend Cristina, who continued to challenge me to integrate my new spiritual learning into my own ethnic heritage.

I was no longer an outsider looking into religion; I had come into the house of the Great Spirit. As Cristina suggested, I tried to integrate what I had learned about Native American teachings with my own heritage and with my other deeply held beliefs. Although my spirit was first engaged through Native American spirituality, I knew I was not an Indian, just a transformed white person of German, agnostic heritage who had become connected to the Mystery. I understood well Ten Bears' hesitance to accept the label "Medicine Man." He would say, "Such an honor is given to a medicine person by the community. It is not something that you claim for yourself. That would be boasting and against the gifts of the Great Mystery. If you run into a person that claims they are a Medicine Man or a Medicine Woman, be careful. They are dangerous to you and themselves." I knew that I would be careful to not to allow myself to be called "Medicine Woman." Ten Bears also reminded me often, "There is no special knowledge available to him or me that isn't available to everybody."

After the Dance, the letters between Ten Bears and me became less frequent, taking on a lightness of tone and relating more of the details of daily life. Our relationship developed the elements of every good friendship: mutual respect, delight in one another's company, and just the right amount of irony. I began to help with the sweat lodge ceremonies at Camp and at Taliesin, where Ten Bears came, a few months after his Dance, to teach us how to build a sweat lodge. The frame still stands, beautiful in the moonlight, shadowed by a giant saguaro at the foot of Taliesin Mountain.

I thought that this building of a lodge almost in my own backyard was the end of the story. But it was just beginning.

Summer

All Things are Sacred.

The South brings us an awareness of the magic of life. It is here we learn all things are sacred, animate and inanimate. The earth, the sky, trees, grass, the swimmers, four leggeds, the rocks, the coral, the ocean, all are creations of the Great Spirit and they are sacred. This does not mean that all behavior is sacred. It just means that all things are sacred. With this realization, we can adjust the behavior in our lives, and live accordingly.
—Ten White Bears

THE SHAMAN'S APPRENTICE

I don't know when or if I actually decided to become Ten Bears' apprentice. I had already called him teacher. My spirit had been awakened. We had made an implicit mutual decision and a commitment to one another; I would be his apprentice, and he would be my mentor. He knew much more about what that meant than I did. From my point of view, I was going to learn the shamanic skills, step by step, and then I would apply them to my work. This was not exactly what he had in mind.

Although I would indeed learn the technology of shamanism, the "magic," the greater lesson for me was that the magic emerged from connectedness with the Mystery. All of the wondrous skills of the shaman derived from one powerful idea: that we are not separate from each other, from other living things, or from the earth and the sky around us. When that idea is fully integrated into one's assumptive world, extraordinary feats seem ordinary. For if there is no separation between ourselves and nature, then we should be able to understand how to use the gifts of nature in healing. If there is no separation between ourselves and other people, then the shaman does not do the healing. Rather, he or she just makes the healing possible by establishing the connection. In fact, most shamanic healers, Ten Bears included, deny that they are at the center of the healing process, but rather that they are simply a conduit for the Mystery's power.

Therefore, during this first part of my apprenticeship, the learning of simple skills was always accompanied by the clear message of Summer: You are the Mystery, and the Mystery is You.

CREATING SACRED SPACE

Shamanic practitioners discover and create environments that have powerful therapeutic and transformative qualities. They seek the restorative elements of nature, such as natural sheltering rock formations and water in motion. They make skillful use of natural materials to create settings that are sacred spaces that comfort the person in need with color, warmth, and yielding surfaces or that challenge all the person's senses and physical capacities. They know how to use powerful symbols to evoke emotion and spirit. They see the spiritual qualities of materials.

One of the first lessons of my apprenticeship was instruction in the design of a healing space—in this case, the sweat lodge.

In preparation for the first sweat lodge that we were do together, Ten Bears and I went down to the clearing in order to see what materials would be needed. I gasped when I saw what had happened.

"Someone has messed it up!" I said. The west end of the structure had caved in, and the entire lodge frame had been moved several feet. To me it was if the shining windows of Chartres Cathedral had been knocked out and the steeples leveled. How could anyone vandalize a sweat lodge?

As I worked myself up, we moved closer. Ten Bears pointed to the odd scratches and scrape marks all over the remaining tangle of wood. "Not people. A stag, removing the velvet from his new horns. Showing his stuff."

"What will we do?"

"Build it again!"

I had never attempted to build anything, although I had watched my neighbor and husband struggle to build a sandbox. And to build anything sacred seemed to be difficult. Where did you start?

As it turned out, you started by letting go of the old structure in a sacred way. We broke down the old frame, pole by pole, and made a stack of the wood. "We will burn these on the fire of the new sweat lodge," Ten Bears said.

It made me sad to see the lodge where I had had my first glimpse of the sacred diminished into a bundle of sticks. I stood there bereft. Ten Bears took me by the hand. "Come over here." He led me to the circle, now a bare round patch, where the lodge had stood. He held his hands down over the earth there, as if warming his hands over a small fire. "Put your hands here, like this. Now close your eyes. What do you feel?"

My hands began to tingle the moment they touched the layer of cool air above the lodge's floor. It was as if waves of light, soft electricity were flowing around my fingers. "What is it?" I said in amazement.

"Scientifically? I don't know," he said. "Spiritually, it's the tears that fell here, the prayers said, the songs that were sung. It's a lot of sacred energy, in one small spot. And it will always be here. We will move the sweat lodge to another place in the clearing to give our mother the Earth a rest here. Now let's find a site."

We walked about silently. Ten Bears turned to the four directions, praying silently. I followed him. There was a place where the doorway would face an opening in the dense growth of trees, letting in the morning sunlight. "Here," he said.

The next morning, we woke early and went down to the shop and warehouse to pick up what we would need for the construction: saws, twine, shovels, rakes, canvases, and buckets, and dropped those off at the site. We went down to the Rainbow Ranch riding stable to get the straw for the flooring. "Wait," I said, "Not straw. Too itchy. Too dead. Can we buy a bale of grass hay?" I asked the owner.

So we left with not one but two bales of sweet, summery hay in the back of my Explorer. A few bright wild flowers peeked out from beneath the twine. The horse in me exulted. How wonderful the lodge would smell!

Then we drove to a nearby small town, to a Ben Franklin for long lengths of red, black, yellow, and white ribbon for the standards around the lodge, and for cloth for prayer ties. Once in the fabric section, Ten Bears seemed to lose confidence. He stood there looking confused. He doesn't know a thing about women's culture, I thought, and confidently discussed types and widths of satin and poly ribbon with the attendant. Now we had piles of satin ribbon and bright red cotton in the back seat.

Back at camp, we arranged for a cord of split wood to be delivered to the site by the maintenance people during the day, so that we would have an ample supply of firewood for the fire. At the eating lodge, we placed an order for sandwiches, fruit, granola bars, and salty snacks to be sent down to us as well.

The final ingredient for building the sweat lodge was the labor, so I returned to the cabins to round up the fourth-year students who had asked to be a part of the construction. Eight students climbed into my six-person car, jammed a Nirvana tape into my tape player, and sang along loudly all the way down to the well site. We met two other students sitting with Ten Bears in the front seat of the truck at the site and conversing to the more sober sounds of a Navajo flute tape.

We all gathered in a circle, and Ten Bears brought out his abalone shell, sage, and raven feather fan. He smudged us before be began work with sage smoke to purify us with just a hint of sweet grass, to call in the spirits. We became silent as the sage smoke enfolded us. For several of us, the sage brought immediate memories of our last stay with the Spirit people.

"The first thing we have to do is go out and collect the poles," Ten Bears instructed us. "We need sixteen saplings for the poles. We do this by asking the sapling if it would like to come with us and be a part of the sweat lodge. It's very intentional. We give it a tobacco offering, and tobacco represents communication, so we are going to communicate with the tree. If you don't have tobacco, you can give it a little spit, because that's a part of you. It's a way of giving thanks to the tree for giving its life so we can sustain ours."

And so we spread out in teams of two and three people. We would spy a tree of the right size and shape. One would lay a pinch of tobacco among the trees roots, and then the other would ask. You could hear the murmurs throughout the woods of the questions, and the whispered response of the trees as the wind blew through. Most of the saplings gave themselves up to us. Once in a while a sapling seemed to have no answer, or to even refuse. In that case, the saw's teeth would not bite, no matter how hard we tried. We learned quickly not to try if the tree seemed to say no.

Soon we had a growing pile of leafy branches. You have to strip off all the branches and leaves, said Ten Bears, and demonstrated with his knife, setting aside a pile of leaves and stems. These things will go into the fire, too, he said.

Now you dig a hole in the center of the area you want covered by the sweat lodge, he said, and several of us began to dig. He got in there with the young men who were shoveling and indicated the depth with his shovel—down to here, about eighteen to twenty-four inches deep. This is where the stones will come. This will be the fire pit. It has to be large enough to hold forty-nine stones as big as a grapefruit.

Ten Bears called all twelve of us together. "How many people will there be?" he asked.

"About sixteen." someone responded.

"All right, sit in a circle as if you were sixteen people," he said. "Sit closely. Then what we do is take four of the poles and build the east west arches first. You do that by setting the four poles into the group, making two parallel arches." We did that. He showed us how to lash the poles together with twine, pulling the twine around into a half hitch and pulling tightly.

"You do the same thing from north to south, except now you lay these arches on top of the other arches. Then you go to the southeast with two poles to the northwest, and lay two more arches down, over the others. Then you go from the southwest to the northeast, and lay the arches down. Now you have sixteen poles in the ground," Ten Bears explained.

This was done with much consternation. Some poles would bend; some wouldn't, and had to be replaced. Some people had difficulty learning to tie the twine. There was much laughter and quite a bit of gentle poking of fun. Ten Bears was remarkably patient through the process. I looked at him askance, remembering his long history of designing buildings and constructing ships.

"Is this driving you crazy?" I asked.

"No," he laughed, "you have to be crazy to do this."

Finally, we had a nice a little dome of green saplings. Ten Bears explained. "When you lay these poles down, north to south and east to west, you are creating entry ways into the lodge for the spirit people. Now if you go around the lodge, there are sixteen poles. If you start in the east, you will see that on the left, there is our grandfather of the east and our grandmother on the right. If you go male, female, male, female all around the lodge you will see that as the poles arch over the dome of the lodge, they change from male to female. This is bringing the balance of the universe into the lodge. Our grandmother and our grandfather, the ordinary world and the nonordinary world, the maleness and the femaleness, the yin and the yang, whatever you want to call it. The simplest and the most elusive lesson here is that one cannot exist without the other. They are not opposites. They are complementary. The ordinary world cannot exist without the nonordinary world. No masculine without feminine. No grandmother without grandfather. No up without down. No right without left. No inside without an outside. It is this understanding of wholeness that we seek."

"Now it is time to make the door. We do this with a flexible piece sapling. In the east, we bend it and place it in a small arch between Grandmother and Grandfather. It is tall enough so that you can crawl under it."

"Then we take some more saplings and make hoops of them, four hoops that surround the dome, which fit around the circumference," Ten Bears continued. "They are evenly spaced and get smaller as they go up the dome and represent the four elements. The first ring and lowest to the ground represents earth, then water and air, with fire at the top. There are some legends that say that the red people were there to protect the earth, the yellow people to protect the water, the black people to protect the air, and the white people were keepers of the fire. With our use of petroleum and nuclear weapons, things are out of balance."

Then Ten Bears instructed us to take the dirt from the hole in the center of the lodge, and we made a little hill outside the east opening. After we did this, he put two forked stakes on either side of the mound to hold the medicine pipe. We put four decorated poles in the four directions, planting them firmly and hanging the ribbons from them. Red to the east, yellow to the south, black to the west, and white to the north to represent the four great nations of people.

We put the covers on, leaving a flap for the opening in the east. The covers were canvases salvaged from old tents and tarps, army blankets, and the students' own sleeping bags. A few people got in to check for holes that showed as beams of light, tapping to show where those holes needed to be covered. We wanted it to be completely dark.

Then we unloaded the hay bales and spread the grass out on the inside of the lodge, leaving a space for the center hole and a cleared pathway for the red hot stones to come in. We built the fire pit to the east of the opening.

Now he had us all stand back.

"See," he said, "It's in the shape of a turtle, our Mother the Earth, Turtle Island." And it certainly was. It looked as if a great, friendly brown turtle had crawled into this green space and settled there for the evening.

This was how I learned to build the lodge: every motion deliberate, every action sacred.

PATHWAYS, RITUALS, AND CEREMONIES

Shamans memorize the words, songs, and actions of the ceremonies of their culture, sometimes mastering all of the ceremonies, sometimes specializing in particular ceremonies that are appropriate to his or her skills or personal vision. Shamans also create special prescriptions of behavior—pathways—rituals and ceremonies that mark passages in life, that honor special events, that bring about healing, that prepare people for meeting challenges and struggles, and that facilitate reconciliation. Most shamanic ceremonies are a blend of faithful cultural transmission and idiosyncratic methods.

Because one of the central ceremonies of most Native American spiritualities is the purification ceremony of the sweat, it was this ceremony that Ten Bears concentrated on in my instruction. It was a long time before I understood that he meant me to actually learn the ceremony. I assumed that he just enjoyed my assistance. The first few times we did these lodges together, I acted either as his fire keeper or came into the lodge with him. Being the fire keeper meant, first of all, preparing the students properly for the ceremony. I was the person who helped the young people to understand what they were about to experience, and it was important to help them to a proper attitude. Sometimes they were overly frightened, sometimes nonchalant.

I would gather the students into a group and say, just as he had taught me, "A sweat lodge ceremony is a sacred ceremony of many traditional people. It has been used for thousands of years as a means of prayer, healing, reconciliation, guidance, and preparation for challenge. In this ceremony, a group of people comes together in a small structure where heated rocks are brought in to create intense heat. Rituals and songs are used to give people courage, to give people an opportunity to reflect, to speak truthfully, to discover a sense of community, to heal psychological wounds and relieve illness, and to make commitments to change and transformation. Some people experience the challenge of overcoming fear, some people experience great peace and serenity, some learn new things about themselves, some see visions that change them, and some just have a good time experiencing a culture and spirituality different from their own."

Sometimes students had objections: "I don't like to sweat! I'm claustrophobic! I don't like to take off my clothes! I don't like to disclose a lot of private stuff! I'm not religious!"

I knew it was important to answer all their concerns respectfully. "It is really very hot, and you will sweat, but you will be safe. We will ask that you drink water frequently to prevent dehydration. You may wear whatever you want. Most people are comfortable in a bathing suit or just a towel; it is completely dark inside and your modesty will be protected. It may feel very claustrophobic, but there are strategies that the leader will teach you to overcome those feelings. In addition, you may leave anytime you wish. It is not a test of endurance. You will not be asked to disclose any feelings that you don't want to. It is not an encounter group, and your dignity will be respected. We ask all participants to respect the confidentiality of everything that takes place in the sweat lodge. You do not have to be religious to participate in the sweat lodge ceremony, and there is nothing in the experience that will offend people of other religions. It may deepen your own convictions and values."

"We perform the ceremony with an attitude of respectfulness and in a sacred way. We encourage all participants to understand that they are being given a gift of a ceremony that was kept secret from non-Native Americans for many centuries because of the fear that it would be degraded and abused. We are all responsible to maintain the proper respect for these rituals, and to use what we learn to be better people."

At first, I probably erred on the side of giving them too much information. As a psychotherapist, I was used to the whole process of informed consent, and felt compelled to answer every and any question. Ten Bears respected my need to do this, but he pointed out that the less information people had about what was going to happen to them, the more powerful the experience would be. "Let the Mystery be," he would say.

In the sweat lodge ceremony itself, Ten Bears began asking me to lead particular songs or to tell the stories he generally told during a round. At first, I would think to myself, amidst the haze that befell me whenever in the lodge, that I didn't know the words of a story, or the rhythm of a song. He would ask me to start the song, and I might falter; then he would prod me gently, saying, "You know the words." And indeed, I would know the words, long stories I had only heard once or twice. Songs in particular seemed to emerge out of nowhere, and I loved bursting into song and hearing the almost instantaneous unison of voices around me. Often outside of the lodge I could not remember those distant melodies. Only when I imagined myself within that space could I retrieve what I was searching for.

In addition to learning the traditional ceremonies that Ten Bears had learned from his teachers, such as the care and use of the sacred Pipe, I was also learning to create spontaneous ceremonies to fit the needs of the moment. I learned to encourage a group to make a talking stick with all of their favorite colors and small objects, and to create a talking circle when a group decision needed to be made. With the principle of noninterruption while one person held the stick, discussions became more dignified and respectful. Any decision-making process could become a ceremony. Ten Bears also taught me how to create ceremonies of greeting and parting, of celebration, and of protection.

He once asked a group of us counselors, "How do you begin counseling?" Each of us went around the talking circle saying things like, "I read my notes"; "I think of my client's welfare"; "I promise myself to do my best with this client." Then Ten Bears said, "Not a single one of you mentioned protection. How do you protect yourself?" We fell silent. None of us had thought of protecting ourselves from our own clients. "You see, if you are connecting with these people in the Mystery, then some of their stuff is going to stick to you. If you take away somebody's pain, then who has it?"

And so he showed us how to create our own protection ceremonies, using smudging, prayer, and the donning of cedar beads, the symbol of protection from ghosts.

After this, I became braver about creating my own ceremonies. It was a long time before I did anything other than mimic parts of his rituals. But my confidence was growing in my own strength of creativity, and my own capacity to connect to the Mystery. It was time to learn to connect on my own.

GOING THERE

Shamans learn to travel between the ordinary world and the spirit world at will. They deliberately alter their consciousness in order to be able to enter nonordinary experience. These states of consciousness may be very low arousal states, such as hypnotic trance or dreaming sleep, or very high arousal states, such as ecstatic dance or even self-induced seizures. They may use herbs or drugs to assist them in creating these states, or they may use the characteristics of their own physiology and brain chemistry to travel in this way.

By this time in my apprenticeship, I was beginning to let go of my categories. I had always made a firm distinction between the ordinary world and the world of the unconscious, as I had been taught to do. Making this distinction had reaped me many rewards, and I was really good at it. However, I saw now that if I continued to make this distinction, the spirit world would recede farther and farther from me. This is what science had done. I honored science, and all that it had done to make the world understandable to us. Science had encroached so far in my culture and in my own psyche, however, that the wisdom of the spirit world was less and less accessible. Science creates a position from which one views the world as object, but only that part of the world that can be seen and quantified. To go to the spirit world, one must find what Ten Bears called a "meta-position"—a place beyond positions, a place above positions and points of view, where the spirit world could be seen as well as the ordinary world. The poet Matthew Arnold wrote of the great sea of faith, receding from the shore as science destroyed those beliefs that had seemed so certain. Now I wanted to call back the sea, to allow the tide of the spirit to rise high again over me so that I could plunge in and become one with it. But I didn't know how to do it. I had indeed gone there in the sweat lodge. But it never felt deliberate. It felt like being grabbed by Jaws as I was swimming desperately along, and being plunged down, down, down, my legs in a vise grip and a big piece of me fearing that I would be swallowed.

I had gone there more gently through the eyes of Ten Bears. He would tell me to look into his eyes, and then as if on a guided tour, through his own soul he would navigate me into the Mystery. Much to my frustration, I would go There, get a glimpse, and then be distracted by something worldly—the beauty of his eyes, or an itch under my waistband from a chigger bite. He would just smile and shake his head a little. I had written to him, "The only way to the spirit world I have found is through your eyes." I wanted now to find my own way. But I didn't have a way of calling the sea back, because I didn't realize that I had to begin with calling deep within myself. This is how my friend taught me to go into the Spirit World on my own.

A misty rain fell over the clearing in the woods where we had performed three wonderful sweat lodges that summer. It was my last day at camp, and I would be flying off that afternoon to St. Louis. As we stood looking at the frame, the hemlocks and beeches around us dripping rain upon us, I began to be restive. I didn't want to leave. I didn't want to return home without knowing how to go to that place I called "There." So I asked my teacher a question, thinking carefully how to frame it. "Ten Bears, how do you know when you are in the Spirit World and when you are in the ordinary world? How do you go there?"

"Where do you want your answer?" This was puzzling. Why did it matter where I got my answer? It was beginning to rain fairly hard. "The Outpost Cabin—let's get out of the rain!" It was the only building nearby, and it was a wreck inside, but it had a nice doorstep with a porch roof. I began to trudge in that direction, and turned to see if he was following me. I realized he had taken off running in the opposite direction.

"Hey," I yelled, "You're going the wrong way!" He ignored me. I turned and ran after him. Where on earth was he going? Did he know some other circuitous path to the Outpost Cabin? I knew his tendency to choose deer trails that went nowhere in particular, so I ran to catch up to tell him that there was a much shorter way—down the road and up the hill. But now he was heading up the great, forested sand dune to the north. I hurried, but couldn't catch up. I reached the top of the dune, very much out of breath, my legs fiery from the sudden exertion. I was much heavier then, and was not used to exercise of any kind. I briefly cursed my feminist belief that only oppressed women exercised. He was nowhere in sight, but I heard the branches snapping on the down side of the dune. Taking a gulp of air, I plunged down the steep incline, crashing through the dune cherries. I saw his receding cowboy hat. "Damn it, Ten Bears, I can't keep up, will you please slow down!" I shouted. Now he rushed down the beach a ways, and suddenly cut back up among the bare sand dunes. I followed, this time finding that as I ran two steps forward, I literally fell a step back as the sand gave way. I began placing my feet in his footsteps, now in a rage. I reached the top of the dune and saw that he had doubled back into the forest. Frustrated beyond bearing, I gave one last burst of energy to leap up a shelf and into the forest. I had finally caught up with him. I stood there, dripping with sweat, lungs bursting, and furious. He spun around and stared at me. He placed the palm of his hand against my forehead and said in a strange, deep voice, "NOW GO THERE."

And I went There. I must have gone down like a tree. I went deep into the Spirit World, far below the lowest level of the unconscious mind, below any hypnotic trance I had ever experienced. Oh it was dark down there, and beautiful, and sweet as a summer night. I was floating, disembodied, dreamy, and calm. I saw a dark hill, and creatures swirling about the hill, entering it like serpents and reappearing on its slopes. Then I heard Ten Bears voice. "Little Horse, you are in the Spirit World now. Go and find all of those you love." And suddenly I was on the floor of the cottage where I lived with my family at camp. I saw my daughter Gracie, and then I was Gracie. I was looking at red and blue plastic monkeys lying on the floor around a red plastic barrel. I was trying to hook the monkeys' tails together. I was thinking, "These monkeys are funny."

Swiftly I changed, and I was in and with my son. I/Sam was at the tetherball pole, wrapping the ball around and around above the head of my hapless smaller opponent, a nerdy little boy who looked like he was about to cry. It was raining hard, and I was thinking this wasn't much fun.

Then I was my husband Chuck. I was reading a book about the Holocaust, but the words were becoming nonsensical as I was drifting off to sleep. I felt the glasses sliding down my nose. I heard the rain outside the window. I heard Gracie playing on the floor in the living room and guessed that it would be all right to drop off to sleep. I was vaguely anxious, but the feeling was a constant companion. I woke several times with a start.

Then there was Ten Bears voice again. "How are they?" A love welled up inside me made of sympathy, and understanding, and gratefulness. I began to weep in this other world, for this lost grace, for this beautiful connectedness with those I loved. I would not lose this. I would stay here forever. I went deeper, deeper, and now all voices and images disappeared, and I rested, above and within the stars. Star People, I think I murmured, over and over. Much, much later, I heard Ten Bears calling me. "Little Horse, you must come back." I organized myself enough to shake my head. No. No. I would not come back. I had found my way, and I refused to leave, and perhaps not find my way back. My teacher was persistent, but to no avail. In the end, he had to lift me up and carry me down the dunes. (And it served him right for running me up there in the first place!). He carried me to my car, opened the door on the passenger side and arranged me there. After a while he began calling again, over and over. I began to weep again, because I didn't want to be called back. He must have reached over and gotten a handful of water, because an icy shower hit my face, and I opened my eyes to see him standing in the rain, the water pouring down the brim of his hat, with a concerned look on his face. He smiled. "Did you get your answer?"

I couldn't speak yet. He smiled and said matter of factly, "Yup, you got it." He drove me back, and as he drove he told me that now I could do this anytime I wanted to, without running up and down the dunes. After this descent into the core of being, I learned a new paradigm for learning: direct experience rather than words. Although I could not describe the path, I knew how to get to the destination. I knew how to get THERE.

THE INTERPRETATION OF WORDS AND BEHAVIOR

Shamans interpret the words and behaviors of others in such a way as to give people insight into their character and actions. Shamans may use simple observation of behaviors in the present, as well as observations of their own reactions in order to make interpretations. Shamans seek to diminish the separateness between self and universe and encourage others toward oneness. They argue with people's beliefs of separateness; they engage in experiential challenges to people's belief in separateness and they use all of their other skills to bring others in touch with the Mystery or transcendent being. Interpretations are made to challenge another toward greater understanding and growth.

I had learned the art of interpretation as a psychotherapist in training. We had been taught to make careful diagnoses based on a rational scheme of observing symptoms, assessing patterns of behaviors, and listening to the ways in which patients used language to describe their world. As I spent more time learning the shamanic ways, I found that my own interpretations became more daring. I remembered how significant it was to me when Ten Bears had said, "You like the hunt, but you don't savor the kill." It had changed the way I viewed achievement, and had given me insight into my own tendency to sabotage my own satisfaction. In all of his letters to me, Ten Bears had made interpretations of my behavior and my dreams, giving observations that were both unexpected and yet accurate.

Now I was learning to interpret more than symptomatic behaviors; I was learning to use my intuition to seek out the innermost conflict that drove a person's behaviors. Too often we censor our first impression, or our first effort at capturing the essence of another's pain in words.

It was in this area that I felt most like Ten Bear's colleague. Before a sweat lodge or medicine circle ceremony, he would often ask me to describe what I thought were the major concerns or personality characteristics of the people involved. He trusted my judgments, and often acted on them. If I told him I believed a young woman who had been recently sent home from college for an eating disorder was too fragile to endure the sweat lodge ceremony, he promptly made her a fire keeper—a way of honoring her current struggle as well as giving her a responsibility that could lead to great pride in accomplishment. When I identified a young man as disrespectful of women, then that young man was set up by Ten Bears to display the behavior, and then confronted with his disrespect.

I once urged Ten Bears to watch another young man trying repeatedly to distract his girlfriend's attention from another guy. He followed her around all day badgering her about her faithlessness until her friends surrounded her in a protective grouping and chased him off. Angry and isolated from the other students, he sat against a tree sullenly while the others chatted and worked on building the sweat lodge. Ten Bears walked over, stood over him, and said, "See how your jealousy is robbing you of your power," then spun around and walked away.

Ten Bears taught me to use my powers of intuitive observation by daring me to predict the behavior of strangers based on my gut intuition. He showed me how to quiet myself, how to place myself in that person's place in my imagination, to breathe, and ask for information. Very odd things would creep into my thoughts, and he persuaded me to speak about whatever images or words came to mind when considering another person. We were watching a crowd of tourists one time, and he suddenly asked me about a man and a woman standing on the periphery. "What's going on with them?" he asked.

"Um . . ." I looked, I breathed, I imagined myself in the man's uncomfortable blazer and long wool pants in the summer heat; I imagined myself my hair tied back as tightly and fiercely as the woman's hair; then I entered their relationship.

"Oh! They're mad at each other!"

Ten Bears nodded. "That's right. In just a few moments they'll come this way."

Sure enough, the woman took a deep breath, angrily said something to the man and marched right toward us. The man walked, then ran behind her several paces. She passed us swiftly, indignant chin held high. The man glanced over long enough to snarl, "How the hell do you get out of this place?"

We pointed silently toward the parking lot and broke into laughter.

LEARNING BALANCE

Shamanic practitioners balance physical, emotional, intellectual, and spiritual aspects of their lives in order to achieve inner peace and harmony with the universe around them and to be useful to those whom they serve. They may practice a physical or athletic discipline to maintain the body's health, but never to the point of obsession. They pray, reflect, seek counsel, and even use herbs and drugs to alter mood states and brain chemistry in order to achieve emotional balance. They guard and tend the relationships that have been given to them carefully. They make deliberate and creative use of their sexual energy, expressing or transforming it in such a way as to affirm relationship or focus creative and spiritual activity.

Before my spiritual transformation, I had developed my intellect at the expense of body, heart, and soul. In fact, I was proud of the fact that I was primarily an intellectual, albeit with better social skills than most cognitive people. It seemed to me that the development of both physical and spiritual capacities would somehow impede the growth of my intellect.

The cross-country race across the sand dunes with Ten Bears in order to "go there" had another impact on me besides a spiritual one. I was tired of being slow and heavy. It was at that time that I began exercising and eating vegetarian meals. I had never paid the slightest attention to my body. When I was a teenager, my best friend developed anorexia, before we knew that there was a word for her crazy dieting. I had started a diet with her, and within a month, my mother had put her foot down and said, no more. But my friend kept going, month after month, becoming sick and skeletal. She nearly died before a doctor was able to get her to stop starving herself. That was when I was fourteen.

After that dieting seemed creepy to me, so I always ate whatever I wanted. That summer, the meat dishes at camp were not so great—lots of corn dogs and Sloppy Joe's—so I began visiting the vegetarian table where the food was fresh and tasty. To my surprise, after a month of that food I had lost ten pounds. I thought I would try being a vegetarian for another month, and another ten pounds dropped off effortlessly. After another month and a few more pounds, I leveled off, lighter than I had been since high school and feeling great. I felt so great that I thought it would be fun to try exercising. I thought about it for about eight months. During that time, I walked more and more. On a trip to Australia, my overly solicitous hosts had a habit of filling every hour of my day. I needed to get away on my own. So I told them, for some crazy reason, that I was a runner. And then I had to run, in order to bear out my ill-conceived fib! My first mile down to the end of the Melbourne's St. Kilda pier nearly killed me. However, the habit somehow took hold, and soon I added workouts at the gym.

I remembered my first magical transformation in the lodge and had seen who I was to be. It was almost as if my body had come into harmony with that first vision. The vision had come to me because in the sweat lodge I could no longer separate myself from my body. Ten Bears said that it was necessary for me to realize the woman within and to recognize that woman in myself.

I had noticed that Ten Bears had a tendency to be heavy like a bear in the winter, and to suddenly slim down in the spring. Because I saw him only every few months, the changes were dramatic. He never dieted, he said. He just knew to hibernate in the winter and become active in the summer, and he naturally did the things that made that happen. How different, I thought, it was from what our culture taught us to do with our bodies. I knew people who punished their bodies into shape, doing marathons, triathlons, weight-lifting endurance contests. They were cruel drivers of their bodies, separating themselves not only from the Mystery in order to accomplish their goals, but separating themselves from themselves.

I became much more sensitive to and aware of the drugs that we use so freely—caffeine, alcohol, and nicotine. I had avoided caffeine for a long time, because it made my ulcer hurt, and I became even more careful when I realized how even small amounts had the capacity to alter my mood. Alcohol, I knew, was the great deceiver, the drug that promised magical powers of kinship and ecstasy and left one robbed of all strength. Now even tiny amounts could make me merry, so I stuck with tiny amounts. I wanted to confine nicotine to sacred uses. I began to be interested in the workings of herbs and the origins of helpful medicines, and knew that a lifetime would not be enough to know all there was to learn. However, the deliberateness with which I managed my body's chemistry was something new and exciting for me. In the coming years, I was to learn a great deal more about the interplay of brain chemistry and life events, and the attentiveness that I learned during my apprenticeship to these things would save me from addiction and self-destructiveness much later.

I was seeking balance in other ways, too, and I again emulated my teacher. I knew he prayed in the morning, and I began to do the same, although I was clueless at first how to start. He had taught me that in the spirituality we practiced there was no supplication, no petitioning. In other words, you didn't pray to God for your team to win the big game or for the object of your affections to fall helplessly in love with you. You didn't pray *for* anything. You honored the day, you gave thanks for the blessings of your life, you remembered with love those in your care and those in need, and you rested in the Mystery. So I made up my own morning prayer: I thank you, Great Spirit for the new day. I am thankful for a body free of pain (or if my ulcer hurt that day, I gave thanks for the reminder that I was alive); for family and friends; for work that is real; and for the teacher who brought me to You. It worked for me. As time went by, the words fell away. Another of the lessons about prayer Ten Bears had given me was that if you are the Mystery and the Mystery is you there is no person, no separate entity to address. Instead, one's gratitude is simply offered without address. More and more, I just listened and looked around me, and caught the scent of the new morning. One day I found that I only needed two words: Thank you. And another day, much later, I would become the Thanks, rather than saying it.

Finally, I was struggling a little, and learning a lot, about the management of sexual energy. During the time of my spiritual awakening, I had discovered the powerful relationship between desire and religious experience. This had seemed so incongruous to me. Brought up in a culture that taught that the sexual impulse was the opposite of religious impulse, I was being led by my own spiritual experience to suspect that the two were not opposites, but also allies. Perhaps Eros is always closely connected to spiritual longing. For me, the strange and immense attraction I had felt for Ten Bears had been the vehicle of my transformation. Perhaps no other force could have unhinged my intellect enough to allow me to accept a new paradigm. That initial infatuation had gently passed as the hoop that was my spiritual awakening closed.

During this early part of my apprenticeship, the challenge to me was to manage the natural growth of our friendly attraction to one another in a way as to promote the teaching and learning experience. It is very rare among indigenous people for apprenticeships to involve opposite sex pairings, for obvious reasons. An apprenticeship like ours presented a challenge of which we were both aware. Ten Bears' behavior toward me had always been very respectful of my marriage, and I had been respectful of his. He had taught me to see the flickerings of desire that pass between a man and woman who are in constant close contact as a vehicle of learning that did not require being acted upon.

Perhaps recognizing that attraction, too, can be sacred is an important part of believing that all things given to us by the Great Spirit are sacred. This vast life force, existing in the tension between masculine and feminine, I knew to be the source of creation. I did not want to lose sight of its strength.

In all these ways, I was learning to live more comfortably with the body that was me, to allow body and spirit to be allies, and to lead a more balanced life. Perhaps, in the end, this is one of the greatest tasks for the shamanic healer. Relentless exposure to others' pain can unbalance anybody. And doing spiritual work does not exempt one from all the crises of love, work, and family life. Since my apprenticeship, I have seen medicine people falling down drunk, engaging in foolish relationships, and abusing their souls with self-defeating behaviors. Nevertheless, in those early days of my apprenticeship, Ten Bears often impressed upon me that balance was the ideal I must strive for, and assured me that this balance was attainable for me.

DREAMSEEKING

Shamans use dreams and visions to guide their own behavior and to assist others. They may seek visions in dreams, semi-dreams, or waking reverie. Shamans are skilled in understanding the archetypes and cultural metaphors within visions, and are able to discern many layers of meaning. They interpret other people's visions and dreams in ways that are meaningful and helpful.

From the beginning of our relationship, Ten Bears had interpreted my dreams for me. He taught me to differentiate between ordinary dreams and spirit dreams. Ordinary dreams, he told me, felt ordinary: you were just watching yourself running from something, fighting about something, crying about something. Spirit dreams felt nonordinary. You always came awake, saying, what *was* that?, and knowing that something significant had happened. You nearly always had the intense feeling of being in the dream, not just a watcher. Spirit dreams give you knowledge that had not been available to you before. "Because dreams do not obey the laws of time and space, they can occasionally be prophetic," he said. "Dreams do not predict the future—because what choices would we have? They do, however, indicate where the current pattern is leading, and the place we might hold in that pattern."

It had been an exciting year of learning new skills and new ways of seeing the world. I was looking forward to the second year of my apprenticeship, which would begin in Michigan during our annual summer conference. Once again, there would be almost a month of continuous learning. At least two sweat lodges, several medicine circles, and lots of conversations that ranged from one end of the Star Path to the other.

Chuck and Sam took the Explorer on the long cross-country trip. I had business in Nebraska, so Gracie and I flew to Lincoln and met up with the rest of our family at the home of our dear friends, the Conoleys. I shared the story of my apprenticeship with my Nebraska friends, and they were amazed that I had done these things. Jane read to me from Joseph Campbell, explaining to me how my journey fit the hero's journey. That led to a lot of laughter from both of our families, who didn't quite see me in the role of a hero. We all stayed up late eating apple pie out on the big front porch, the two oak trees on the lawn whispering in the warm breezes and the fireflies bubbling up from the new-mown grass. I went to bed that fragrant summer night safe in the loving embrace of my husband, surrounded by the sounds of our sleeping kids on the floor and the kitchen noises of our friends below. This is what I dreamed that night.

The Lake was frozen, and our Camp friends had been having a good time skating and sitting around the bonfire. I looked up from my conversation to see Ten Bears crossing toward us over a part of the lake I knew to be thin ice. I cried out him, but he had already fallen through. I shouted to the group in alarm, but everyone laughed and said he would be fine—after all, he was a great swimmer. Unable to rouse them, I ran to the side of the lake nearest the place where he had gone under. He surfaced on the far side of the lake, and struggled toward a log where he sat and shivered miserably. I ran to him and placed my big stockmen's coat over his shoulders. I worried that I was too late, and that he would die of the cold. As I tried over and over to get him to speak to me, I eventually woke up from this terrible dream.

It was a bright July morning in Nebraska—how strange that I should dream of winter! I told my dream to Chuck as we drove north, and he could make nothing of it.

The next day upon arrival in Michigan, I learned shocking news from our friends Mark and Jeff. Ten Bears would not be coming to Michigan this summer. Ten Bears' wife had died suddenly, the night before.

Fall

Respect and Maintain the Differences

The West brings us lessons of strength. Here we can learn to respect and maintain the differences with grace and honor. This means to allow all things to be as they have chosen and respect them. If a spirit has chosen to be a woman or a man, then we should allow it to experience the choice to the fullest, without intervention. If a spirit has chosen to be black, white, yellow, or red, so be it. If a spirit has chosen to be a coyote, bear, wolf, eagle, so be it. We can respect the choices made, observe, learn, and become alike if we choose. By being so, we are not burdened with the need to make others like us. We are then only responsible for changing our own lives. If people need help, they will seek those that can help. If you are not sought, you cannot help regardless of your talent and skill.
—Ten White Bears

RESPECTING THE DIFFERENCES

I was thunderstruck by the news, in the true meaning of the word—stopped, stilled, and afraid. The next days were days of confusion and stern revelation. Chuck and I went to the memorial service in his town, leaving Michigan for several days for the trip.

I saw Ten Bears for the first time in his mourning, in a black suit, sitting in folding chair next to his eighteen-year-old daughter, veiled, beautiful, and enfolded alone in her sorrow. I had searched the first row over and over to find the man I knew. But my eyes had passed over him several times, for the man who sat there was shorter and smaller than Ten Bears. When we shared our condolences with him at the reception, his voice was almost inaudible. He did not look at me, but looked down and whispered, "I am between the wind."

The service, combining both Christian and Native American elements, had been beautiful. And the nephews and nieces with whom we sat down to dinner were thoroughbreds, articulate and graceful in their speech, showing a family heritage of careful attentiveness. But, but . . . it was all so ordinary. The Midwestern town, the co-workers in their Sunday suits, the funeral banquet we sat down to . . . where was the richness I had come to expect of every situation involving this man? Here is where I first learned about his conventional life, the quiet life he had led outside of the sweat lodge.

Although I did not know entirely what he meant by being "between the wind," I understood that he would not be teaching me for a long time. A few weeks later, when it was time for our students to have their sweat lodge, I was in a dilemma and did not know what to do. People had begun to turn to me and ask if I might be able to lead the lodge. It seemed unreal, impossible. I could not imagine doing it without him. However, when I telephoned Ten Bears to see how he was doing, he told me that I must lead the sweat lodge. "But I don't even know the Creation story," I said. "I wouldn't know how to begin."

Then, very quietly, he said, "This is how you begin." He began the story. I wrote the words at a furious pace on an envelope.

"Long ago our first Grandfather lived by himself in the Star Nation. One day he reached into the stars and gathered a bunch of them together. He made them into a flute with his hands and he began to play it. He made music for the first time in the Star Nation. As our first Grandfather continued to play music other stars came together and began spinning like a great pinwheel. As Grandfather made music these stars formed themselves into our first Grandmother.

Our first Grandfather and first Grandmother lived happily together in the Star Nation. They had children and gave life to the four great nations of people; the red people, the white people, the yellow people, and the black people. They taught their children in the ways of good living, being balanced, living in harmony, and in all the sacred ways. It was a happy time.

One day our first Grandfather gathered all the family around him. He told them that he was going to leave them and live beyond the star path. The star path is what you know as the Milky Way. Grandfather's family was very upset because they would not see him for a very long time. Grandfather gave his family a gift. He reached into the stars and created a great turtle. He blew into the turtle's nose to give it life. Then he touched the turtle's heart to give it love. And he touched the turtle's head to give it wisdom. Then he put his family on the back of the turtle and told them to live in the sacred ways that had been taught to them. He told the turtle to bring his family to him across the star path. The turtle stuck its head out and then its tail and legs, and began the long slow journey across the Star Nation towards the star path.

Our first Grandmother lived happily with her family on the back of the turtle. The family grew. There were grandchildren and great-grandchildren. They grew into the four great nations of people, as we know them today.

One day our first Grandmother gathered all of her children together and told them that it was time for her to join our first Grandfather across the star path. She reminded them of all the sacred ways they had been taught. She told them to live this way forever and if they did there would always be balance and harmony. She told them that when she went to live with our first Grandfather, they together would become the Great Mystery. She gave her family a great gift. She laid herself down on the back of the turtle and all of the oceans became oceans. The mountains grew, the moon rose in the sky, the rivers and creeks ran, and the wind blew. All of the trees and grass grew on the land, the swimmers came into being, the crawlers came into being, and the four leggeds and flyers came into being. All of creation happened. It was very beautiful and there were no dark corners. This is the story of creation. And this is the story of the Great Mystery."

He finished the story. Very softly and firmly he said, "I cannot do my medicine for a long time," he said. "You must do this work."

I walked about the grounds in tears. How could I do this? I went to stand on the bridge over Stony Creek, not far from the gazebo where we had smoked the Pipe together for the first time. Coming over the bridge was Rosie Holmberg, a warm hearted Ojibwa social worker who had visited and helped us with our diversity workshops. We did not know each other well. I was shy with her, because of her quiet dignity. She was a respected elder in her community and in ours. We talked a while about the kingfishers in the creek, and then she asked me why I was there. I told her that I had been asked to lead the sweat lodge, but that I did not feel ready. I explained that my teacher was in mourning for his wife and could not come. "Well, then, I'll help you," she said. "I know a little ceremony. We can put together our ways."

After the anger I had encountered among some Native Americans about my participation in this spirituality, I was surprised that she would offer to do this. But I should not have been surprised at the workings of the Mystery, and was thankful that she had been sent to walk down this bridge. At dawn the next morning, she met me and the students in the clearing. She smudged us as she taught us a song to Manitou, the Great Spirit. I opened the flap of the lodge for her when it was time to go in and she laughed and said, "No, I have kinda high blood pressure. So you go in and do this, and I will stay out here and help you. You will be fine." And so I did my first sweat lodge. I don't remember much, except that I tried to do exactly what Ten Bears did. I told the stories just as he did, and I sang the songs at about the right times. The students went on talking much longer than they usually did, perhaps because I did not know how to help them complete their words. Or because I had not so much given up my self to the Great Spirit as just mimicked Ten Bear's words and actions when he did so. It is little wonder that my intuition could not work very well. I felt clumsy and illegitimate; but Rosie encouraged me in between every round, and sat with her back to my back on the other side of the canvas, occasionally hinting at a song. I did not perform the sweat lodge; I survived it. And the students seemed to benefit and to feel grateful. When I returned from the lodge, I was quite late, and my husband was angry with me for my inconsiderateness. I was confused and tired, and crept into my bed to rest.

When we returned to Arizona, there was a large insured package waiting at the Post Office. I took it home and opened it in the family room. It was Ten Bears' Pipe, with a note saying that I must keep it for him and use it, because he could not practice his medicine.

I ached for his loss and felt helpless in the face of its enormity. The Pipe made me feel bereft and frightened. It was wrapped in a long buckskin bag, with jingles made of bullet casings swinging from the bottom, and intricate beading over the flap. It smelled exactly like Ten Bears, as if his being was somehow captured like a genie in this bag. The Pipe had too much power for our suburban home and I did not know what to do with it. I wrapped it carefully in red cloth and put it in the back room. I did not open it or use it.

There comes a time in the relationship of the apprentice to the teacher when it is important to learn that the medicine man is first just a man. They are human beings just like the rest of us. The lesson was beginning for me. I had now seen Ten Bears as an ordinary man for the first time. I did not yet believe it. There were to be many other lessons, and three more years would pass before the message got through. This was the first of those lessons.

It was a very difficult time in my life. I had an accident with my horse that left me with an injured shoulder and back. I don't know exactly how it happened. I was trying to make him stand still in the cross tie while I groomed his ears and forelock. He jerked suddenly and reared, and I was pulled along with him as his head flew up. My back hurt so much that I had to sleep on the floor.

My husband became ill again and was very depressed. He was struggling with his own demons, and I tried to help him. All of my energy was taken up in the attempt to bring balance to our family and to go on working. Things went badly at work again, as students sometimes complained of my inattentiveness. My writing suffered, too, as I tried over and over to write a simple chapter. I would work very hard to get ten or twelve pages written, and then somehow accidentally delete all my work from my computer. More frequently, I would simply reread what I had written and see that it was uninspired and poorly constructed. I did not feel like I could do anything well.

Meanwhile, the Pipe sat there. I could not use it. I didn't want to smoke it alone, without my friend. And I didn't know how to use it to make things better. If something so immense and terrible could happen to a good and holy man like Ten Bears, then what horrors were not possible in this world? I wondered when my dreams and visions would return to help me on my way.

I did not realize that I was still being taught, and that third great lesson was beginning to take shape. The lesson of fall, the lesson of respecting and maintaining the differences, was all around me. With Ten Bears deep in his mourning and out of contact with me, I saw that I could reach out to the people around me for friendship and new wisdom. I was learning a new way to be with the people around me. I was making new friends, creating relationships that were deeper and truer than I had been able to create before. I knew my old friends in new ways. And I was allowing the people that I loved the most to be different from me, and deepening our love in the process. All of these relationships would help me through the sadness.

My first new friend had been Sandy. I had never met him before coming to Arizona, but he had been an invisible angel for many years. In the first years of my career, when I got up the courage to do research in the area that truly interested me (rather than what was fashionable), I found very quickly that there were few other psychologists who shared my concerns for gifted and talented people. My colleagues assumed that having already won the genetic and environmental sweepstakes, people with extraordinary intellect needed little help in planning or changing their lives. At that time, most schools had eliminated their programs for gifted children because of the opposition to special tracking. Everywhere brilliant and creative children languished in regular classrooms, nodding off in boredom or devising antisocial schemes to keep themselves stimulated. Far away from the Midwestern university where I searched fruitlessly for support for my plans to help these children, a group of faculty at Johns Hopkins University had taken matters into their own hands and created classes for mathematically and verbally precocious children. Like a monk illuminating manuscripts in a distant Celtic land, I assumed that I was unknown to these other keepers of knowledge. However, one day there appeared on my desk a huge package containing a binder labeled, "Study for Mathematically Precocious Youth." In it was every paper and article I needed to justify my work; clear directions for developing programs for gifted children; and a letter of encouragement from a man named Sanford Cohn. It was a treasure trove; it was a dream come true. There were others who cared about the marginalized children who struggled with their burden of their own genius; and there was one who cared about me.

Five years later, I wrote my book on smart girls, and my publisher sent it out for review. When the book was printed, there on the back cover was a glowing review by none other than Sanford Cohn. He called it "a splendid book." In the next year, I read several other warmly praising reviews of my works so far by this unknown colleague.

Another five years passed, and my husband was being recruited for an administrative position in Arizona. The possibility of us moving was remote, because as a dual career couple, we had decided we would only go where the two of us were equally valued. It was most unlikely that a university would be interested in two psychologists of the same type. In addition, Chuck didn't want to be a dean; he wanted to be a full professor. However, the unlikely occurred. Chuck returned saying there was an associate dean there who was hell-bent on recruiting me for a position at the same level and same salary as the one that he was being courted for. This particular dean had trumpeted throughout the college that we were a very talented couple and that we must be snapped up immediately as a package deal. So, against all odds, two attractive full-professor positions were created, with secondary responsibilities for administering the two counseling programs. When I arrived in Arizona, I found out that the associate dean, the angel that Chuck had not named, was none other than Sandy Cohn.

We did not become friends immediately. He was just too forbidding. Sandy was a large man with red curly hair and a thick beard, and glinting thin-rimmed glasses that gave him an impossibly intellectual visage. He was the quintessential academic psychologist, who spoke in polysyllabic words and convoluted sentences in meetings, intimidating people with a just-about-to-be-pissed-off voice tone. He was doing research in a rather esoteric area of intelligence studies—speed of information processing and chronometrics—and he was known as a pioneer in the use of the new computer technologies with gifted children. There was really nothing about him that I could connect with, except our mutual interest in gifted students. I really didn't understand why he liked my work so much, which had nothing to do with the workings of brains or computers, and everything to do with the dreams, choices, and compromises of bright people. I also heard that he was very ill and had had severe diabetes for years that impaired his mobility and often confined him to bed. What could someone like that have in common with someone like me, so full of nervous energy and action?

So it was two years before we finally found ourselves at the same conference in Iowa. It was the spring of my spiritual transformation, and it was the week of Ten Bears' Sun Dance. I was on my way to Michigan, where I would visit my sacred site. I was wearing my medicine coat, and I had changed in appearance so much that my Iowa friends from two years before did not recognize me. I was in a state of mild religious ecstasy, going in and out of trance-like, fleeting visions. I could barely concentrate upon the proceedings. I found that I wanted to get out of the conference and walk beside the river where I had walked so many times when I lived there. However, I felt strange being with my old friends, who kept responding to me as if I was my old self. Seeing Sandy sitting at a table in a breakout room, I had an overwhelming impulse to invite him for a walk.

"Come with me, Sandy! Let's get out of here! I want to show you the river and the park—they're just beautiful, and everything is so green here!"

He picked up his briefcase, got slowly into his raincoat. He was coming along! We walked through the student union and then across the long bridge to the other side of the river. And as we walked over the old stone bridge, something changed. I looked at him at he walked carefully over the cobbles. Head down in the mist, droplets of moisture in his beard, a bemused smile on his face, he no longer looked very intimidating.

Suddenly I knew that I would tell him who I was. "I want to tell you about an experience I have had," I said. "I've become a spiritual person. I met this medicine man, and I wrote him all this year. And he has changed my life. I am so different to myself that I don't even know how to describe my new self to other people."

He smiled at me and I continued. I told him my whole story, the first sweat lodge, the second, the letters, and my awakening. We walked, he nodded, and I continued to compulsively narrate my story. When I got to this weekend, to the Sun Dance, I stopped.

Almost under his breath Sandy said, "I have shape shifted. I have had a vision. My name is Bee Wolf."

You could have knocked me over with a twig. I stopped and stared at him, and we both laughed. "Yes, I'm a recovering logical positivist, too, and nobody but you knows it."

Sandy went on to tell me his story, which converged and diverged with mine in an interesting braid of narrative. He, too, had been a bright child and soundly rejected by other children. He, too, had come to trust his intellect above all, and to separate his mind from the rest of his being. He, too, had a long string of achievements, followed by a vast hunger. Sandy had suffered through greater challenges than I had: a life-threatening disease that several times had brought him to the brink of death in insulin shock; a terrifying and long case of writer's block. However, his time of illness and break-down had sent him to a Jungian analyst, who had taught him how to search for his true Self in his dreams and his stories of his life. Now he was on a path of learning to live in the moment and to trust in the Universe.

From that moment, standing on the path by the Iowa River, Sandy and I were soul mates. He was not the kind of person I would have sought as a friend before my change, nor was he the kind of person that I could have connected to. I had learned to respect and maintain the differences. By allowing myself to be transparent to a man who I assumed to be very different from me, to take the risk to divulge my secret to one who I thought could not understand, I had learned that we were alike in a most extraordinary way. I had been biased against him because of the way he looked and the mask he had created. I realized that by respecting another's persona and simply being my own self in a giving way, that little miracles happened. Sandy was my guardian angel and I was his. He preferred to think of himself as my Foo Dog, my guardian Wolf spirit. He was all of these things, and more.

During my apprenticeship, Sandy was fascinated by every event. I shared all of it with him. And when Ten Bears went between the wind, Sandy helped me to see that I was still being taught.

Among the old friends that I found a new way to be with was Roseann. I had known her for so long that being with her was like being in my childhood room. The colors of her clothes and her furniture (black and red); the smell of her perfume (expensive, urban); and the feel of her small waist when we hugged were the elements of the whole construct I called Roseann, and that meant to me, best girlfriend. Like me, she had somehow escaped the beer-drenched, baseball-obsessed vortex of our South St. Louis neighborhoods to enter a world of ideas. She had worked in a factory and in various awful businesses in order to put herself through school as an art history major. It was years before she could find work in art galleries that was suitable to her talent for finding, understanding, and educating people about contemporary art. We were like Snow White and Rose Red. She was dark-eyed, pale skinned, dark haired, and I was blonde and blue-eyed and rosy cheeked. She was graceful and deliberate and I was impulsive and enthusiastic. Her attitude toward me was one of absolute acceptance and fierce protectiveness, so that throughout our life adventures, she listened philosophically to my wild schemes and stood ready to combat anyone who might think that I was not serious about achieving them. I felt protective toward her, too. Until she met her husband—she married in her mid-thirties—I believed there would never be a man who could understand her mysteries and love her as I did. But her husband, a funny, brilliant journalist in a baggy gray sweatshirt was her perfect mate. My heart soared that first time I ever heard him say, "Aw, Rosie . . . I love you."

I had a new reason to feel protective of her now, because she drove herself relentlessly, working long hours by day and devoting most of her evenings to her work raising funds for the AIDS Foundation. The AIDS crisis hit the art world at the beginning of her career, and her passionate concern for the dying and the dead led her to become the leader in her city for the fight against this disease. Sometimes she was so weary when she got in at night that she couldn't eat, but sat curled in her red cushions eating a few olives and drinking wine and whispering about the most recent deathbed she had attended.

I thought I knew everything there was to know about my friend Roseann until I began telling her about my new spiritual life. Only then did I learn about the visions she had seen as a young Catholic girl, and the vivid spiritual life she lived now. How could it be that we had discussed everything under the sun except these mysteries? Now a universe of possible connections opened up to us. Of course, she continued to be suspicious of Ten Bears—that was her role, to protect me from men who might hurt me. But because she respected my choices, she continued to encourage me in my development of my new faith, and shared her own with me. It was wonderful to see how once again, we were Snow White and Rose Red: she quietly exploring a personal, mystical life, and I loudly living my new adventure in the spirit. It was how we respected and maintained the differences, and it was how a friendship already rich in love became richer, greater, and stronger.

Over the course of my apprenticeship, there were to be other new friendships formed and old friendships renewed. Sharing my story with others led them to share their stories with me. Then we had a new language for describing our shared reality. We could talk easily of things of the spirit. And we could do ceremony together, to celebrate our relationships.

Perhaps the greatest change in the way I related to other people was in my relationship to my husband. During the year of my awakening, I bore a dangerous combination of heightened spirituality and secretiveness. My eyes shone brightly with the excitement of my new knowledge. I felt alive; yet I also felt a vast sadness.

My spiritual exploration seemed to have alienated me from my husband. What marriage wouldn't suffer when one of the partners has a hidden life? I had made two mistakes in the course of my transformation. The first was my assumption that what was happening to me had no effect on my husband. I had thought that because I had continued throughout the year to be affectionate and careful of my responsibilities to my family, that it had not affected them. When I had first been freed from the eerie attraction that had held me while I wrote the letters, I was able to feel in full measure the real loss of trust and intimacy that had occurred when I failed to share with Chuck all that had happened to me. There are the inevitable evasions and gaps in the long-running conversation that is a relationship, but also a certain, insidious absent-mindedness that comes with a secret so great.

I burned with grief at the loss of that innocent, trusting relationship, but to everyone who met me that summer after my transformation, I believe it looked more like some kind of ecstasy. I was lonely for my companion at the same time that I was filled with the joy of my newly discovered spiritual life. It was like going to the best Party ever given, alone. The strange charisma that I had begun to radiate soon after the last sweat lodge had grown, and I didn't seem to be able to control it. When I asked Ten Bears why this was happening, he shrugged and said, "Well, people are attracted to people who are gaining their balance. Respecting that is part of your growth."

This new interpersonal power actually got in my way, because it sent the wrong message. Men and women were drawn toward me as irrationally as I had been toward Ten Bears, and I didn't handle it as gracefully or wisely as he had. I was surrounded by people who wanted to tell me the secrets of their lives and who were eager to hear my story—but it didn't make me any less lonely for Chuck, to whom I believed I could not tell it.

That was my second mistake: believing that while I was going through all those changes that he was standing still. How silly of me, to believe that the man who introduced me to Walt Whitman's poetry and whose eyes filled, like mine, during Mozart's last clarinet concerto could not understand what had happened to me in the sweat lodge. I expected him to be contemptuous of my "irrationality," sure of his reality, and impervious to change. I was wrong. As we grew further apart, his depression deepened and my inability to help him broke my heart. One day we knew it was time to talk about it.

For many days we hardly ate or slept, and we talked constantly about what had happened to us. There was so much to tell, as if we had been away from one another for a long time. And there was so much hurt, on both of our parts, because we had failed to believe in each other's wisdom and love during our darkest time. I told him about the sweat lodge transformation of my body: yes, yes, he remembered when that had happened. He had seen me walking out of the Shoreham Hotel in Washington, a few days after the sweat lodge, walking toward him in a new way, a way that seemed beautiful to him as he sat and watched from the sidewalk cafe. I told him about the embarrassing, consuming attraction I had felt for Ten Bears for almost a year; and he said, yes, he understood, he knew what it was to feel a crazy desire, and to feel shame about it. Finally, I told him about my conversion, and how painful it was to believe something different than what we had believed together, and to know that I could not go back. But, as it turned out, Chuck had been on his own journey into his soul, his own odyssey to which I had been completely oblivious—but that is his story to tell.

We got back on track, with the help of our friends. One of the friends who helped us was Ten Bears. When I asked him, "What should we do?" he simply replied, "Love each other with reckless abandon." That's what we did. And one day, I looked into the eyes of my husband, my brother, my look-alike, and discovered the possibility of a new marriage, one very different from the one we had first made. So much of our marriage had been made up of subtle and not so subtle attempts to change the other. I was the messy one, he was the clean one, and we were forever criticizing each others' sloppiness or compulsiveness. I was the easygoing one, he was the bad-tempered one, and so I made him feel like a brute while he made me feel like a coward. I wanted him to be more protective, he wanted me to be more self-sufficient. I wanted him to be more emotional; he wanted me to be less. As the truth of the lesson of respecting and maintaining the differences sunk in, I began to realize that I could not change him, that I could only change myself. I even realized that I didn't want to change him. He was my friend, and we would find a way to live together with our differences. He was coming to exactly the same conclusion at this point in his journey. Perhaps every true marriage has this miracle hidden within it, this possibility of a new love between two changed people.

Now we each went down our own paths with even greater enthusiasm. To outsiders, I believe we looked like we had a rather strange arrangement, because our ways diverged immensely. He continued to be known as a firm atheist and a wry and skeptical scholar; I was increasingly known as the wide-open one out on the edge of spirituality and alternative therapies. He pursued his interests in classical Greek and his relationships with his friends at the Malta Center, where he volunteered as a counselor for people with AIDS. He began a new work-out regimen, at a place called, rather improbably, the Warriors. I enjoyed his new enthusiasms, and he was proud of mine, much to the confusion of our colleagues. He kept the totem animals I made him on his desk, and wore the spirit beads I put around his neck when I wanted to protect him from my bad dreams. He came to the sweat lodge site when I needed help hauling wood, and sometimes even acted as a fire keeper, although he never came inside. We both knew that was not his direction. Our greatest common interests continued to be observing the remarkable development of our children, our delight in telling of our travels, and of course, the knowledge we fed to each other lovingly every day.

Many tests lay ahead, but we had been strengthened, and we were ready.

As that year went by, the new friendships I had formed and my renewed marriage supported me in making changes that were long overdue.

Ten Bears came to visit many times that year. How daunting it was at first to have him in our house. I was a little embarrassed for him to see the frequent disarray of two people who were leading hectic lives. However, he was a perfect, gentle guest. He fixed everything in sight—the door latches, the showerheads, the light switches. He made big salads that were ready when we arrived home from work. He held Gracie on his lap and told her stories, and taught Sam how to fix things.

I took Ten Bears for rides out into the desert, and showed him my favorite places: the quartz outcropping high on the ridge, the little canyon where I prayed, and the place where the sage grew in thickets around a wash. Once we sat high up on the mountain, and I forced out the words that I needed to say: that I did not know how to be with him now, and I was so very sorry. And that if I had at any time taken any of his energy away from his relationship with his wife with my constant demands for instruction, that I was so sorry about that too. He comforted me, and mused about how it was quite often necessary for him to comfort his friends who wanted to console him! He explained a little to me about what it meant to be "between the wind"; that it was like grieving, except that it involved being in the Spirit World most of the time.

Chuck and I brought him to our classes with us, and he would speak to our students about his ways of healing. He would perform small feats of medicine that left them surprised and delighted. He would give a young woman tremendous strength by teaching her how to connect with the earth's strength below her feet. Then he would remove the strength from a muscular young man with a wave of his hand and a simple command, later instructing a delicate young woman to push the behemoth over. He would patiently explain how the magic was in the Mystery—in each one of us, and in our capacity to connect—rather than the Mystery being in the magic. It's no mystery at all, he would say.

It's just refusing to be separate from Creation. I noticed that even though he was functioning with such low energy, his medicine power was still there, and still great. Sometimes I think I pushed him to do too much, and he would be very fatigued. How strange it was to see him tired and empty. His silence was not the powerful, waiting quietness that once cloaked him. It was the silence of a man who was stunned. It was an ordinary man's sadness.

Ten Bears would stay in the guest bedroom when he visited, and I hoped for a long time that he would take the Pipe with him when he left. He repeated to me often that it was mine to use, but I knew that I was not ready.

Nevertheless, the Pipe was having its effect. My dreams became much more vivid, and visions came to me to guide me as I helped my friend through his time of sorrow. I had learned to respect and maintain the differences with new friends, old friends, and my family. The greatest challenge was to learn this lesson with Ten Bears. However, because my teacher could not teach me this himself, it seemed as if the Spirit World took up my instruction, for dreams and visions came to me more vividly than ever before. Because the most difficult task of all for me in learning to respect and maintain the differences lay in creating a new relationship with my teacher, the Spirit People came to my assistance. My greatest impulse was to remove his sorrow; but I was to learn that it was not in my power to take away his winter.

I was becoming alarmed about Ten Bears. I knew that he had given away a great deal of his wealth in the traditional way and that he had provided for his daughter so that she would never have to worry financially. Death stalked him; shortly after his wife's death, several of his closest friends passed away. Gary, his good friend and neighbor from when he lived in Kansas, died suddenly of a heart attack leaving his wife and two daughters. Spirit Wind, the man who made flutes for Ten Bears, passed away suddenly as he took a nap. Then, Ten Bears' medicine teacher passed away and his close friend Norma, a medicine woman from South America, died in an automobile accident. And a young man who Ten Bears helped to raise from childhood when his father left the home, died needlessly in a motorcycle accident. When he visited us, I saw that he walked around with the soft step and spoke with the muffled voice of a man who had already decided to leave this world.

I conceived of a number of schemes to interest him in life, such as workshops on our campus and projects at Taliesin. I noticed that his passivity was so extreme that he no longer seemed to have a will of his own, but went pleasantly wherever he was guided and did whatever he was asked to do. "This is not good," I told my husband. "At the very least, someone who is interested in his wealth and protection will take advantage of him. At worst, he will simply neglect his own self-care until he has an accident or becomes seriously ill. He is on the wrong path," I said. I knew that Ten Bears' daughter was probably fighting the same battle to keep him in this world, and sent her my prayers, but I could not alarm her with my fears.

I wanted his friend Jeff's advice on how I might help him. Jeff seemed to know Ten Bears' heart so well; he could humor Ten Bears into taking care of himself, and challenge him to action. With his awful jokes and pranks, maybe he could make him smile again.

I called Jeff up at Miniwanca. Mark answered his phone. "I have bad news," he said. "Jeff became dizzy and lost his balance. A few days ago, he began to have difficulty being coherent. He began speaking a kind of gibberish. We took him to the hospital. Jeff has been diagnosed with a brain tumor. There's not much hope. He can't speak very well, but you can call him at home."

Jeff was at home. I nourished the hope that it was all a mistake, that he would be fine. It was not conceivable to me that another member of Ten Bears' closest circle could be leaving us. And at first he seemed all right; he remembered who I was, he guffawed as he always did, and with an audible leer said, "Kerr, you're up to something . . ." Then, however, he started talking a kind of doublespeak. My heart ached as he struggled to make sense to me. I listened hard for a pattern. The words he kept coming back to were, "Go North! Go North!" North on the Medicine Wheel, to the time of closing the hoop, the time of ending? North to Minnesota, where Ten Bears lived? North to some other winter?

With no one left to consult, I sent up my prayers and asked for guidance. Only a short time after these prayers, I received a visitation.

I saw Her for the first time in a waking vision while crossing a busy street on my way to the office. Horns honked as I scurried to the curb so that I might sit and gaze upon this image that had formed in space right in front of me, and came into focus when I closed my eyes. She was the liveliest, the sweetest, and the most beautiful and loving woman I had ever seen. She was young and small, with shaggy golden hair and laughing blue eyes. She wore a short dress of white doeskin and feathers and a circlet of gold and white feathers around her forehead. In my image, she knelt over a sleeping Ten Bears, with a look of such complete and radiant love that I guessed, in my naive way, that this must be somebody who would be sent to him to care for him and heal him, perhaps a young girlfriend of some kind. How funny, that to my spiritually immature mind, this incandescent Angel—my guiding spirit and the manifestation of the Great Mother of us All—should appear to me as a friendly coed.

She said, "Ten Bears will have the love he needs to get well. Go North and you will see. Go to him with this message." I thought I understood the message, but much later, I learned that my understanding was superficial. I went to the North to his home in Minnesota, to take him the message from the spirit people. I had a new scheme, too. We would edit our letters to one another, and create a little book from them. That might interest him.

I had driven all the way from central Wisconsin, where I had given a speech at the Marshfield Clinic. The last of the winter light had faded from the sky and a deep chill was now rising from the frozen streets as I left my car. His house was a pretty house near a lake in the suburbs of St. Paul. Oh, it was cold. I shivered in my crepe professor dress on his doorstep. He opened the door and there he was, my familiar friend, in his own home. He stood in a pool of yellow light. A warm scent of tobacco, spices, and beeswax reached me. After a warm embrace he led me into his house. My high heels tapped loudly on the floor, like a horse crossing a bridge.

Here was the richness that reflected his soul, in this winter house. Candlelight glittered off of shining clean windowpanes and the reflecting surfaces of polished hardwood floors. Photography of the Southwest showed me familiar canyons and ruins. Most of it was a male home—books on aviation, hearty woolen blankets over the furniture, and lots of clever kitchen technology. One room I sensed instantly was her room: a parlor with Edwardian furniture, tiny bibelots, and a few pretty antique dishes. He had made this little room into a sort of shrine to a graceful, feminine spirit. I could feel a delicate presence there, sweetness in the air. Everything in this house was simple, elegant, and gloriously clean.

I visited Ten Bears in his den many times that winter. Each visit was much the same for the first few months, except for the visions and dreams that coincided with my stay. We would begin with talk and a glass of wine in the kitchen where he cooked wonderful meals, pasta with pesto, or a delectable soup. The small dining table was set perfectly with ceramic goblets and plates he had made himself. He took my hands in his across the table and gave thanks for the food; I whispered along. "Let us give thanks to the Mother Earth for the gifts that nourish us in the heart of a Great Spirit," he would pray. We ate quietly, and then he would spread his medicine blanket by the fire where we talked until late. I would show him things I had written about our experiences and we would read the letters together. Did it happen that way? What did you feel? What was it like for you? When we were too sleepy to continue, he would carry my things to my room upstairs and we would say goodnight.

The first night I was there, I told Ten Bears of what I had seen crossing the street—my vision of the beautiful young woman. "It came to me that she had the name of a bird . . . but I don't know who she is," I said.

Ten Bears stared deeply into my soul. "I know who she is. She is Medicine Swan. She is as much myself on the other side as I am myself on this side. She is more than that, too. And her message is right, Little Horse. I have what I need to be well. Listen to her message carefully. It is for you, not for me." I did not understand what he meant. Surely it was a message of hope for him. I wanted him to have hope. I wanted him to live. If he would not have hope for himself, then somehow I would find a way to give it to him.

Ten Bears went on to bed. I knew I would be up late; I was three time zones removed from my home. So I wandered into his library, poring over his books. A marvelous, eclectic collection of books on all manner of healing; shelves of anthropological and linguistic studies of Native Americans; and to my surprise, on a lower shelf, quite a few of the texts from my own graduate education. I read for a long time, and then looked out the window. It had begun to snow again.

I went back to my room. I slept in a maple bed stacked with Hudson's Bay woolen blankets drawn to military tautness. It was an ordeal just finding my way in. I lay there, listening to the sounds of his breathing down the hall. I thought I heard him groan right before I slept. I fell to dreaming precipitously. I was in a lodge of men I did not know. Ten Bears was there, in the West of the lodge, and he was sitting there in a trance. I was given to understand that he was being made to relive the struggles of his life. He was groaning and crying out, eyes closed. He writhed in misery. The men sat around him silently. I remember a stout, red-haired man; a handsome, wiry man with bright blue eyes; and a dark bearded man. "How can you let him suffer like this?" I asked. I lunged forward, to wake him, to embrace him, and suddenly a man leapt out of the shadows, a huge knife in his hand. He pushed me back, holding the knife to my heart. "You don't belong here. Get out." He shoved me out roughly, and I woke. I lay awake a long time, and many times, I thought I heard sounds of distress from the other room. I was too scared by my nightmare to move. I lay there rubbing my hand over my heart, which hurt where the knifepoint had been, until I fell asleep.

The next morning, I told Ten Bears my dream on the way to the airport. "Yes," he said, "you saw my lodge of men. You saw Thunder Wolf, and Red Crow, and the guy who kicked you out was Iron Knife. He is my protector. And he was right. You didn't belong in there, not even in your dream." I sat there feeling like I always did when told I couldn't join the boys' club. I was frustrated. I had come to help him, and I felt shut out from helping him by people I didn't even know.

On a deeper level, however, I knew that I was receiving an important lesson in respecting and maintaining the differences. Somehow, both Medicine Swan and Iron Knife were giving me the same message: that I could not struggle for him. I needed to respect the process he was going through, and allow him to do it. Allow him to be between the wind. But how could I do this? The only answer I could come up with was to just be with him, to be there. But it didn't seem like enough.

So I contrived more ways to visit him, accepting any lecture engagement that took me up his way, and it seemed as though a great many lecture offers were made to me that spring in Minnesota, Wisconsin, and Michigan.

On my second visit, it was raining an icy rain, and the Mississippi River was iron gray as Ten Bears drove me to his home. But the fire was burning brightly in his house, and our letters were there on the kitchen counter ready for us to read and work through. We had a delicious dinner, and we talked animatedly about our ideas for a book. Around midnight, Ten Bears and I again raided the kitchen and found Dove Bars. With our manuscript between us on the kitchen counter, arguing some point while licking our ice cream bars, we both began to smile. "This is good," Ten Bears said holding up his Dove Bar.

"This is good," I replied.

"Dream well, it will be a long winter night," he quietly remarked.

That night I dreamed that the Horse and the Bear ran together down the beach. I felt my hooves drumming the sand and the glorious wind in my mane and tail. I looked over at my friend, the shaggy brown bear with a great smile on his upturned face, who loped easily beside me. Ah it was good to run together like this! I stretched my nose and galloped even faster. The Bear fell behind as the Horse galloped joyously into the wind. Suddenly the Horse became aware that the Bear was not at her side. I turned and saw that he was down on the ground. Suddenly, he was surrounded by a ferocious rabble of men and women with long knives. Then I saw to my horror that he was being skinned alive! The Horse whinnied to him, and stamped her feet, telling him to GET UP, but he refused. He just lay there passively, allowing them to pull long ribbons of his brown fur from his body. "Go on, Little Horse," he said to me, "Go on without me. Go on without me, and we will meet again." I cried out in frustration and terror, and wheeled again and again back toward him. But the wind called to me, and the Bear was flayed and lay still. I reluctantly ran on, slowly at first and then faster and faster until I woke. The dream made me sad, but in the dream Ten Bears had nodded and simply acknowledged the truth of it. "You cannot follow me where I need to go, Little Horse", he said. "But where are you going?" I asked plaintively. He shook his head.

This time, in the dream, he had told me himself that I could not help. So once again, the message was that I could not help him with his struggle, or save him from conflict, or persuade him to run joyously next to me when it was not yet his time. Again, I tried hard to understand and accept the message. I must find a way to be with him that allowed him to be sad while I was happy; that allowed him to stop time while I rushed along into it; that allowed him to slowly work through his sorrow while I thought I had everything figured out for him. I realized that I really had a pretty small repertoire of roles that I knew how to play with the men in my life, and rescuer was high on the list. I was good at it; I was resourceful, and quick thinking. My supervisors of my psychotherapy training had told me that I was a natural-born helper. The trouble with being a rescuer is that it separates the helper from the helpee; it immediately creates a chasm of differences. I didn't want this, and I knew that an alternative existed, because I had read about it in the writings of the phenomenological and existential philosophers—the I-Thou relationship, a deep empathic bond that allowed for both respect for the uniqueness of each self and the possibility of union.

I wanted to learn; I was ready. I had learned thoroughly the lessons of respecting and maintaining the differences. It was time.

SHARED BEING

It was my fourth visit to Ten Bears' home and once again, it was snowing. After a nice dinner and our usual late night chat, I retired to the guestroom. I had only been asleep a few minutes when I again heard the muffled moans from his room. Worried that he was ill—he had mentioned that he had had some heart problems—I struggled out from under my covers and quietly went down the hall and into his room. He was fast asleep, but moaning haltingly. I tiptoed up to him—his eyelids fluttered, and he sighed and gulped for air.

Like Psyche gazing for the first time upon the sleeping face of the immortal, I felt both curious and fearful. His countenance was like a flickering light. Ten Bears seemed to dwindle, his spirit nearly extinguished by the battle he seemed to fight under a distant sun.

Oh Creator, I murmured, what should I do? I saw again in my mind the icy lake; his shivering form huddled under my great coat. I sat beside him in the rocking chair next to his bed and lay my hand upon his cheek. He did not wake, but he quieted.

The icy snow fell hard on the windowpane. It muted the sound of the wind in the branches just outside the forest that surrounded his home. It fell around the panes of the glass behind us, blowing softly into triangles, which glowed in the light outside. It was so quiet I could hear the flakes accumulate on the windowsill.

Every forty-five minutes, he would begin to make one low, groaning sound and his eyes would begin to move rapidly beneath his lids. I would grasp his hand softly, or lay my hand upon his cheek, his shoulder. His distress would last about fifteen minutes. Ever the psychologist, I noted that he had an aberrant sleep cycle—a long burst of REM sleep followed by a longer deep sleep cycle, repeating every hour. Most people have two four-hour sleep cycles, with a short REM phase during the period of shallow sleep. I considered what this might mean for his adroitness in modifying his consciousness. I considered it in spiritual terms as well.

In his language, he was being drawn down into the Spirit World for what looked like fierce, agonizing struggles, only to somehow drag himself back to the safer shoals of ordinary sleep . . . over and over again. No wonder he seemed so spent, so blank sometimes.

I watched and waited, and the snow fell. I held his hand in the darkness, and he finally slept heavily.

I heard the furnace below switch on and off every few minutes, working hard to hold back the cold. Ten Bears had left a stack of CDs in the stereo in the living room, and I heard the music playing faintly. His skin seemed feverish and he trembled occasionally, but there was no other sign of physical illness. Dawn would be coming soon. Outside, the wind died down. I was so very tired, but I was afraid to fall asleep.

My eyelids became heavy with sleepiness, and I began to lose consciousness. I shifted toward him, still holding his hand and facing him so that I could see if he began to wake. I drifted again, down, down toward the depths of sleep, and then suddenly saw that his eyes were open. Open but not awake. He was looking straight at me, but he was in the Spirit World, just rising toward consciousness as I sank away. So we met there, for a moment joined in precisely the same in-between place, quietly gazing at each other's souls, adrift in the great Ocean. Floating there, I experienced a timeless, serene Oneness. I suppose this experience is the only real glimpse we have of the elusive promise of all faiths: that we might someday join with the souls of those we love and care for in the eternal grace of the Great Mystery.

He had his raven feather dance bustle hanging on the wall, a polished silver concha in the center of it, placed in such a way that the first rays of the sun would strike it. It was beginning to glow with the faint light of a winter dawn. It was time for me to go. I carefully and gradually withdrew, rose, and backed away. I walked softly back to the guestroom, and slept perhaps an hour. Then Ten Bears stood before me smiling and telling me to come to breakfast, pack my bags, and get ready to go to the airport.

This is how it was all through that long and cold winter and into the much-delayed spring. Whenever I heard his moaning, I went to him and sat beside him until the dawn. I thought that he never knew that I joined him at night and sat vigil as he struggled against his darkness. A few times, he entered my room after I had returned to rest, and stood watching me. Once I saw him shake his head and then shamble out, hesitant and bear-like. Somehow, he knew.

So the weeks past, and he labored through his winter. I had arranged—or it seems as if the Universe and Northwest Airlines had arranged—for a stopover in Minnesota every few weeks on my spring lecture tour, just as in winter. As the spring at last came to that northern place, I began to sense a change in him. He moved more quickly than he had before, and he smiled more often. I saw that the bear was moving slowly out of his den, sniffing the air and carefully considering whether he might come forth.

In April, Ten Bears called me, and there was excitement in his voice. "Little Horse, I have been invited to perform the sweat lodge for the Sun Dancers. It will be Memorial Day Weekend. It's a great honor. And I believe that I just might do it. I am thinking of doing my medicine again."

A rush of excitement filled me, happiness about the thought that he might return from his time between the wind.

"Ten Bears, that is wonderful! And I have been invited to perform a sweat lodge for the professors at the Wakonse conference in Michigan the same weekend. Perhaps I could stop through Minnesota afterwards, and we can compare notes!"

A few days before he was to perform the sweat lodge at the Sun Dance, a joyous vision came to me for my friend as I was climbing a mountain near my home. In my vision, the Horse was trotting up a mountain, higher and higher. The terrain changed from desert to chaparral to pines. All the way, I was searching for my friend, the brown bear. I noticed that to my side ran a dingo dog. But I saw no bear. Near the top, great granite boulders formed a cave. I stood square on my hooves outside the den and called, "TEN BEARS COME OUT." Where was my friend, my gentle bear? I waited all night. Just before dawn, a burst of rock fall and a ferocious roar shook the mountaintop. I backed in alarm, eyes wide. From the mouth of the cave emerged an enormous, white bear. It raised itself to its full height and roared a deafening bellow of joy. I looked in its eyes. It was my friend and my teacher, and he had transformed.

Not long after my vision I received this letter from Ten Bears.

Maplewood, Minnesota
May 28, 1996
Dear Little Horse,

So much to do and so little time to do it. A clear and concise message from the Sun Dance and sweat lodge. The fourth world is coming to an end and preparations for the New World are happening deliberately. It is happening all around us. It is going to be wonderful. It will be a time of peace and prosperity for all.

Of course, my arrival to the dance area was accompanied by a good old-fashioned Kansas thunderstorm. It happens every time. People accuse me of bringing the rain.

Lightning, rolling thunder, heavy rain, just what was needed to purify the earth and ready the people for the ceremony. There were 16 dancers this time with 16 sponsors. Stumbling Deer had a sweat lodge for the dancers and sponsors on the evening before the ceremony began. He asked me to be a fire keeper for the two lodge ceremonies along with a fellow named Tim. Encouraging 16 people into each lodge was subtly humorous. The lodge holds about 12 comfortably. "Mushed in" comes to mind. We got them all in and the lodge looked nine months pregnant bulging at the sides, more than ready to give birth.

In the third round of the first lodge an anorexic black woman who calls herself Rainbow emerged for a brief rest. She was hyperventilating and dehydrated. Tim, an EMT, and I together nurtured her back to health. She claimed she had been fasting for 21 days. All she could talk about was man-energy and how much she missed it. She said she had been 9 years since she had been close to a man. She revived quickly and returned to the lodge. Tim and I decided we men must be worth something, but we were not quite sure of what. I am reaffirmed it has to do with interloping. All went well and the ceremony ended with wide-eyed participants quietly emerging from the Mother Earth.

The second lodge went well also. A young man named Vic expressed himself in such a loud vitriolic, angry way that Tim and I thought we might have to go into the lodge and get him out for a bit. We brought really hot rocks for the next round and he calmed down. I think he found his humility for a brief moment. Interestingly, he carried the anger on his back like a packhorse through out the dance until almost the very end. At least it was not inside him.

By the time we cleaned up after two sweat lodges ceremonies and hauled our tired bodies to a place to sleep it was 2 a.m. Considering the late evening the night before, this was getting challenging. I recalled a method of getting the self out of the way. A Medicine person will have the initiate carry a heavy rock back and forth between two points until they are no longer in need of what your call the ego. I thought to myself, "here we go Ten Bears, your rock is sleep deprivation. Get it out of the way. Something is going to happen and you need to be alert." The dance began at dawn, just 2 hours after my falling into fitful sleep with vivid un-recordable flash dreams of my life.

The day was beautiful for dancing, mostly cloudy, cool, with occasional sun. I could see into the spirit of each dancer and each told me her or her own story. Stumbling Deer seemed irritable, vibrating around the centerline of his balance. He was clearly disturbed by some of the behaviors of the dancers. Especially, the young man Vic, who continued to express his anger while he danced. He would dump it off his shoulders and it would jump right back on to him.

Just after noon, I began the process of getting the fire and stones ready for the afternoon sweat lodge Stumbling Deer had asked that I do for the visitors. The fire would only start in the south. When I would bring coals around to the other directions, they simply would snuff out and wait for the south fire to consume all of the wood and stones.

In the early evening all the participants gathered to enter the lodge. Three men, eight women, and myself entered the lodge. Four people were new to the lodge ceremony. At least two of the women were overt lesbians and the others were in various states of change in their personal lives. Some to be married soon, some in-between relationships, others ending the divorce process in addition to one wide-eyed 15-year-old young lady. Everything from, "been there done that," to "this is new for me." It was a broad eclectic group.

I was in all candor, explicit with the group about my recent history before we went into the lodge. I told them about my wife, Wee-zee, and I told them that I had been between the wind for almost two years. I explained the invitation from Stumbling Deer to do this lodge was to me an invitation to come from between the wind, back to this reality. I told them this was the clearest message from several encouragements from this side and the Spirit World that it was time to come from between the wind. I also said, "I would be changing in the lodge. Because of that, if anyone wished not to come in, they were wise to make a good decision." All said they would come into the lodge with me.

And so it goes; four rounds, four stories, four songs, shape shifting, and the four lessons. It made for a good day to die. Your message about the White Bear was affirmed. I was told by the spirit people to add it to my name. So Ten White Bears it is. . . . I became the White Bear.

Emerging from the lodge was the most unique experience. I knew I had changed a lot. I remember looking around; my eyes were sharp and the colors brilliant. I had the feeling of "how ordinary." Is this what I came from between the wind for, the struggling dancers, angry Vic, the horny self-consumed anorexic black woman? Yup, sure enough. All of it: the people, the trees, the sky, the rocks, the creature, and the earth. When I regained composure, I looked at myself. I had changed. So will all of this. Because I am better, it will be better.

The dance went on until dawn through the clear night skies and a bright half moon. Another beautiful Kansas thunderstorm to early in the morning to cleanse the earth, and life begins again.

All that I am,

Ten White Bears

What a joyous meeting we had in the airport after his transformation! I bounded off the plane, the pipe bag jingling at my side. I had just performed a sweat lodge for the professors at the Wakonse Conference, and it had been very, very good. I glowed with pride. I caught sight of him before he spotted me. The crowd swirled around him on the Gold Concourse, where he stood, smiling, radiant, bouncing on the balls of his feet. We laughed and hugged, then trotted down the concourse to his waiting car. We had both been fasting, so we feasted at an Italian restaurant and talked long into the night of our recent experiences.

I woke under those heavy blankets of the guest room bed to a lovely May morning. Ten White Bears called me to breakfast from the bottom of the stairs. I arose sleepily and went to the kitchen. Looking out the sliding glass door, I could see the trees he had planted leafing out and feel the warm breeze through the open screen. On the plate before me were fat strawberries sliced thin, honeydew melon crescents, eggs and bacon and muffins. I sat cross-legged on the chair in a blue-striped nightshirt he had found for me, sleepy-eyed and tangle-haired. We were comfortable as cousins with each other now, and I no longer felt the need for grooming before breakfast. As we ate the sumptuous breakfast, I spoke about my dreams. He listened quietly as he ate. When I finished my stories, he became very serious.

"Little Horse," he spoke, "the role you have played was to remind me about a life over here, in the ordinary world. I had a choice to make, to live in the ordinary world or to live in the Spirit World. I know it is hard for you to understand, but you must know that the other side is a very compelling place. It's very beautiful and peaceful and magical. It would be so easy to stay there. The spirits of my friends are there, my wife is there, and they all love me very much. In a sense, my wholeness was being forged there, in the Spirit World, with my friends and loved ones. There will come a day when you, too, if you have the courage, will be challenged. If you accept the challenge you will understand what it means to be whole by first understanding what it means to be apart. Then you will go between the wind, and learn about Wholeness."

His prophecy was ominous. I'm sure I looked puzzled for a moment, but then I dismissed the thought. On this sunny morning, I could not imagine such a thing.

He went on. "The vision you had for me was a true one. Ten White Bears is the spirit that emerged from between the wind. The Spirit people told you about the White Bear because you were fretting and worrying that I wouldn't come back. It was an important step—your unselfishness led the Spirit people to want to comfort you, to show you what I was about to become."

Now he smiled broadly. "Your vision was exactly right! Thank you for this wonderful vision, Little Horse! Now I would like to wash your hair!"

"It's that bad?" I laughed. "Sure! Do we have to do the dishes first?"

"Yes. Go get some towels and the shampoo I have in my in the linen closet, and I'll put these in the dishwasher." I giggled when I saw that it was Mane'n'Tail shampoo for horses.

A few minutes later I was seated beauty parlor style at the sink, several cushions stacked on the kitchen chair below me. Nobody except my hairdresser and my mother had ever washed my hair, so I felt a funny sense of dislocation as his calloused hands swept my hair back and under the stream of warm water. What a sweet service it is to have one's hair washed! I closed my eyes and yielded to the warmth and fragrance of the shampoo, the May morning, and this warm kitchen. I opened them once, to see his face close to mine, eyes squinting and his tongue held tightly between his teeth like a boy sorting Legos.

This time, when I returned home, I remembered, as I sat on the plane, his eyes, his breath, his fingers in my hair. And I knew I had crossed a line. For the first time in our relationship, I was having feelings that were familiar to me. Not the infatuation that had held me in its grip during the first year of our correspondence, the vehicle of my conversion. Not the bond of the apprentice to the master. Not that mysterious blending of souls that had happened as I guarded him in his sleep. This was just ordinary love, the love of a woman for a man who was strong and good.

And that meant I had fallen into a trap, a device of intricate capture and torment. If I should let him know that I loved him in this way, I would lose him. He would act immediately to protect my marriage. If I deceived him and did not let him know, then I would betray the honest relationship we had built; the relationship would wither, and I would lose him anyway. There was no way out. It was the end of the twentieth century, and I was caught in a Victorian drama. I chose the slow torture, rather than the quick demise of my happiness. I was on my way to my ruin, and my career as a liar had begun. Or, in the considered words of my sister Cindy, who listened to my whispered fears on the phone: "I would say you are in the waiting-for-your-life-to blow-up-in your-face-phase of your life."

My initial naive attraction to my teacher had grown into a profound love, a love so great that I could not bear for a day to go by without a word from him. To me, our relationship was of a degree of intimacy and power that it seemed to surpass all ordinary bonds. Yet I was so very unhappy and confused. The goal I had cherished for so long—that Ten White Bears would return to his medicine work and to this life—had come true. He was healthy and fit, and his sweat lodges and ceremony had great power. He was tentatively beginning a new life, fixing up his house, looking for a second career after his retirement from the business he had worked twenty-six years, and beginning to have new friendships. All of this I had known would happen, and I was glad for it. And yet, I continued to feel a terrible sense of loss. What was deeply illogical about my feelings was that they came at a time when my marriage was stronger and happier than it had ever been, and when my family life was richly rewarding. I did not want to give up the home I had helped to create. Nevertheless, I felt an overpowering sense that I must somehow persuade Ten White Bears to keep me by his side, even though I knew in my heart that he couldn't. He would make me grow beyond it if I had the courage, and I knew it.

Although I had looked forward to the day when he would again be able to practice his medicine work, I now realized with horror that this would also mean that he would be subject to all the humiliations that any single man his age must endure. The thought of him going through the ludicrous rituals of courtship that our society requires of men when they want the company of women made me sick at heart. To have to package himself not only for this purpose, but also in order to find a new job seemed outrageous to me. And yet he set about both tasks with a willing heart, even enthusiasm, sometimes asking me for advice on dating or on job hunting. "You are a medicine man!" I wrote him when he told me of his executive firm search. "Why not find work that allows you to be who you are! The spirit world grows impatient!" Only I did not realize it was I who had grown impatient, and frightened, and miserable.

I hid my feelings from Ten White Bears, and from everyone else. And deep within me, the ulcer that had lay dormant became active again, causing me daily distress. Nevertheless, I maintained a cheerful demeanor. I knew that soon my family and I would leave for Michigan, where Ten White Bears and I could return to our work. Only in Michigan, in that sacred grove in the meadow, would I feel safe again. At last our summer school duties were over, and our family made our annual pilgrimage to the sand dunes.

It was a summer full of learning. Ten White Bears seemed to be accelerating my education, making up for lost time. He seemed driven to a goal with me and he worked me hard. I learned the many symbols that were used in the ornamentation of sacred objects, and I learned how to make objects sacred through preparation, purification, offering, and mindfulness of use. We always prepared the pipe for use by unwrapping it and burning the small piece of sage that had been wrapped with it. The pipe was smudged and purified in this way. Then I would give an offering of the tobacco still in the pipe to the fire pit near the lodge. Ten White Bears would explain how the stem of the pipe was the male part and the bowl the female part; together, they created the Mystery, a balance, and the power of the pipe to carry our prayers to the Great Spirit. Finally, I would fill the pipe four times with tobacco (the tobacco had also been blessed beforehand), and we would smoke the pipe together.

There were many sweat lodges that summer, and therefore, many opportunities for me to see the variety of personalities that each lodge took on. Roseann came to visit, and I had the thrill of sharing this, my most precious experience, with her. Oh, how she watched Ten White Bears in the firelight, her black eyes flashing. I felt her waves of suspicion, but I also detected her hopefulness. And as I sat next to her in the lodge, I saw her fierceness give way to a glimmering, dulcet quietness.

He taught me many useful ceremonies besides the sweat lodge. When a group of women approached me and asked to do a ceremony of togetherness and healing, he suggested a medicine circle. One at time, a woman would enter the center of the circle, and speak from the heart a sorrow or need. Then, around the circle, people would speak from the Four Directions, giving new perspectives, solace, wisdom, and nurturing. We performed the ceremony in the light of the late afternoon sun under the pine trees. How quickly the tears flowed in this group of strong and capable women! Many years after that circle, women who had barely known each other that day were still bonded in friendships that spanned many continents.

We practiced "going there" until my consciousness was supple and responsive to my own cues. Sleep, dreaming, deep trances, and light trances: each form of consciousness had its unique mode of perception. Each released the spirit from the pull of the body in a different way. For me, the deepest sleep was associated with kinesthetic experiences of soul travel and body transformations. It was in deep sleep that I could change my appearance. Actually, I really wasn't very good at controlling it yet. I just knew that I would wake up some mornings thinner and more muscular and some mornings soft and rounded. Certain sharp eyed people like Beth and Sharon, best friends who had fox-like capacities for sensing small changes, teased me about it. Beth was a tough-talking hairdresser who was likely to go from Parisian Red to Swedish Crystal Blonde from one day to the next. Sharon was in training at the FBI academy in forensics, and had perfected a long slow gaze that took in everything about you. They would stand on the lodge porch, arms crossed, watching me walk towards them. "So . . . you lost weight?" or "Got water-retention issues or do your boobs just look bigger in that shirt?"

I could not yet guide my dreams, either, as some people apparently could, but I had become skillful at using their content to question my own behavior or to prod myself to change. Trances I could induce and use for intuitive work. Ten White Bears showed me how to use my intuition while touching an object or a part of a person's clothing, sharing existence with that object until it yielded useful information.

One time, on a long ride in the truck to pick up materials for the sweat lodge, he began to talk to me a great deal about how metaphors could be read in illness or physical appearance, and the uses of those metaphors in healing. This was familiar territory for me; psychoanalysis had shown the many ways in which inner conflicts were converted into physical symptoms. It was so familiar that I was barely listening to his lecture as we rode along. I was spacing out, as I used to in class. "Your ulcer," he was saying. "Perhaps you could ask yourself what it is that you cannot stomach." I was suddenly unaccountably annoyed with him.

As long as I had known him, Ten White Bears had borne a scarred area beneath his cheekbone that occasionally erupted into a rash or an open sore. I found myself leaning toward him, lips compressed, eyes narrowed and suddenly pointing, touching his cheek. "So tell me, Ten White Bears, tell me about the wound that will not heal." He recoiled, swerving a bit as he drove, and yet I pressed on. I flicked some sort of inner switch, and suddenly saw him embattled, saw an owl fly over him, and said, "Tell me. Do you think I don't see? Do you think I don't know?"

He stopped the truck and rubbed his cheek. He said in a low voice. "Yes, it is the wound that doesn't heal. And you are correct. But I can't talk about that now. It has to do with the owl of death. I will tell you later when you are ready."

"And I can't talk about my stomach. It's something I have to work out myself."

"Little Horse," He spoke sternly.

"Okay."

There were a few things that Ten White Bears tried to teach me that I just didn't get. I wasn't very good at the auras thing, probably because people who insisted they read the colorful halos of energy around each being could still engage my skepticism. It seemed like such a cheap claim to authority, like palmistry. Only once outside of the sweat lodge did I see an aura. Ten White Bears and I were walking along the west Michigan beach at night.

"Ten White Bears," I said. "I think the aura thing might be crap. I mean, sure, we all generate a little electromagnetic stuff, and some heat halos, which I suppose if you are really sensitive you can pick up, but auras—really, I don't see anything like that in Black Elk Speaks, you know what I mean? I have never seen an aura—" I gulped. A blue cloud of light surrounded Ten White Bears. He was grinning "—except that blue one around you right now. Cut that out!" I howled.

I also found shape shifting not only implausible, but also impossible. Ten White Bears had told me the story of how he taught his first apprentice, Thunderwolf, to shape shift. I found it an interesting story, but I just couldn't see it. To lose a few pounds overnight was conceivable. To change into a crow or a monkey was not. And so of course, I could not do it, although Ten White Bears tried very hard to teach me. He believed that the fourth round of the sweat lodge was most conducive to shape shifting, and he had a special rattle given to him by a holy man that was known to induce mass shape shifting. But I could not do it. One time I almost felt myself becoming horse-like, as I had when I was a child, but I could not complete the feat of shape shifting despite the encouragement of my friend.

"It is one of the last lessons of apprenticeship, Little Horse," he said.

"Ah," I thought to myself. "Perhaps that is why I cannot learn it."

However, as the summer bloomed, the magic of the place and the people took hold, and I forgot my fears. Each day began with the dawn prayers or lessons in the medicine ways with my teacher; then breakfast in the Eating Lodge. While Chuck and I taught our morning classes, our children ran wild and free, building sand castles on the beach and hiking Old Baldy, our most massive sand dune. I was a co-director of the leadership conference that year, and my friend and co-director, Leon, and I would circle the grounds, "managing by walking around" in the afternoons. We watched the community of four hundred adolescents develop from an anonymous, motley mass into a harmonious, merry international city of youth. Not a single discipline case marred that conference, and small miracles seemed to happen in every gathering. In the evenings, our cottage rocked with laughter as old friends gathered with our families to create sumptuous cookouts of fresh-caught lake salmon and to play games and tell stories around the fireplace till late at night. At night, as Chuck and I drifted off to sleep to the sound of rain and wind in the pines, he would murmur, "This is our golden summer."

There was a place where the older folks took you only when you'd been around a long time. Most people who came to our camp never knew the place existed. The Upper Meadow was a rare micro-environment: a true Alpine meadow perched on the top of our tallest dune, a place of lush grass, wild flowers, lichens, and dried moss—an island of the Glacial Age left behind by the retreating sea of ice.

To get to it, you climbed up an almost vertical game trail through dense woods up to a forested ridge. You trotted along a long, level ridge trail, until it suddenly disappeared into a thicket of staghorn sumacs. Then there was a period of wandering through the sumac, bearing to the right, and hoping for a break in the red branches that would give you a glimpse of the breast of the hill. When at last you spotted the first tussocks of grass, you walked another great circle of the tall grass perimeter of the meadow and found yet another game trail leading up into the meadow itself. There at the top was a stunted oak.

You could sit under that oak and see for miles in every direction. To the south were the treetops of the north end of the grounds, then the beginnings of fields and orchards. To the west lay the majestic Lake Michigan, its waves so distant that they could only be heard as a whisper. To the north, the whole camp and Stony Creek, and to the East, Stony Lake beyond the trees stretched out, dark and shining until it dissipated into cattail marshes.

Morning arrived in this sacred place iridescent and veiled in mist. Wisps of mist seemed to cling to the crown of the upper Meadow at all times of the day except the hottest afternoons. If you were there at dawn, you would see creatures stepping out of mist that you saw nowhere else on the property: a young buck; a tawny fox, one tiny paw raised; an awkward tern blown here from a distant cold sea.

It was to this place I came in the last year of my apprenticeship, when I needed quiet to piece together all that I was learning. I had packed in my green sleeping bag with the checked flannel lining, and a pale emerald rain fly that I suspended from the branches of the crowning oak, water, a candle, the sacred pipe and a cache of a candy bars. I would lie upon my stomach, peering out the triangle of light, at eye level with the fragrant grass, breathing in the ancient aroma of the meadow. Above me, my lovely tent puffed in and out with the breeze, beating like the green heart of summer.

And it was here that my teacher found me, to teach me about shared being. I knew his footstep, although I only heard it as he came within a few feet of my mosquito netting. He peered in from one side, and then climbed in the other, lying like myself upon his belly and facing the waving grass. We did not speak for a long time, but breathed in unison with one another and with the gently billowing silk above us. When he looked at me, I gazed into his eyes calmly. Time passed.

"What are you doing?" I asked.

"Shared being," he stated.

"Shared being? Is this what we have—this feeling of sort of blending consciousness—is this shared being? It feels to me as if I know what you will say, what you feel, and sometimes as if I am seeing through your eyes. It flickers in and out, but it truly seems as if there is some sort of exchange of mood, of imagery, of kinesthetic sensation. So shared being is literally sharing the being of another?"

"Yes and no—your mistake is in believing that it is only with me, or only with other people that you can have shared being. You can share being with all of creation. This blade of grass can share being with me, and I can share being with it." He looked at the blade of grass, cupping it in his hand. He quietly looked into the heart of the spirit of the grass as it shivered in the wind. Suddenly Ten White Bears became still and rigid as if he was and alarmed like a deer. "What do you hear?" he said. I listened. The wind was rustling the grass all around us; the green rain fly beat more intensely and more rapidly. But beyond this green heart, the conversation of the grass people was now apparent to me. And they were speaking words of alarm. And suddenly the wind too was whispering in alarm.

"I must go," said Ten White Bears. "It's time to go. I hear Jeff's voice in the wind. It is his time."

"I want to go too," I said. And so we quickly went down the hill. We went to his room to get his eagle feathers and then straight to his car. On the way to the hospice he handed me a red cloth and tobacco asking me to make a medicine bundle. But I did not know how.

I fumbled with the red cloth and the tobacco pouch, and tears began to flow. Jeff was dying. I hid my tears. My friend Ten White Bears had lost his wife, and now his best friend. And he drove now, quietly, forehead wrinkled in concentration. He said, "It's okay to cry. You don't have to be brave about this."

We arrived at the hospice, in a stifling, treeless, run down part of Grand Rapids. The hospice was a refurbished old hotel. It was horrible. As we entered the corridors, we immediately heard moaning, and were struck with the chemical smell unique to those dying in institutions. We went to the fourth floor, and passed room after room of supine figures. "This place is a charnel house," I whispered angrily to Ten White Bears.

We reached the receptionist. She was talking loudly on the phone. She said, "Yes, we think this is it. He seized and fell out of bed so many times last night that we left him on the floor. Yes, we've called the family." Ten White Bears and I looked at each other, knowing immediately that she was talking about Jeff.

The receptionist turned toward us. "If you're here to see Jeff, it's family only now." I began to say something but I stopped.

"*We're not here* to bother you," Ten White Bears said very carefully and slowly, looking into her eyes . . . and then he suddenly vanished in a mist before my eyes. The receptionist turned away as if nothing had happened. I had gotten caught in the backwash of his hypnotic suggestion, but I didn't know it. All I knew was that he was gone, the receptionist was at least temporarily distracted, and I had no idea how to find Jeff. I hurried down the first of three corridors, not sure of where I was going. The dreadful moaning and sighing was everywhere. Most of the figures were alone in their beds, all wasted, all still. Where was Ten White Bears? I knew he was with Jeff now, but how was I to find him? The corridors went on and on. Now I was running and weeping at the same time, in a panic. Then I remembered what he had taught me about shared being. If I could somehow slow down, go There; go to Ten White Bears, share being with him, I could find him. I took a deep breath and sat down in the hallway, my back against the wall. I breathed in more slowly, closed my eyes, and went into the Spirit World, to Ten White Bears, whom I suddenly knew to be sitting on the opposite side of that wall I was leaning against. I quickly rose up and opened the door right next to me. This was Jeff's room. Jeff lay like an enormous child, in a great diaper on a pile of wrinkled sheets and blankets. Bruises covered his body where he had seized and fallen repeatedly. He lay curled on his side, his eyes closed except for slits, and his breathing labored. Ten White Bears sat against the wall, crouched, his hands hanging in front of him. I felt his bleak sadness and a momentary hopelessness that frightened me more that anything else I had experienced with him to date. Then I felt him gathering his strength. He suddenly rose, crossed over Jeff's body and lay next to him on the floor, facing him. I knelt behind Jeff, my hand lying lightly on his head. Ten White Bears took his great bruised body in his arms. In a low voice, he said, "It was a good road, brother. You were a great warrior, and now your time is done. You are my best friend. We have run together with the wolves. I love you. It's time to walk forward. I'll see you on the other side."

Now Ten White Bears sat up and reached into his pouch. He brought out his sage, his fan, and his eagle feather. I lit the sage and smudged all of us. Ten White Bears took the eagle feather, and held it a few inches above Jeff, sweeping it gently in the air above him from head to foot. He prayed for his spirit to be taken quickly, and for Jeff to join all of those he loved on the other side. He praised the life Jeff had led in a few words, and urged the spirit people to guide him into the next world. I placed the medicine bundle in his hand. Then we were silent a long time.

We both raised ourselves up at the same time, ready to leave. We both turned around at the same time. Jeff, almost entirely paralyzed, was waving his little finger in farewell.

It was still early Sunday morning. Ten White Bears and I went to a coffee shop and sat watching the people on the street. I was still stunned from the events of the morning. I tentatively asked what had happened in the reception area. "I was really upset," I said. "But it seemed to me that you just disappeared into thin air. I had to go There to find you, I had to be with you for a while, and that was frightening. What was happening?"

My teacher explained that he knew we had to get past the receptionist in order to do the dying ceremony, and it was his experience that hospitals did not deal well with this sort of situation. He had spoken to her spirit, rather than to her mind, and she was willing to allow him to disappear. "You could think of it as the creation of a negative hallucination," he said, "like when you can't find your car keys when they're right in front of you. But I wasn't really being deliberate, I was just acting in the moment."

Now I knew that while he had been resting this last year that his powers had grown, and that soon he would be much stronger than he was before. I had been worried that he would be too out of balance from his grief that we would not be able to do the sweat lodge we were to do that night. But now I realized that he would be strong enough; his time between the wind had forged him anew.

The sweat lodge that night was unlike any I had experienced. The young people were almost manic with excitement. They sang and shouted and Ten White Bears seemed to fan their rowdiness. He turned to me between rounds and said, "It's a heyoka lodge, the lodge of the clown. The coyotes are laughing outside and we are laughing inside. It's for Jeff." In the fourth round, the young people begged for a fifth round. "A fifth round?" I asked. "Can we do that? Is it okay?"

"Sure," said Ten White Bears.

"If the other rounds are spring, summer, fall, and winter," said one guy, "then what is this one for?"

"This one," said Ten White Bears, "is for Detroit."

The young people roared and broke into song again, something about in and out the window, a chant that went on and on into the furthest realms of hilarity, until at last they all tumbled out of the lodge laughing.

"Jeff was here, wasn't he?" I said to Ten White Bears as we stood on the crest of the fore dune, watched the young people diving into the moonlit waves of Lake Michigan below us.

"Yes, he was. It was the kind of fun he liked," he whispered.

Jeff lingered on for a few more days, but he never regained consciousness. Each night, Ten White Bears prayed for him and drummed. A friend who was there the moment he died said, "When he died we heard the drums."

The day after Jeff died, the conference ended, and my family and I flew home to Arizona.

I was happy that Ten White Bears was coming to visit several times in the fall; it made the parting at the end of the conference less difficult for me. And, when he came to visit, we did workshops together. We found that we worked together extraordinarily well, and we were invited for a number of speaking engagements. He would amaze the audience with his feats of "magic," which he said was no more than acknowledging that we are all related, that there is no separation between us. I would explain, in scientific terms, what the audience was seeing. He wore his usual cowboy clothes and silver. I wore pretty professional dresses. Together we created a dynamic polarity, an electric tension between male/female, science/spirit, and listening/experiencing, and the audience felt the excitement.

Rather than being joyful about this new way of working together, I was sad. It was just one more thing to lose when he went on with his life without me. I thought I had become skillful in hiding my feelings from Ten White Bears. It was part of the growth of my new powers. Nevertheless, he sensed some part of my sadness in my increasing silence and in the diminishment of my laughter. When we would hike or ride horses together, he would say, "Talk to me, Little Horse. Tell me why you are sad." But I could not. There was no comfort for me. I think he knew and was just provoking me.

One day, the day of our speech at an international conference on healing architecture at my university, he suggested we go out before the dawn and see the sun rise on Taliesin Mountain. For once, I had awakened feeling well and balanced. The October dawn sky was indigo blue and the new air sweet as we drove toward the desert. Once at Taliesin, we quietly passed through the gates and parked on the road below the mountain. We watched the lights in the great Valley of the Sun below twinkling in the morning haze. We made our way up the slope slowly, climbing over chollas, barrel cacti, and great slabs of the distinctive red quartzite that jutted everywhere out of the ribs of the mountain.

The air was perfectly still, and all I could hear was the sound of our breathing and our footsteps, which gradually began to rhyme. Step, breath, step, breath, and all the way up we went. Ten White Bears took my hand at the top and we walked together onto the level crown of the mountain. I felt peaceful, regal, my hand lifted gently in his, approaching this summit, ringed by the morning stars. At the same moment, we dropped to our knees over a soft mat of new desert broom grass. We faced each other, the sky gathering toward sunrise around us. Our breathing continued in unison, our hands touched, fingertips to fingertips. I looked into his eyes, and I heard his voice in my mind, saying, questioning, "Now?"

"Now," I replied, silently.

We flew into each other's spirits, faster than the light could travel between our eyes, and we went THERE together. The image of my friend disappeared into that of the mountain below and around him, but I held fast to him, to his inner light. Our selves seemed to blend first together, and then into the Great Mystery. This was peak experience, flow, transcendence, and the I-Thou relationship all at once. It was the fulfillment of our mutual creation. Together, we went into the Great Mystery.

When we returned, there was a look of grace in Ten White Bears's face such as I had never seen. His eyes burned bright. "You became the Sky," he whispered. "Your eyes . . . became the sky."

"And you became the Mountain," I said, "and I became you."

"It was—"

"Beautiful."

A hot beam of heat and light now flashed from the east, and the sun rose all at once, looming yellow from its birth in the cloudless horizon. We stood, stretching our arms to the sky in the traditional way, to the morning, praying in those wordless whispers that come from the depths of the soul. A few gold-lit tears of gratitude sparkled in my eyes. Ten White Bears had taken me into the Great Mystery.

That was my final lesson in shared being. I was surprised that afterwards, he did not seem to want to talk about it. I did not see how he could ignore such an astonishing experience. But that night he laughed and talked with old friends as if nothing unusual had happened.

In the next weeks, he did not call or write, and I became agitated about what seemed to me to be neglect. I became angry, and my ulcer flared up, worse than ever. In desperation, I called him and asked if I could visit.

Ten White Bears said that now I should be able to understand how to heal myself. "I'm not comfortable with the word healer," he told me. "It implies a separation between the person healing and the person being healed. But there isn't one. Healing happens through shared being. Healing happens when both people are connected in the Mystery. Now you know how to do this."

Soon after I arrived that late fall night, Ten White Bears said, "Would you like to work on your stomach now?" I said that I supposed so, but I was a little wary. I was afraid for him to touch me, because I did not want to feel any sensations of attraction. He explained about healing touch, and he made the connection between the work of the Native American shaman and the chakra work of East Indian traditions. He had me visualize my pain, and then step out of my body. He asked me to leave my pain behind when I stepped back in. To my surprise, and perhaps to his as well, it did not work. I did not want to disappoint him, but I could not hide the fact that my pain continued. I smiled at him in apology, and said perhaps I should get some rest.

"Well," he said, "You know how to heal it when you want to."

That night, lying in my bed, I realized that if I was to heal the pain in my stomach and the pain in my heart, I was on my own. Ten White Bears, even with his great power, could not heal me, because I felt so separate from him—and from myself. With that bleak realization, I struggled on to sleep.

When I returned home, I took a turn for the worse. As I worried, my ulcer was growing unbearable. Ten White Bears was not making it any better. His conversations were full of cheerful references to, "closing the hoop," and "completing our work." How could he speak so blithely about such things?

Over the years, I had gotten used to the pain that would begin under my sternum in the late afternoon, grow in intensity, and peak around dinnertime. I would often eat starchy and bland foods just to buffer the pain, but it didn't help. Just at the point where I was exhausted from hiding my pain, it would let up, and I would lie down to sleep hoping that the next day I might be spared. Now, however, the pain was beginning even when I first woke up, and it lasted all day long.

My doctor was frustrated. She thought that perhaps I was doing things to make my ulcer worse, but I didn't know what that could be. New antibiotic treatments had become available, and we tried them, but without success. In fact, one of the drugs stopped my stomach motility entirely. I tried dietary changes, but these didn't work either. My doctor warned me that people with my pattern of stomach disorders often developed stomach cancer. This frightened me even more, and I tried ways of calming myself and increased my exercise. The ulcer grew, and began to bleed. Now there was only one option—surgery to remove the lesion. But my digestion would never be quite normal after that. It would be a drastic step. "I've done everything I can," Dr. Susan said. "Now it's up to you."

I decided to take a day to go out into the desert and think out my situation, maybe seek a vision that would help me understand and remove the pain. Chuck was taking Grace and Sam to a movie that afternoon, so I would have the whole day. I woke up that morning in a great deal of pain. I went to the stable to saddle up my horse, and found that even those movements hurt. I sat curled in pain in the saddle, letting Ragtime take me up the mountain and into the canyon on a path he knew well. We came to my favorite place, a place where the canyon walls almost met, and where palo verde trees and sage bushes form a kind of glen. A large, gray schist outcropping jutted into the glen. I liked to think of it as Brynhilde's rock, the place where the warrior Brynhilde lay sleeping for twenty years. I was really too ill to enjoy the drama of climbing up on that rock; I just wanted to stop now and rest, and there was a good place to halter and tie Ragtime where I could see him if he got restless.

The late November sun was already warming the rock, and it felt good under my back. I rested my hands on my burning stomach, and closed my eyes. I was so tired of the pain, and wished I could get used to it. I began to cry, and it seemed as if pain of my ulcer had come to represent all the pain of what I had gained and then lost, my apprenticeship gone bad, my marriage threatened by my perpetual dissatisfaction, my work all but stopped. And if this really was going to be the death of me, it seemed such a cheat, to have had a glimpse of what I might have become and then to leave everything behind. I cried until I slept.

The vision emerged slowly, seeping into the spaces of my dreaming consciousness until the image was fully formed. I sat in a lodge of women. The lodge was not exactly a sweat lodge, but more like a hogan, the octagonal structures built by Navajos for ceremony. Sitting in a circle around me were all the women I had loved and who had loved me. They were grouped in a way that made sense to me. I sat in the east. To my right and left were my most trusted confidantes: Roseann and Pipp and my sister Cindy. To the south were my wild and crazy girlfriends: Esther, inventor, dazzling creator, star of American Gladiator; lovely Gina, who looked like an Italian diva, founder of a rape crisis center; Mary Ethel, wild haired, hard-drinking, brilliant journalist; Susan, poet, actress, seducer of Jesuits. To the west were my motherly friends who had simultaneous pregnancies with me: soft, nurturing Terry and delicate and sweet Nukhet. To the northwest were my wisdom keepers, Sharon, my colleague in research and companion in spirit in my office; Kay, who called herself my "Jewish mother"; Susan, my elder, artist and sage of Taliesin. And in the far north, my women friends who were ill but unconquered: Marcee, who directed a shelter for abused women despite a ten-year struggle with Hodgkin's disease; Felice, whose autoimmune disorder didn't dampen her creative spirit, and Cleo, whose work as a pediatric cardiologist fellow was cut short by an accidental inhalation of chlorine that led to permanent emphysema.

To my surprise, my mother entered, much embarrassed by the surroundings and unsure of herself. I asked her to sit in a place of honor in the west right across from me, and I gave her many necklaces of shells and turquoise beads to show her my love. My Grandmother Barbara, gone since I was a teenager, entered and smiled at me, and sat next to my mother. Then there was a cry from outside as my older sister Beverly stuck her head inside. "Why don't you invite me in?" she asked in a wounded voice. I had the same feeling of confusion and jealousy I had when we were teenagers, and snapped, "When are you going to get in touch with your strength and your sexuality?" and she replied, "And when are you?" Oh, she was right. I reached over and handed her into my lodge, bowing my head in apology, and placed her near my mother.

Now my women friends and family members began to give me their advice. They talked to me a long time, and I can no longer remember their words. They told me how I should begin to care for myself. They said that a dark time was coming, and that I must prepare. I wept when they told me this, because I knew it to be true. I learned from them that each represented a part of me, and that I was a collection of the parts: Scholar, mother, wild child, wounded warrior, jealous sister, and loyal friend. There would be a time, they said, when all of these parts would be cast into the wind, and that I would either become whole and integrated or die—the choice was up to me. My intestines now began to writhe in pain, peristalsis halting, ulcer flaming. Then someone said, "There is more."

A glow outlined the door flap. It grew, a bright golden light, and the flap floated open. On hands and knees, the most beautiful woman I had ever seen, someone I thought I might know, entered and then raised herself up, with the bent knee and knowing smile of a DaVinci angel. She had curly, tousled golden hair that lifted almost imperceptibly in her own breeze as she tilted her face toward me. A circlet of soft white feathers and plaited gold held back her hair from her face. Aquamarine eyes danced as she glanced about the lodge of women. Her face was heart shaped, sun kissed, and filled with humorous delight. She wore a large white scalloped shell at her throat. Her body beneath her white doeskin sheath was small and sensuous: round breasts, sweet full hips, and dusty, perfectly arched little feet. Just the sight of her filled me with such love and admiration that I felt my heart brimming. Who could this be, this person who made me feel the love I felt for my daughter, the gratitude I felt toward my mother, the longing I felt for my grandmother? Who gave me the strange and awed surge of hope like the promise of the Annunciation? And so I asked, "Are you my daughter, grown up?" and she replied, "Yes"—and no, the little maid must wait outside until she is a woman." She laughed at my confusion.

"Are you my mother?" I asked.

She replied, "I am all the Mothers, and the First Mother, and all the daughters and their daughters. You can call me Medicine Swan. It is just one of my names."

"Why are you here?" I asked.

"To heal you, of course!" she replied, and took both of my hands.

"Little Horse, you have been ill a very long time, and have not been whole. Now it is time for you to learn about healing. I am going to take away this pain, because you have much work ahead of you."

Now she knelt before me on both knees and asked that I lie down before her. I lay looking up into her radiant face, in complete trust. She reached into my stomach. I gasped, because I felt considerable pain, from sternum to bowels. My eyes suddenly flew open, and I saw my intestines churning a half-inch above the horizon of my stomach, like a scene in Alien. I snapped my eyes shut to bring back the image, and there she was, laughing and holding up high in her right hand an enormous black claw, dripping with blood. "You see," she said, "this is what has gotten inside you!" With a determined look and a wrinkled nose, she threw the claw into the fire pit. My eyes grew wide and relief began to flow only to be stopped short when the claw flew out of the flames and right back into my stomach. I yelped in pain, and she reached into me immediately and pulled the claw out again. Now she held it in the hot rocks of the fire pit until the claw sizzled, scorched and fell into ash, "Ha!" she said, "Not so fast, Old Claw!" She held it until it had all disappeared except one tiny tip of a talon. She took this tip, no bigger than a seed, and placed it back in my stomach.

"Wait," I cried, "What are you doing?"

She smiled mischievously. "Don't you think you should do some of the work? And shouldn't we leave something for Ten White Bears so he can make himself useful? Don't worry. If you care for yourself, and you call for your lodge of women when you are in need, you will be well."

Now the glow around her expanded into a golden mist, and she faded, along with the entire lodge.

I woke, and saw that the sun was setting over the western rim of the canyon. A cool breeze blew the first scent of evening. Ragtime was stamping the ground impatiently, having eaten every branch and tuft of grass in sight.

The pain in my abdomen was gone. I tested myself gingerly, touching above my pelvis, pressing on my navel, massaging under my rib cage. The sharp agony had vanished.

I clambered off the rock, and fumbled with my horse's lead rope. I took off his halter and returned it to the saddlebag, and then bridled him. I began to lead him away, but after all that impatience, he now balked and lay back on his hind legs. He stared at me, ears back, and began to scrape the earth again with his hoof. Thinking that he had a piece of cholla stuck in his fetlock or his frog, I lifted his hoof. There, under his hoof, was one soft white feather. I picked it up, almost laughing at how wild, how incredible, how over the top this little sign was, and placed the feather in my medicine bundle. I knew it was the most powerful medicine I would ever be given.

The pain never came back that day, or that month, or in all the years that have fled since that day. A few weeks after my vision, an x-ray of my stomach, that had once shown ugly cankers, now showed a clear stomach wall, without any scarring.

This was the story of my healing vision. I did not know that it was to be my last incandescent evidence of the love of the Creation and the power of the Mystery. Now I understand that it was like the quarter that your mother puts in your hand before she sends you out into the night. "It's just in case," she says. "In case you need to call home." I was about to be launched into the night, and did not know it.

Not long after the first days of creation, the people lived happily in their village. They hunted, fished and gathered food. All was well and they lived a prosperous life in those first days of creation.

There was a group of warriors led by Iktome who had been banned from the village by the Council of Women because they were bad spirits. Iktome had sworn he would find the people and conquer them. His warriors had names like Guilt, Anxiety, Jealousy Anger, Frustration, and Fear. They were full of bad medicine.

So the Council of Women instructed the young warriors of the village to scout around and be on guard to protect them from Iktome and his band. The warriors did their job well and in time they spotted Iktome coming towards the village. The Council of Women asked for volunteers to do battle with Iktome and his warriors so that the village would have time to move, to find a place where they could live in peace, and Iktome would never be able to find them again.

Forty-nine warriors volunteered to face Iktome and his warriors. They rode out of the village on their horses and out to the battlefield. They engaged in fierce battle and fought for four days and nights until word came from the Council of Women that the village had been moved. It had been moved in such a way that there was no trace. They left the place in a natural way as if no one had ever lived there.

The forty-nine warriors had a problem. How could they get back to their people without Iktome and his warriors following them? They discussed and argued how to leave the battlefield all night. None could come up with a way to leave without Iktome fol-

lowing them. As dawn came one of the warriors stood up and told his brothers that he would ride out to the battlefield and fight Iktome alone. He would do this so his brothers could steal away and get back to the village without Iktome following them. His brothers were upset and argued with him not to sacrifice himself, but none were willing to go with him or had a better idea

So this brave warrior put on his eagle headdress. It had many eagle feathers because he was a courageous warrior. It had so many feathers that it had two tails. The tails were so long they hung down below his knees to the ground. He mounted his horse and rode out to the battlefield. Iktome and his warriors stood on the edge of the battlefield and stared at this warrior as he got off his horse and staked it. Then he lanced one of the tails of his headdress into the ground and let out a war cry. This warrior stood in the face of Iktome and his entire band while his brothers got away. As Iktome and his warriors charged, they turned into shadows in the light of his courage. He exposed them for the illusions they are.

When the warriors got back to the village the people gathered around and cheered. They had defeated Iktome and gotten away. Iktome and his warriors would never be able to find them again. As each warrior walked into the village the Council of Women had the people sing a song for each one of them. All but the forty-ninth warrior came into the village. The people waited and waited. Finally, the Council of Women asked the warriors where their brother was. They all hung their heads in shame as they told the story of his courage and sacrifice for the people.

So this is why we have forty-nine stones in the sweat lodge. The first rock into the lodge reminds us of the courage of the warrior that stood alone before Iktome. The other rocks represent the other warriors that helped the people escape from Iktome and his bad medicine.

Ten White Bears

INTO THE NIGHT

I felt good enough the next day to go to the gym with Chuck, and I decided on a vigorous workout. I got on the treadmill and began to run as fast as I could. I pushed the controls to steeper inclines and faster and faster speeds. I panted and pounded the treads. I looked at myself in the mirror, ashen with sweat, muscles quivering. Suddenly, I saw an apparition coming at me from the mirror. She had tousled blonde hair, so at first I thought it was Medicine Swan. I reached out eagerly, still running as fast as I could. She slouched closer, I saw to my horror that it was not Medicine Swan, not my shining guide, but a ferocious, dirty woman in panther skins. She pushed my outstretched arms away, knocking me down. She stood there snarling at me, saying, "You little fool. You pathetic little fool. I came here to protect you, not to love you." I lost consciousness. I woke-up on the floor of the gym, surrounded by worried trainers and my staring husband.

I began to go crazy, at first secretly. Weeks passed, and the holidays came and went. I tried to remember to smile. I tried to concentrate on wrapping presents and baking cookies. I had constant hallucinations of the panther beside me. After the holidays, I began to go without sleep and food. Ten White Bears did not write or call throughout the holidays, and I was in a fury. "He has forgotten you," whispered the Panther. "He never cared about you."

My sabbatical, that I had waited seven years for, began. It had been a time that Chuck and I had looked forward to; when we would finish writing projects and enjoy time with our children. Now, however, I was too unbalanced to enjoy the freedom. I needed structured activities to keep my angry thoughts at bay. I had been training for a long time for the All Arabian Horse Show, so I used this as an excuse not to eat and to spend hours at the stable. I would ride around and around the arena, spurring my horse into a state of frenzy when he would not perform properly. My trainer Nancy was shocked at my behavior, and reprimanded me. "Your hands are too harsh! Why are you using your spurs, he's trying to give you what you want! Stop that right now!" I practiced the dressage patterns in my head night and day, because it was the only thing that kept the panther at bay. I tried very hard to listen to Nancy and to go easier on my Ragtime. The show took all the effort I had left. My friends all came, and Chuck held a beautiful birthday party for me out at the stable. I saw his love through a haze of exhaustion, and clung to him in my sweaty breeches and habit, saying, "thank you for this, thank you for this." I apologized to my sweet horse, and promised him a long rest.

Everywhere I went I began to see the panther again, and I began to think of her as an ally. I was very angry with Ten White Bears. He was busy with a new life, and had only called briefly to wish me well in the show. But being with the panther made me feel strong and independent of him.

I thought I would go to the leather shop and find something to make a medicine bundle for her, a kind of offering. A stranger approached me there and asked what kinds of skins I was looking for. I said I wanted to look at all kinds of fur. He gave me the name of a taxidermist, and said I should go there right away. I went to a small house on the edge of the Pima reservation. A wiry man with sharp, small eyes met me at his door. I told him I needed a variety of furs for a craft project. He led me into his workshop. It smelled of death. In a corner, on a stool sat an enormous Pima Indian, absolutely still. Before I could stop myself, I said, "Are you real?"

The taxidermist laughed scornfully. "Yeah, he's real. Real fat." The mountain of a man laughed, too. The taxidermist took out a large bag of scraps. "Here, you can have these," he said. "I have something for you to see." He took me into his garage where he has skinned a mountain lion. She was splayed on a ping-pong table, tacked down. I walked around, mesmerized, and stood right in front of her dead eyes. I stopped. She leapt into me.

"Well, I guess you really connect with that cat, huh? Look, I can't sell you that skin, because it belongs to someone else. But here," and he handed me a piece of her. "Her throat was spoiled, because some asshole tagged her under her chin instead of in her ear." He gave me a collar of her fur, and some other bits of her skin. I wore the skins under my clothes.

My friends and family became concerned. I wrote and called Ten White Bears frantically, but he did not return my calls. Sandy intervened, spending long hours consoling me as I raved that Ten White Bears had forgotten me.

Sandy called Ten White Bears to express his concern. Ten White Bears spoke to Sandy as if he knew everything that was happening to me. "She has been exercising herself mentally, physically, and spiritually, so she is breaking through. The panther represents those parts of her that she needs to get out of the way or to integrate so she can move on. There has never been any doubt in my mind that she could leap forty feet and kill with one stroke of the pen. The aggression is a part of her she has never acknowledged. She is beginning her metamorphosis, Sandy. I must get out of her way."

Ten White Bears called me and told me to come and visit, that he had good news for me. So I arranged a flight to Minnesota.

The snow on the ground and the steel gray river were the same as they had been the year before when I had first visited Ten White Bears in his winter den. But I was different. The year before I had been glowing with health and warmth as I entered his home. Now I felt sickness in my limbs, in my stomach, in my aching head. I could not keep my thoughts on track. I wore a man's black coat and hood and a tawny-colored sweater over dark slacks. Under it all I wore a collar of mountain lion fur. I no longer remembered how it had gotten there, but She had told me not to remove it.

He greeted me as usual when I stepped off the plane, but I backed away from him. He smelled strange. Was it too much cologne or some unpleasant man scent? I fingered my collar, releasing its comforting feline odor. I walked beside Ten White Bears, not touching him. I felt afraid and angry, and I didn't know why.

I don't know what happened the next few hours. I remember eating meat, which was strange, because I had been a vegetarian for so long. But I don't remember where we ate, or any of the conversation. He kept asking me if I wanted to finish something. I couldn't hear him. Instead, I remember Panther beside me whispering to me not to listen to this man, because he would betray me. I felt tired, and my head hurt.

After dinner we went to his home. His house was different. There was a strange feel about it. The pretty little parlor was stone cold and as empty of life as a tomb. The curtains hung limp and the little books had dust upon them. I saw the dust on my fingertips.

I remember that later that evening he stood behind me and had me look into the mirror over his piano. "You are a beautiful person," he said, lifting my hair and setting his hands upon my shoulders. "But tonight you look like an old woman, because you won't rest." How cruel of him, I thought, to see me this way. I growled low to myself, and a hum began in my mind at that frequency. Then I could not hear his words at all. He was trying to teach me something; he was saying something about resting, that I needed to learn to rest. Resting was necessary because I needed rest for my final lesson, in which I would learn to take a different shape.

Rest! What a fool, I thought. I hadn't slept for so many days that I could not remember the feel of rest. How was I supposed to rest when I had such an enormous problem to solve?

The growling sound was becoming louder in my mind.

I was speaking to him in a brittle voice, and I was trembling all over. My eyes closed, and I fell back, back into some dark place.

His scent was making me sick, and he was now in an old gray tee shirt. He was trying to get my attention, but my eyes were wandering all over the living room, as we sat on the medicine blanket he had purposefully laid on the floor. I tried to focus on his face, but I did not like the look of it. His eyes were red, his face flushed. I looked again, and tried to tune him in. "The apprenticeship is over. You are done. You will have to go away from me."

What was he saying? I must have heard wrong. I tilted my head and looked at him from another angle. I licked my lips. "What did you say?" I inquired.

"Our time together is over. The hoop is closed tonight. Tomorrow I will give you the Pipe, and you will go home." He spoke with no emotion.

"That's not what this is about, this is not about my apprenticeship! I'm an inconvenience to you and you want to get rid of me. You can't do this!"

"You knew that this moment would come," he said. "This is what you have been working towards. Your independence."

I heard a keening voice of the Little Horse coming through me, a terror filled shriek. Little Horse! Where was she speaking from, from what abandoned corner of my soul was she crying? "This will kill me!" she cried.

He had heard her. "I can't be responsible for that. Isn't this what you wanted— for me to go forward with my life. Remember?" he spoke firmly.

"But not without me!" The Little Horse was in my throat again, crying,

"I cannot live without you," I yelled at him.

In a voice tight with scorn, he said, "Have you forgotten who you are?" In those eyes, which had never held anything but love and kindness and the secrets of the universe, I now saw contempt and anger. He was making me go away and I was terrified.

Now the sound of the Little Horse within me was silenced, and all movement within me halted—heartbeat, breath, blink, bowel. A pitiless calm descend over me. A second passed. Another. And then a rippling began as my body suddenly loomed in the air, claws unfurled, teeth lethal and bright, powerful haunches pitching me up, up above this Man, this foul-smelling, dull-toothed, slow-moving two-legged. I roared and crouched low, tail moving slowly, scenting the air through wide nasal passages. This was a Man-den! I was trapped in this horrid little box, a place lit by a strange light and filled with stifling hot air. I exploded in rage and anxiety, snarling and leaping about, tearing the strange furniture and ripping at the walls. There was no way out! This puny creature had entrapped me! I leapt back to where he sat, and flung him on his back, claws at his throat. I saw his surprise, and I savored his alarm. The alarm made him smell better to me. I wanted to taste it; I wanted to taste his blood. I considered. If I held him with this paw, then one swipe with the other and he would be lying in a wet bloody nest, his life pumping out of his torn throat. That would be a good thing. Just as I raised my forepaw, just as I expected him to cringe back, he leapt forward instead, sending me off balance.

He rolled over with me clinging to him, and taking my two front paws in his hands, he shook me somehow and then he shaped shifted into a giant white bear. The bear had pinned me firmly to the floor and I could feel the huge pads of his clawed paws. The bear's hazel eyes stared directly in to mine. I was helplessly pinned below his great furry weight. His huge round head shook and reared back, pointing his black nose to the sky. His jaws opened, baring yellowed teeth and a roar came from deep within the spirit of the bear, a growl so loud it shook the earth. I was a small woman being held down by a great white bear, his paws over my wrists. I screamed at him, "Let me go!" He shook his head, staring at me fiercely. I was suddenly aware of a whole pride of mountain lions, she-lions, surrounding us.

"Give her to us. You have no use for her," they demanded, as they hissed and twitched their tails. "Give us the Little Horse." He looked directly at them, challenging them, where they stood in a ring around the blanket. Drool slipped from his open jaws as he growled low and gutturally. He watched them circle us and with a low growl, he again challenged them. He had the strength to kill them all and he knew it. Still holding me down, he looked around the circle, shaking his head, saying firmly, "No."

Now I was crying, whimpering, "Let me go, oh please get away from me, please. I didn't mean to hurt you. Please don't hurt me." He held me down with all his weight, glaring at the panther people and me. I sobbed, and gulped for air. He was so heavy that I couldn't breathe. The tears streamed down my face and neck. For a long time there was no sound except my weeping and his heavy breathing. I waited, and struggled for air.

And then I sensed another presence in the room. A brief glow, and the shadows of lions faded. I heard a familiar voice, an easy, melodious Western accented voice calling softly, "Ten White Bears. Listen to me now. You are responsible for her in these last moments of her life as Little Horse. Her spirit is wounded mortally, and it will die here tonight as you have been told. The panthers would like her for their own, but we must not let them have her. She is wearing a collar of panther fur. You must remove it. If you don't remove it, you will never see her again." Then the panthers disappeared.

Now human again, he released me, and quickly unbuttoned the top button of my sweater, revealing the stiff and decaying collar of fur knotted around my neck. "Barbara, help me get this off you. Come on now, let's get this off of you, quickly, before they return and I have to kill them." I fumbled with it, and his fingers helped pick the knot.

"Wait," I reached for it briefly, sobbing, and touched the place where a metal ear tag had somehow been accidentally fastened to the flesh of her throat. "This hurt her so badly. They tried to staple this to her ear, but she struggled and the agent missed. It got infected, and she clawed at it all the time. She hated men, oh she hated them for this, for capturing her over and over and giving her this pain." He nodded, pulled the necklace from my neck and left the room with it dangling from his hand.

When he returned I had already found my black coat and pulled it on. I stood there in my coat and bare feet, dizzy and disoriented. "I need to go. Now. I need to go home."

"Barb, it's the middle of the night, and it's snowing. You can't leave now."

"But I have to. There's not a moment to lose. I have to get back to my life. You said it yourself. I forgot who I was. Now I must remember before it's too late."

"Wait until the morning. Don't go yet. Stay here until it is safe."

And so, against my better judgment, I spent a miserable night wrapped in my coat on the floor on the medicine blanket. I would not let him comfort me. I lay awake till dawn. I fell asleep for only about thirty minutes. But when I woke up, my soul was dead, just as Medicine Swan had said it would be, and Ten White Bears was gone. I picked up the phone, and called Sandy. I would need his help to get home, because I could no longer remember the way.

I was weeping even before I could get out the first words. "Sandy, I can't find my way home. I need to come home. Please help me Sandy."

"Barb, what has happened?"

"The worst. The worst has happened. He is gone; he's left my life. I need to come home, and I don't know how. How will I get there?"

"Oh Barb. Oh Barb," Sandy's voice broke with concern.

Through my agony, I suddenly realized there was something wrong with his voice. "Sandy, why do you sound so strange?" I asked.

"I don't know how to tell you. . . . I nearly died last night. I went into insulin shock and my heart stopped. I was revived, but I'm still weak."

And so it had happened—the breakdown of his system that the doctors had warned about. He had died, and I had died, and we were together, completely alone.

"I've been so careless of you, I left you when you were sick, oh Sandy, I'll come back and take care of you, if I could just get back."

"Antonio is here to take care of me. But Little Horse, your work is done there." Sandy spoke in wisdom.

I began to gag, and covered my mouth. "Don't call me that, I'll never be that name again. How do I get home?" I was wailing again, long low groans I had never heard from myself. Sandy carefully went over my predicament, giving me possibilities, explaining that I could change my airplane ticket, explaining how to get a cab if Ten White Bears did not return. He suggested how I might speak to Ten White Bears.

"I can't, I can't, and I can't be with him. He is making me go away. Why? Why Sandy? Why?" I felt a wave of nausea.

"Now listen to me. You are traumatized. Be gentle with one another and part as well as you can. Accept his help this one last time, so you can return safely. I'll call Chuck to meet you. I'm so sorry I can't get out of this bed."

I said goodbye as I hung up the phone, lying on the couch in the den, utterly out of control. I had not known it was possible to be like this. I had suffered the deaths of friends and family members with simple tears, and the loss of early romances with the briefest of heartbreaks. I had come back to consciousness after having been run over by a car with my bones broken and my skin flayed. But I had held back the groans of pain in order not to frighten my mother and father who held my hands on either side of me in the emergency room. I had labored quietly and in good humor. Never had I known creaturer-cries like the ones pouring from me, and the sounds of my own alarm kept igniting my terror. I screamed and screamed.

Ten White Bears was standing beside me, with the Pipe in his hand.

"No! Please go away, I didn't want you to see me like this." He looked puzzled and worried. "Come, we will have some breakfast. I repaired the Pipe so that I could give it to you. You have the courage we spoke about. You will need all of it. Your time to learn wholeness has come. You will do it by coming apart. Like all the medicine people before you."

"No, please, don't give it to me, I won't be praying any more. Don't you see I am dead?"

With a quizzical look, he took me by the hand and led me to the kitchen. It was still early in the morning. He had fixed a breakfast, but of course I could not eat. I sat and trembled. He led me away from the table, and seated me on the floor. He wrapped the medicine blanket around me, and held it there.

I believe we smoked the Pipe. I believe I said some words like, "I relinquish this man," but immediately realized the absurdity of the words. He had relinquished me, and nothing I could do could change that or recover my lost honor. He gave me the Pipe, and told me to take it. "You are finished now. You don't need me any more to mediate between you and the Spirit World. You will do this for yourself. You will be the medicine woman you have sought. The Pipe is yours. Take it."

I took it but I did not want it. This sacred Pipe, the symbol of his power, seemed to me a shabby consolation for a life without my teacher.

"I will watch over you. I will love you as I always have," he said.

We sat silently until it was time for me to go to the airport.

At the airport, he waited while I went from airline to airline begging for a seat. I got the last seat on the last flight, which left in just a few minutes. When I returned to him, he spoke softly. "I am sad," he said. "I wish I had more wisdom for you."

And head down, sorrowing, I walked onto the plane, and into my long winter.

Winter

Only the earth and sky last forever.
Make every day a good day to die.

The North cleanses us. It makes us pure. The North renews us and reminds us of how fragile life really is. We live in a fragile environment. As such, all things will eventually change and return home to the Great Spirit. To understand this allows us to be our own selves at our very best all the time. It is an old saying: Make every day a good day to die.
—Ten White Bears

Chuck picked me up at the airport, but was uncomprehending of the immensity of my disorder. I found I could hide it by staying silent, and speaking in carefully planned answers to his questions. He knew that something was very wrong when we entered the house and I fled at the sight of the furs, drums, feathers, and Indian art. "Get rid of that stuff," I cried, "I can't look at it."

"What has happened?"

"My apprenticeship is over. And I'm done with it all. I don't want any of these things in the house."

"All right, but what about the things that you and Ten White Bears are writing?"

In reply to this, I rushed into the room where I kept the letters and our manuscripts, grabbed a pile of them and headed for the fireplace. I picked up the pipe on the way.

"What are you doing? Stop this. You're being melodramatic. Put that stuff away. You wouldn't want to hurt the pipe, would you?"

That stopped me. Even in this state, I did not think I could destroy the pipe. "I need to find someone to keep it for me. I need to get it away from me!"

"All right. Now calm down. Do you want to go see Sandy? He keeps calling."

"Yes, yes, I'm going to Sandy's, he's sick."

I flung down my baggage and rushed out to the car, soon finding myself driving blindly toward Sandy's house. When I arrived, I pushed through his door and found him lying on the couch, very pale and expressionless until he saw me. Then his expression was a strange mixture of horror at my appearance, relief at seeing me, and an exhausted realization that we may have both reached the end of the lives we had known. "It is zero hour, Barb. From here on, it is just the unknown. Whether I will live, whether you will be well again, it is up to the universe and to our efforts. We start here."

But I had no energy to start anything. I fell into his arms and wept uncontrollably. "Listen, Barb. You know that our fates are intertwined. I will call you, every night. I will call you and talk you to sleep, or just listen to you, or just be quiet with you. We will talk, every night at ten thirty, until we are both well again."

"I may never be well again, Sandy. I do believe that I am crazy."

"Then we will be crazy together."

Sandy's promise was good. He called me every night after that.

That first week of my illness, Chuck became more and more alarmed. Ironically, as psychologists, we had made little use of psychological services. Where does a psychologist who has a shattered mind turn? Fortunately, we had friends like Sandy and Sharon, my colleague with whom I could be completely open. There was also our friend Cleo, a physician who offered to evaluate my condition. So the next weekend, while my parents babysat the children, Chuck drove me down to Tucson to visit Cleo and her husband Peter. Peter and Chuck turned in early and Cleo asked me to stay up and talk with her. We sat at her dining table in the dark, and I told her my story, in a flat voice, tears streaming down my face. I was too depressed for drama; I just wanted the pain to stop.

Cleo asked one question after another about my depression. She asked when I had last slept, and I couldn't remember. She asked when I had eaten, and mentioned that she saw that I had pretended to eat at dinner. Again, I couldn't remember. I hadn't had an appetite for a long, long time. She asked what was going on in my head, and I tried to explain about how Ten White Bears had killed the Little Horse. Now, I said, my soul was dead, and I wasn't sure how to live without it.

We were quiet for a while when Cleo said, "Have you told Chuck that you are a danger to yourself?"

"But I didn't tell you that . . ."

"That is what you are thinking. I know you, Barb, you are clever, and you want to hold a secret option in case the pain gets to be too much, and your intellect is impaired. So, I'm going to intervene, and we're going to tell Chuck together and you're going to tell a few other friends, so that we can keep you safe. And now we're going to get you something to help you sleep, and on Monday, you're going to your doctor."

On Monday, I went to my doctor. I was barely able to speak. I mumbled as well as I could my self-diagnosis of depression, of traumatic stress reaction. She took both of my hands in her small hands, and looked in my eyes. "That would not be my diagnosis."

I looked up at her through the fog of my despair.

"I would diagnose a soul in torment."

I hung my head, and nodded.

She agreed with Cleo's concerns, and gave me something to take to calm the ghosts who shouted at each other in my head; it gave me two or three hours of sleep.

My disintegration was not a dramatic storm that cracked and shattered with the weight and fury of its ice. Rather, it was a long, muddy winter like we had in Missouri, with sleet and thaw and slush following each other in a monotonous serial misery. After my initial collapse, my depression took on an almost routine agony. Most days I saved all my strength for the hours when my children were home. There was one shaky hour in the morning when I got the children ready for school, filling lunch boxes and checking homework. When they and Chuck left, I could collapse into bed where I lay for hours with conversations in my head. Perhaps if I had said this . . . if I could only say this, then I might have peace . . . if he had said this . . . I would have been well. Perhaps I would have been satisfied with this . . . I remember groaning and thrashing about, and sometimes getting up to look at my strange gray ashen face in the mirror. Somehow the sun crossed the sky and it was time for the children to return home. I would take my medication so that when they came in I could ask, "Did you do well in tennis? Did Jeannine give you that cute little barrette?" I would make dinner carefully, and make dinner conversation even more carefully. My love for my family was like something I could see through a thick and weathered pane of glass. I am here, I thought, and they are here, and I can do this for them because I have done it so far. When the children went to bed, I would go to bed myself, exhausted from the effort of hiding my affliction. If I could not sleep, Sandy would talk me to sleep on the phone, soothing me with stories and assurances. Chuck alternated between fear, loving care, and impatience; he had never seen me incapacitated.

Pipp came down from Flagstaff for a visit, and I gave her the Pipe to keep for me. I gave it to her in the sacred way, placing it in her hands four times, but I could not pray with her. She told me she would keep it safe as long I needed.

Sometimes I would have a few days of functioning, in which I might paint one little corner of my shelter at Taliesin. Even out there in the desert, I was not alone. My friend Susan, who had first brought me to Taliesin, and who had helped me to create the sweat lodge there, often came by my shelter to talk and to engage me in the various activities of the community. So some days I went with her to help students with their projects or to attend the teas where the community gathered. These days were made possible by heavy sedation, two or three phone calls to Sandy or Roseann, and some kind words from Chuck. A few days of coping always led me to believe I was on the mend, so of course, I would announce this to everyone, and then try to go back to "normal life."

Astonishingly, I insisted on keeping two of the out of town engagements I had made many months before, and my family and friends allowed me to go. Both engagements came after a flurry of reassurances from me that I was well now. In March, I tried to do my lecture tour in Michigan, but I fell asleep between lectures right in the middle of lunch with my hosts because I had overmedicated myself. Later, I tried to drive to the airport in a snowstorm and drove almost a hundred miles in the wrong direction. Finding myself in Kalamazoo rather than Flint, I somehow remembered that some camp friends were holding a meeting there to which I had been invited long ago and had declined. I showed up at the elegant Fetzer Institute in the middle of a blizzard. I believe that I looked so very strange and disheveled that they immediately assigned me a room in their Seasons Lodge. I was given the room F in the bottom of Winter Building, and my friends took me in hand. Mark was there and another friend who seemed to know instantly that I was not well. They isolated me from the others, and alternated holding my hand in a downstairs room while I wept and raved that my soul was dead, that my faith was gone, and that I could not go on. Yet, I could not tell them what had happened to me. They asked no questions, and did not attempt to pry the details out of me. I remember the words that Mark said to me: "Your soul is in the Tomb now. Rest there. Even Jesus spent three days in the Tomb. Are you any better than him? Even if you cannot feel Him, God is there, and his love will guard you through the night." I do not remember how my car was returned, or how I managed to fly home from the wrong airport.

In April, I wanted to attend the planning meeting for camp. For the first time in many years, Ten White Bears would not be there, so I thought I might be able to manage it. I was wrong. I got as far as O'Hare Airport and got spooked in the United Terminal. I had entered the great underground passageway lit by the strange musical and light spectrum when I was struck by a wave of grief that Dante's dying multitudes must have felt as they passed the gates of Hell. So here, in the center of the walkway in the busiest air terminal in the world, with thousands passing me by, I abandoned all hope. I simply collapsed in a heap upon my luggage as red, pink, violet, and indigo flashing lights surrounded me and I wept, sick and angry. A despair flowed from me that had no bottom to it. There were moments when I had those strange, lucid thoughts that come even in the middle of a complete breakdown. "What will they do with me?" I asked myself. "Will they take me to a nice hospital in Oak Park near that pretty Ravinia Festival where we saw the opera? Or will they take me to Cook County with all the poor crazy people?" Nobody stopped, however, to examine the woman who lay curled and crying upon her bags. I wept there for hours, missing several planes. Then I must have gotten up, and walked to a gate where a plane took me to Michigan.

My friends greeted me, and once again, without questions, shepherded me through meetings, helping me to keep up the appearances of normality. We planned the schedule, but I could barely speak. It was a rainy, cold weekend. I could not get warm, and the nausea that had begun in the airport increased by the hour, as well as strange deep pangs in my lower belly. When the meeting broke up, I rushed outside to get fresh air, and ran down the beach in hopes of warming myself with exercise. I ran until I could not run anymore, the rain beating in my face, my clothes soaking, and my stomach sending sharp cramps to signal me to stop. When I did, I was seized by a wave of nausea so intense that I began vomiting uncontrollably. I fell to my knees, the cold waves lapping and soaking my jeans, and retched into Lake Michigan. A great wave pushed me over in the sand and I lay there waiting for whatever came next.

It was Medicine Swan. Medicine Swan, walking over the waves toward me, in company with another woman-spirit, curly-haired, thin and dressed in a gauzy India-print dress. I had never seen a picture of Ten White Bears' wife, but I knew immediately that it was she. I remember feeling the warmth of Medicine Swan's radiance, and I had a thought that perhaps they had come to take me to the other side. I wept in relief, because my pain would surely end there, in their sweet company. "We have not come to take you," she said. "We are here to take your dead soul from you. We are here for the Little Horse." I knew then that I would have to deliver the stillborn soul out of me. And so I labored, a harder labor than I had had with either of my children, great wrenching contractions followed by more vomiting and the release of fluids from my terrible infection. Throughout, Medicine Swan stroked my forehead with her warm and gentle hands, and said in her lovely lilting voice, "It's all right. It's all right. You were such a good little horse. You worked so hard. Now let her go. Let her go. Let her go." And so with one last groan, I let her go. I saw the little gray shape lifted from me; I saw the curve of her neck and the swinging wet mane. I saw Medicine Swan enfold the tiny dead filly in her arms, kissing her lightly. She passed the foal to her companion, who turned and walked with her into the waves.

Then she knelt beside me. I touched her golden curls. I looked into her dark blue eyes, where there was nothing but the infinite love of the Mystery. She touched my hand to her lips. "Barbara, you will have everything that you need. But you must be strong, beautiful, and loving, so that you will be ready. The Panther will never return, because you have won the struggle with her. I will always be with you. Go and do your work now, and live without the Little Horse. Her work in this world is done."

So I got up and went back to the dorm, where I showered and climbed under a woolen blanket. Later I drank a cup of tea.

On the way home, I flew through St. Louis in order to avoid the nightmarish underworld in the O'Hare Airport. Roseann was there to meet me, and take me to a restaurant, where she asked me to speak all the words that had been spoken, and tell all that had happened. As I told my story, her bright eyes filled with tears. We huddled together in the bistro, surrounded by Jamaican music and our big bottles of Jamaican beer. "Thank you for crying for me, Roseann. Thank you so much." I gave her all that was left of those terrible memories, an agate panther fetish I had picked up during my madness. "I don't know if I should give you this, it's such a terrible thing, but I can't keep it . . ."

"It's not a terrible thing to me," she said. "It's a symbol of strength, and I'm not afraid of it. Thank you for it."

But as I have said, there was monotony to my illness. I was almost well for a few weeks. I went into my office at the University for the first time in months, and began to work a few hours a day there. I began to sink again, and rather than concentrating upon Medicine Swan's message of hope, I could only think of how beautiful it would be to be with Medicine Swan, to have her soft fingers upon my forehead always, making me forget. When a janitor came through our offices at work with a key to open our windows for cleaning, I was fascinated. Why, I could climb right out there on the ledge and fly straight into Her arms! My body could fall down there below onto the sidewalk, crushing this awful skull that held such terrible thoughts, such unhappy images. So one very hot, sunny afternoon I stepped quietly out the window onto the ledge, holding on to the frame lightly with one hand. A warm, sooty breeze blew over me. The palms swayed and a few clouds puffed by overhead. I looked at the sidewalk below, and wondered, would it do the trick? I felt such relief, that

I was finally here at the end of the story. I stood there and breathed the thick air for a long time, getting ready.

Then something caught my eye—flashes of sunlight upon a car in the parking lot perhaps—a glint of golden light precisely the color of my little girl's hair. Images began to flood my mind. Gracie's hair. Gracie's face. Sam. Sam's eyes. Gracie's eyes, full of tears. Chuck. Chuck alone. Dear God, I thought, what am I doing? I can't do this. I love these people! I have responsibilities. I stepped back in. I shut the window, tight.

It was the bravest moment of my life. Not because I decided to live, but because I decided to live with the hell in my head for the sake of the people I loved. I knew that it might be thirty, forty, or fifty more years in which I would wake up each day to an unfeeling body, a bleak heart, and an empty soul. For a lifetime, I might continue the conversations in my head that always ended in unanswered questions: "How could Ten White Bears turn his back on me? What happened to me? Was any of it real, or was I crazy? Why was my mind taken from me?"

For all I knew, I would never get better. But I decided to take Medicine Swan's words and make them real. I would build the strength of my body through better care for myself and I would build the beauty of my heart through acts of loving service. I would find a way to heal my mind, even if my soul was dead.

I picked up the phone and called my HMO. "I need an appointment with a therapist now. Any therapist."

And so I became a psychotherapy patient, a very docile patient, one who filled out depression inventories, set goals for each day, performed little tasks of recovery, and took her medication faithfully. Each week I set a small goal to achieve: to get through an hour without a memory of that terrible night; to touch a small cat without trembling; to carry on a conversation with Roseann or Sandy without obsessing about my loss; to go all day without crying.

My therapist, a clinical psychologist from India, would show me her notes and my scores on the depression inventory every week. "You see?" she would say in her clipped, cheerful voice, "Much improved!" I could not discern any improvement. Every morning I woke to my injured innocence, and every evening I tried to dampen my anger enough to sleep.

However, just as the seeds lie restless beneath the snows of winter, change was occurring somewhere below the level of my awareness. As my sabbatical ended, I turned with relief to the students who needed advice concerning their research. Although I could not write, I could help them with their academic problems. I found that I could give them insightful guidance about their most difficult clients. Now I knew what it was like to be hopeless and to be helpless to change, and could teach my students a little about the darkness. When summer school came, I found that I was eager to do a good work as a teacher. My course topic was creativity and self-actualization. Despite the irony of an extinguished soul teaching self-actualization, I decided that I would use the best teaching techniques. For the first time, I taught a class that did not depend completely upon my knowledge and enthusiasm. I drew upon the students' knowledge and resources, used role plays, case study debates, and brought in guest speakers representing different domains of creativity: a famous novelist, a Juilliard violist, an inventor. At the end of the class, I read to my students some of the letters that Ten White Bears and I had written to each other, and they were moved to ask me if we might have a closing ritual. The class ended, surprisingly, in a beautiful medicine circle in a darkened room, each student having contributed something from his or her own spirituality or philosophy to the group. I can do this, I thought. I am still a teacher.

Soon afterwards, Grace, Chuck, and I visited Chicago. Instead of venturing out sightseeing with them, I chose to stay behind, and as I sat in our hotel room, I began analyzing the data and writing up the results of a research project my students and I had performed the year before. My writing was a bit stilted, and I had to calculate my statistics by hand, but it came back to me. As the answers to the research questions appeared before me, I was happy. Science had not abandoned me. Nor had I abandoned science.

Long before my disintegration, in a shop owned by Navajo people, I had seen a beautiful antler white pipe with long white feathers hanging from it and red and black beading in a pattern just like my medicine coat. Now my family gave me that pipe. "I know that you're not doing your spirituality right now, but maybe you will feel like it again someday," said Chuck. "This can be your pipe, without any of the bad memories."

"It's prettier than the other one, too," said Grace.

I decided to take it to Michigan with me.

* * *

Ten White Bears speaks:

All the while Barbara was going through her transformation, and outside her awareness, I was always with her. I was with her in the Spirit World, helping her to her destiny. I was watching over her as I had promised.

Her people reminded her of her value here in this world. I knew that her old spirit must die so that she could be reborn whole, and I knew that I could not go with her. She must do it on her own as all have done before her. She must come apart so that she can get what is important and bring it back together to be whole. To understand wholeness you must come apart.

I would get a sense of her in her struggles and I would do ceremonies with my personal pipe, the one I do not share with anyone. I would help her battle with Iktome's warriors. I would go into the Spirit World and find her. To find her, I would drum and pray with my feathers. Once when I was doing this I walked through the darkness. When the dark became light there were ugly flying things all around. They were fierce, like fierce-looking barn swallows. The further I walked into her spirit land, the more these things would fly around me. Huge animals like dragons or monsters would attack me. If I stood without fear, they would come at me, charge me, and then just disappear. I was in full war regalia, face painted with two yellow lines under my eyes and seven red dots around my right eye.

I found myself looking down into huge meadow of tall grass. There on this vast plain she was wrestling with this huge monster. It was four-legged and hairy, human and bear-like, Sasquatch-like. This Spirit wasn't getting the best of her, but she wasn't getting the best of it either. It looked up at me and paused. She hit it with her fist. It went right through it. She had a desperate look in her eyes. There were also reptilian snaky kinds of monsters hissing and biting at her. They were all trying to defeat her. None of those spirits could do anything. She had a blouse and skirt on and was scratched up and pretty muddy. Determined and terrorized.

I ran up to her and the beast heard my war cry. She hit it in the chest and then grabbed it and wouldn't let go. She had stunned it. "Now what?" she asked. She was beat up and had tears in her eyes. "If I let go of it, it will hurt me," she said. I told her to let go of it. "I can't," she replied. I told her to let go of it four times. She pulled her hand away and the beast disappeared. Suddenly, we were in a tall yellow meadow, with the grass blowing around our legs and the blue skies above. Her war with herself was over and that was the end of the vision . . .

Ten White Bears had taken a position as director of our conference center. When summer came, I steeled myself for the ordeal of seeing him daily. When we would meet, I was always angry or sad; Ten White Bears was subdued and gentle. My conversations with him seldom went well.

"This is about wholeness," he said to me in one of our conversations. "You must come apart to be able to be whole."

"And who asked you to take me apart?"

"You did, Barbara. You did. When you decided to be my apprentice. All medicine people must endure their own death. Get their egos out of the way. Prepare themselves for a new life. It is the way that they are born. You said that you wanted to go all the way, that you wanted to complete the process. I told you that you would have to be willing to give up everything. I asked you four times if you wished to do this. That night you said yes four times."

"I have no memory of that. This was all your idea for me to be a medicine woman. Not mine. And I would trade all the medicine power in the world for just one more day of the relationship we once had, for you to be my teacher."

"Be careful when you speak those words. It is not your power to trade away."

"Don't lecture me. You are not my teacher any more."

And another time, I suddenly became aggrieved again when he began to tell me how much I had grown as a result of our separation, and how glad he was to see me getting well. "How would you know?" I asked. "You have not been around to witness my growth or my lack of it."

"I knew that the only way for you to come into your own was for me to separate from you."

"Yes, but I took all the risks. What did you have to lose?"

"This—that if you do not win this struggle, I will never practice my medicine again." His statement stunned me. Could it really be true, that if I failed it would put an end to his medicine days? I didn't know why he would do that.

The women students in the conference approached me, asking if I might lead a women's lodge while Ten White Bears led a men's lodge. To do these lodges separately seemed the only way that I could go forward with them. I was very apprehensive, because I didn't want to have any flashbacks or bad experiences. But I looked into the hopeful eyes of the two young women who brought me tobacco and asked me to lead their ceremony and realized that this was a service I should give, no matter what the risk was to me. I wondered if I could lead a lodge without a soul. I walked down by myself to the sweat lodge site to think about it. There, on the site of the first sweat lodge, in the place where I sat as my soul was born, a delicate albino vine was growing, with one white flower. I looked closer. Yes, it was almost entirely without chlorophyll. The leaves were of such a pale green as to appear white. And a flower was growing, from a plant that had virtually no way of transforming the sun's energy into sustenance. And yet it lived. It was the sign that I needed.

Gracie had helped me to sew a beautiful garment of white rabbit fur and doeskin. The night before the ceremony, I went alone to my sacred place in the Upper Meadow to try to remember how to pray, and to seek a vision to guide me in this work. I hung a pavilion of mosquito netting from the branches of the oak at the crest of the meadow. I built a medicine wheel around me as I had been taught, in the sacred way. I lit a few candles and set them between the roots of the tree. I lay down in my garment against my mother, the Earth, and wept for one of the last times into her arms. I thanked the Mystery that I still had life to give those who needed me. I vowed to do my best to heal. I asked for a vision, if only a small one, to see me through.

I was given just a glimpse, but it was enough. The candles around me had almost burned down, and the night breezes made my mosquito net pavilion billow. Through the mist, I saw a golden horse, a mare with powerful haunches and a long curving neck, gliding noiselessly through a silvery woods. She had wisdom and serenity, courage and strength. She had powerful medicine. She was the Medicine Horse. She was somewhere in my future, and I would find her.

Ten White Bears arrived at sunrise. As usual, I did not hear him coming. He stared at me through the netting as my eyes opened. "Medicine Horse," he said.

I was shocked that he knew my vision, that he knew my new name. "The Little Horse has died. Shonkawakan Ketala has gone," he spoke in his soft tones. "You know, there comes a time when you look at your students and you say, 'You're a doctor.' It is like that. I came up the hill, and your aura was breathing and glowing. The hoop is closing on this time of coming apart, and you are emerging to live well."

He reached for my medicine pipe and did the awakening ceremony, handing it to me four times. It was like he was handing me a diploma, except more, he was honoring my courage and my life. We smoked the pipe without saying a word. Then he spoke, "The Mother Earth and the Father Sky have awakened you. You are the Medicine Horse. Go and do your medicine." He disappeared down the hill. We did our separate lodges, and they were very good.

I had a new spirit. I was on the road to wholeness and was ready to seek healing in earnest. I was still in winter, but it had a different quality. The winter had blown through me, cleansed me, renewed me, and purified me. I sought help from a medicine woman named Mary Delaney, who took up my instruction. One day she helped me "peel." It was a process of using one's intuition to identify and cleanse the emotions. She asked me to pick a place on my body where there seemed to be a lot of emotion centered. I pointed to my throat. "And what is it?" she asked.

"Fear that something bad will happen."
"And what is under that?"
"Defiance!"
"And then?"
"Regret."
I went down through the layers of anxiety, fear, and outrage.
"Then what," she asked?
I stared at my inner vision in disbelief.
"Then what?"

To my astonishment, what was under all that was a pure, cool, tranquil pool of the purest Love. I smiled, and told Mary what I had seen.

"Yes, of course, because love is the only genuine emotion. The rest are just shadows."

My newborn spirit drank from that pool again and again from that day on.

A few weeks later my friend Sunnie called me to tell me that she and her husband would like to have a ceremony to celebrate their commitment to preserving the land and sacred site around which their home had been built. "Susan tells me that you are a pipe bearer. I didn't know that. How have you kept it such a secret?"

I didn't want to get into the difficulties: my sensitivity to cultural appropriation issues, the fact that I felt I had pretty much flunked out of my apprenticeship, and the fact that the Pipe had been sent to live with Pipp until it was safe from my rages. I felt self-conscious because, except in Michigan, I had never been asked to do ceremony. What would I do? However, I thanked Sunnie and agreed to come out to her house on a Sunday evening in September.

Usually, September nights in the desert are dark and miserable. The sun sets early, but the heat, humidity, and dusty monsoon winds make every movement uncomfortable. That evening as I drove to Sunnie's, the sun had not set yet, but the breeze was almost as cool as late fall. Sunnie's house is an extraordinary glassed-in heap of mammoth boulders, and has been featured on the cover of *Architectural Digest* and just about every other journal devoted to architectural beauty. It was built over and around a paleoastronomical site once used by the ancient people who lived in these foothills. She and her husband spent considerable time researching the past of the area and fighting for its preservation against rabid development. On this night, local activists, City Council members, journalists, and friends gathered to dedicate the site as a paleohistorical landmark.

Sunnie greeted me as soon as I arrived and led me to a magnificent catered buffet. "I'm so happy you could be here," she said. "And we were able to persuade Delmar Boni to come as well to help us with the ceremony."

I jumped. Delmar Boni! I remembered this Apache medicine man from the memorial service he had performed for one of
our Fellows at Taliesin. Several hundred of us had sat on the
mountainside, surrounded by towering prayer flags in the Apache
holy colors, black, white, yellow, and green.

I certainly was not going to perform any ceremony. It
might offend a Native American to have a white woman speaking
of the Medicine Wheel. So when it was my turn to speak I just
offered some words of thanks to Sunnie and her husband for preserving this land, and I held up a few little pieces of Hohokam
pottery my great uncle had given my mother, and said, "I have
brought these potsherds to right a wrong that was done to the
people of this land, and to the land itself. I will give them to the
children here to go and bury all over this area—to bless this area,
and perhaps to confuse future archaeologists!" The crowd
laughed, and then drifted back toward the drinks. The sun was
setting, and Delmar was now playing a drum. I noticed that he
played a drum made of a bucket, a chamois, and a bicycle tire
tube—a far cry from the lovely hand-painted drums manufac-
tured in Taos for yuppie displays. His clothes were similarly modest and eccentric, just a cowboy shirt and jeans and his big black
top hat. He was playing his heart out and singing a joyous song
to the setting sun, but nobody was paying attention, because the
hot canapés had been served. I didn't like this, so I began sidling
up to people and saying things like, "Listen to how the drumming
changes rhythm with the sounds of the crickets!" and, "Listen,
the coyotes hear his singing and they're calling back to him!" As
several people began to be attentive, I encouraged them to move
closer toward him. Soon at least fifteen people had set down their
wine glasses and had wandered over.

I turned to the group and said, "Perhaps it would be a
courtesy to our friend if we would dance to his music." They
looked puzzled, but I took the hands of my little girl and Sunnie's
granddaughter and showed them how to go forward and back as
I had seen at the pow wows. They were delighted, and soon the
rest of the group joined in. Others wandered over, and it wasn't
long before most of the party was dancing or listening politely to
Delmar's zealous singing and drumming. The sun set, the song
ended, and we all applauded. I took Gracie to get some cookies,
and then headed for the parking lot. As I was approaching my

car, Delmar stepped out from behind a pickup truck. He walked straight toward me, smiling, and then reached forward, indicating that I should put out my hand. I did so, and he placed a small cotton sack of tobacco in my palm. "Do you know what this means?" I knew that tobacco was a gift that was given to medicine people. I looked up at him and his eyes crinkled in fun. "I know what you are."

"You do?"

"Yeah, I know what you are, so why are you dancing in the shadows?"

I was dumfounded, and had no answer, but I must have looked pleased. He then said, "Hey, thanks for what you did. Thanks for helping. Maybe we'll be working together sometime soon." Then he shook Gracie's hand and introduced himself and did the same with me. I introduced myself, and he hugged me. "Be seeing you soon!" he said, and hopped in his pickup.

So had he really seen something? Was there a power awakening in me that I could not sense yet?

Winter continued, however, but now I needed a therapist who could help me to get rid of my last clouds of my depression, to integrate what I had learned, and to find my new power. I asked the psychiatrist and author of books on Native American spirituality Carl Hammerschlag to be my guide.

Even though I had not cried in a long time, I cried for most of the first therapeutic hour that I spent with Carl. We discussed my ideas about what had gone wrong with me. I told him that I thought I had some kind of bipolar disorder and carefully described how well I fit into that diagnostic category. My wild desires and passions, the religiosity of the last few years could all be explained as mania; the out-of-proportion devastation I experienced after Ten White Bears's abandonment must surely be bipolar depression.

He shook his head and laughed. "Oh, you don't believe that at all. You chose the Red Road, and you chose your spirituality. Now you want to use the medical model to explain your experience. You can't do that. You can't turn back."

"But I am depressed, I'm classic, I'm the kind of person I used to diagnose in five minutes, and I can't get over it. And I'm suffering from obsessive thinking as well. My mind is so full of garbage I just want to medicate myself into oblivion. For six months, SIX MONTHS, night and day, I just relive that night, the things he said to me, and the terrible things I did. I'm so tired of having to go over and over it in my mind. I'm just so tired. I need help!" I started weeping into my wet Kleenex again.

"I think you gave this depression to yourself, for reasons we will discover here. I will work with you, but I will not use the medical model or listen to your scientific explanations. That is not why you came to me. You will heal yourself, and you will do it with the sacred ways. Do you know how to make a prayer tie?"

"Of course I do." I was thinking of how Ten White Bears had taught me to fold a pinch of tobacco in a red square of cloth, and then place it above my head in the sweat lodge. I had done this for each ceremony. Yes, I was an old hand at making a prayer tie.

He smiled, a little obnoxiously. "Well, then, you are going to make a thousand of them. You will find kinnick kinnick; I know you are resourceful and will find it. You will find the proper cloth. You will make ties of red, yellow, black, and white, symbolizing the Four Directions. Do you think you can do this?"

High achiever and good patient that I am, I automatically replied, "Oh yes, I can, but it might take me a few weeks."

He let out a few sonic booms of laughter. "It will take you a lot longer than that. It will take you until spring. And when they are finished, you will sit vigil surrounded by them, all night, in a place I will determine at that time. You will be safe, although you will be uncomfortable. Until that time, I will work with you here, once a week. And you will also have the assistance of my brother and friend, Delmar Boni, if he agrees to help you. Do you know Mr. Boni?"

Yes, I knew Delmar Boni! But it would be embarrassing to ask for his help; maybe he would be offended by my request for help. On the other hand, perhaps he wouldn't be offended. He had given me a pouch of tobacco. He had said, "I know what you are."

"I do know him."

"He can help you with your healing. Call him."

I waited a few days, thinking of my strategy. No strategy occurred to me. I was preparing for a trip to St. Louis, where there would be a camp planning meeting. I assumed that Ten White Bears would not be there, because it was just my own team. It would be a comfortable, pleasant meeting in my own hometown. I reflected happily upon the fact that I was now able to travel without emotional incident. However, a few nights before leaving, as I pulled out of my closet the black camel coat I had last worn that dreadful night the spring before, several pink tissues fell out of the pocket. I remembered for the first time the plane ride back from Minnesota. A girl, perhaps seventeen years old, sat next to me as I sobbed uncontrollably. She said, "Here, here are some tissues. Are you all right?"

"Someone died," I had said. She had reached over and placed her small, polished fingertips over my hand. "Then you just cry. You just cry."

How long would it be before I could express the simple compassion that arises from a quiet heart like hers? How long before I would be able to give, to listen to another, to love? I was sick of myself, sick of the blood-sucking selfishness of depression. And I was going to beat it, I was going to get well. I looked up Delmar's name, a few tiny letters, in the fat Phoenix phonebook. "Mr. Boni? Delmar? This is Barbara Kerr. Do you remember me?"

"I was wondering when you would call."

"Oh, did Carl tell you I would call?"

"No. I was just thinking you would call. Because you know, we kind of met at that lady's house, what was her name? The one with the finger sandwiches?"

I laughed. "Sunnie's. Yes, I remember, you gave me some tobacco."

A long Indian silence (longer conversational latency time, I was thinking, principle of noninterruption, just shut up, just shut up, oh wait a minute—it's actually my turn) . . .

"I need your help. I'm having this depression, and it has to do with some spiritual experiences I had, and Carl is helping me, and he says I need to make a thousand prayer ties. But I really don't know how, and I need to know the proper way . . ." and now I was afraid I was going to start to boo-hoo again and blow my chances to present myself as a person with some dignity.

"Then you need to come see me tomorrow. At noon, at the Metro Center, at the Indian counselors' meeting at the Embassy Suites."

Wait. That was too soon, I couldn't fit that in my schedule.

"I'm sorry, I have to take these Hungarian visiting schol-ars to lunch."

"Tell them to go away."

He had hung up, and I was in cross-cultural hell, because I knew I couldn't reschedule a healing. I would just have to make the Hungarians go away.

I did make the Hungarians go away, by having Sandy take them to lunch. (Sandy was excited to have a mission. He, too, had been healing nicely, and was eager to assist me in my cure.) By twelve noon I was in the courtyard of the Embassy Suites, where about sixty Native Americans were gathered under a gaily striped pavilion set up on the lawn to handle overflow meetings. I peeked into the opening and saw Delmar clear on the other side of the tent, in a tall black cowboy hat bent over an easel, where he was sketching the AA-like meeting that was occurring. Everyone within forty feet turned clear around and stared at me, and I felt audibly blonde and profoundly out of place. I smiled brightly and began to back out. I had backed as far as the door to the lobby when Delmar showed up at my side, took my arm and said, "Let's go in your buggy."

This was unexpected, but so was everything else that had happened so far, so I let him in to my Explorer, got behind the wheel, turned on the ignition and was hit by a blast of the Doors singing, "Break on through to the other side, to the other side, hey, hey, hey, hey . . ." I started to turn it off.

"Doors. Yeah. Break on through to the other side. You know what that's about?"

I turned it down instead of off. "What?"

"Breaking on through to the other side. You know what happens when you break on through? You're dead. I have seen a lot of people trying to break on through. Gotta be careful."

"Um . . . Where are we going?"

He started calling out directions, up this avenue, down that street. I wondered what I should be telling him. He didn't seem to have much curiosity, but he listened attentively as he fiddled with the radio dial. I was saying that I was going to Carl for help because I had suffered a depression after my spiritual teacher cut me loose. He taught me some of the medicine ways, and showed me how to go to the Spirit World, I said, but then I saw and did things that were very frightening to me, and my teacher had left me all alone to try to make sense of what had happened to me.

"A medicine man is just a man. It's about just breathing and walking. Pouring the water. Talking to the Stone People. He's breathing now and he's walking his road. You're breathing. You're walking."

A few minutes later we were at the entrance to a desert mountain preserve, I think Shadow Mountain. "Park here. We're gonna walk up there, get a little closer to the mountain." He had a big brown paper bag with him I hadn't noticed before. I was wearing a velour skirt and sweater, and got stickers in the fabric as he hiked me up the hill. We stopped at a crest and stood a while in the noontime sun. He spread a red cloth on the ground, and placed black, white, green, and yellow symbols around me. "Sit on this."

I sat cross-legged on the red cloth. I stared down. Oh goodness, I recognize this fabric, I thought, this is one of those nice tablecloths they sell at Dillards, this is his wife's tablecloth, and I shouldn't be sitting on it on the ground. I looked up, and standing over me was a medicine man, a medicine man who grew out of the desert like the creosote and cholla that surrounded us. Two hawks circled far above his head in the cloudless sky. This is it, I thought. This is where I was going. His eyes were closed in his broad face. His raven black hair, which hung down to his elbows, was lifted by the breeze. He whispered words in Apache as he drew pollen from a little sack and blew it in the four directions. He held his hands high in the four directions. Then he leaned over me and pressed the pollen into my forehead, my chest, my shoulders, and finally on to my tongue. He sang in this strange language, full of whispers and hisses, treble and bass, sustained dark vowels and resonant tones.

Now the tears began to flow again. He lifted me up and patted me all over with his fingers spread wide and continued to sing. My heart understood and heard his words. I knew that he was telling me that he walked in the Light, and that his fingers were Light, and that I would be filled with Light. And in those moments, I knew for the first time since my soul died within me that I would be healed, and that the life and happiness that had been taken from me would be returned. I was also learning, in the marrow of my bones, what Ten White Bears had tried to teach me: that he was not the source of the power that he wielded. Here was another, who spoke a different language, and performed a different ceremony, but whose healing power was as familiar to me as a friend's face—familiar because it was my own healing power being stirred up within me. It had not been the man, not Ten White Bears who had given me my new life and my happiness. It had been the Mystery, working through my own Self. I had drawn down the power of the Great Spirit myself, because I had found Ten White Bears, and I had found Little Horse, and now I had found Delmar. Standing there I felt like Dorothy in her ruby red shoes, finding out that she had always had the power to go wherever she wanted to, even after the wind whipped the Wizard away. Delmar now took me in his arms and hugged me long, and then longer. In fact, it was a beat too long for my cultural upbringing. It was that extra beat to the measure of contact that affirmed the healing that had begun taking place in me. I finally relaxed into it, and an idiotic grin spread across my face. I looked up at Delmar to see that he was grinning, too. Then he bounced me around in a little waltz, singing "Ha naa na na ni yee, Ha naa na na ni yee, Ha naa na na ni yee, Ha naa na na ni yee . . . Twinkle twinkle little star, How I wonder what you are . . . Ha naa na na ni yee, Ha naa na na ne yee . . . Happy birthday to you, happy birthday to you . . . Ha na ee ee ya! Ha na ee ee ya!"

Then, to my amused horror, he got out a big scissors and cut a square out of the nice red tablecloth. He laid two pouches of tobacco next to it, and blessed them with pollen. Taking a pinch of tobacco, he twisted it in the tie and then looped a string around it tight. "This is how you do it. You know how. When you begin to work on your ties, you take four steps before you get to the place where you do your work. You pray at each step, 'Creator, help me out here,' or something like that. Now this tobacco is blessed, now it's sacred. You can do those ties now." He folded up the cloth, the square and the two pouches of tobacco.

I knew I still had a lot of work to do, a lot of hours of therapy. A lot of prayer ties. There would be more tears as I patched up the story of my life. But after that day with Delmar, I was never in doubt that I would be whole again.

I was in such a rush to finish the prayer ties before spring that I took them with me everywhere. They even came with me to a planning meeting in late November. To my surprise, Ten White Bears was there after all. But I felt neither animosity nor attraction. Chuck was protective, but did not need to be. A new calm had settled over me and I sat contentedly through the long meetings, tying the ties and cheerfully participating. Ten White Bears looked at my prayer ties during a break and I told him of my task. He smiled and showed me a quick little knot I could use to tie them faster.

I enjoyed doing the prayer ties during the holidays, in between the festivities. I took them to my visit to my alma mater at the beginning of the New Year, where I was being honored with a visiting scholar award. Before one of my speeches, I sat with my favorite college professor, Joe, now a dear friend, who was to introduce me. My hands were busily wrapping pinches of tobacco and tying knots. By now I was quite expert, and my fingers must have flown over my task as Joe looked at me in wonderment. He questioned me closely, and I found myself admitting not only that I was in therapy, but the reason why. It had taken some courage to explain to Joe, the mentor to my intellect, that I had become, of all things, an apprentice to a medicine man, but he responded with supportive curiosity. I realized then that one of the purposes of the bulky mass of fabric and string and tobacco I had carried with me everywhere was a sort of coming-out process. Carl had given me this task so that everywhere I went I would be compelled to answer the curious questions of my friends and family and to tell the truth about the person I was becoming. I might as well have been wearing a large feather headdress.

The prayer ties, and the prayers that accompanied them, did their work. And the sessions with Carl, who listened carefully to my stories, poked fun at my self-dramatization, and suggested new ways of seeing the events, were helping me to create a new narrative. A sort of crystallization was occurring, where all the elements of my story lined up in a new way, clear and beautifully faceted.

Beginning with my childhood, he showed me how the Great Spirit had been preparing me for a long time to meet Ten White Bears. The wild and lonely childhood of an eccentric little girl; the intellectual curiosity that led me to science, and to the study of extraordinary people; the hunger for connection and the fulfillment I found in the role of student and teacher; all created the apprentice. The fear of abandonment, the rejection of the aggressive and powerful aspects of the feminine, as well as the loss of faith in the Mystery led directly to my darkness.

He repeated what all the medicine people had said: that my disintegration was necessary, and that if Ten White Bears had not precipitated it in the way that he did, that the Mystery would have sent another devastation to take me apart. He helped me to see what it must have been like for Ten White Bears, how difficult and also how necessary it was for him to let me go. "Delmar is right," he said. "A medicine man is just a man. And Ten White Bears is a good man."

He challenged me to take up my work again and to come out of the shadows. It was not my path to go off into the desert as holy hermit or to run off to Sedona to live among the crystal shops and vortices. Rather, I should do my medicine in my own home: the university and the academic world. There is much to be done, he told me, and, "You will not have the luxury of being bananas forever."

So it was then that I knew that my time of being bananas was nearly over. I was ready to start writing letters to the medicine man again.

Scottsdale Arizona

Ten White Bears,

I wonder if you've ever seen horses in the winter. I used to love to visit my horses in their pasture in January. Their thick coats stand up for warmth, frost tipping their manes, tails, and fetlocks. Horses are so enterprising in winter, scuffing up the snow for the tender green shoots below, stripping the bark off of trees, and galloping from one end of the meadow to the other. Their hooves striking the ice sound like flint on steel. I have been enterprising, too, during my winter, reflecting, working hard to make changes in myself, and learning from everyone I meet. I think this is the time to share the lessons that I have learned. Mary, my doctoral student; Delmar, who is a San Carlos Apache ceremonial healer; Carl Hammerschlag, who was my psychotherapist; and Sandy and Susan, whom you know as friends, were all helpful to me in learning these lessons. And in visions, Medicine Swan has been there to show the way.

Love is the only genuine emotion. The rest are shadows. This is the lesson I learned, both from the sweat lodge, from the "peeling" exercise, from conversations with Medicine Swan. In these experiences, where all emotions are experienced and then cleansed, what remains when the all many forms of anger, fear, and sorrow are washed away is love. Love is the unexpected, invincible foundation of our experience, and the other emotions are just incomplete reflections of it.

Ignore the shadows and they grow until they engulf you and your loved ones in darkness. If you try to forget your fear, deny your anger, repress your desire, or put away your sorrow, then they will consume you and hurt everyone you love. It is not enough to face Iktome's Warriors: it is necessary to allow them to run their lances straight through you and out the other side.

No relationship with another person can heal your wounds. The only way to heal one's wound is to complete the pain. This is a lot like the last lesson, except for the implications for relationships past and present. I learned that we all carry around some unhealed wound for some period of time, because all parents are fallible in some way. So we go through a lot of our lives trying to find the all-loving parent or replicate the youthful romance to heal the wound. Even the Great Spirit will not heal us without our doing the hard work of understanding the nature of the wound, experiencing it fully, and allowing all the emotions arising from the injury to pass through us unchallenged, unhindered, unquestioned.

Just consider for a moment that you are exactly where you need to be. When you are really miserable, uncomfortable, or in a tight situation, maybe that's where you are supposed to be. Stop struggling. When you are content, fulfilled, alive, maybe that's where you are supposed to be. Be happy.

You are going to get everything you need. However, the Universe is on Universe time, not your time. Nevertheless, you, Your Self, will be provided with everything you need to be complete, and then you will rest in the heart of the Creator. Stay strong as you can be. Be as beautiful as you can make yourself. Learn and fill your mind with all the knowledge that is available to you. Love as much as you can as many people as you can. Then you will be ready.

These are the lessons I learned during this very hard year, which is now almost behind me. I have stayed away from recovery groups—because what am I in recovery from?!—but I am afraid these lessons may sound terribly like those self-help manuals used by the twelve-steppers. I know that you, and lots of people, know these things, but they are hard won lessons for me, and therefore very precious. The prayer ties that I began during the St. Louis weekend in November are almost done. Did you know that I didn't know you were going to be there? I am glad you were there to show me how to tie the prayer ties so efficiently. It is such a satisfying experience to put in the tobacco, the prayer, twist the bundle, open the loop, slip the knot and move to the next in line; after close to a thousand, I'm an expert! Next month I will do a sweat at Taliesin, climb the mountain, and make a circle of prayer ties with the opening at the yellow ties. I will keep a vigil through the night, and in the morning, will leave through the doorway to spring. These are the ceremonies that Carl and Delmar planned for me, so that I can be healed completely and can go on with my work in this world.

I hear the Pipe calling sometimes. Perhaps you do too.

I want you to know that I have no expectations about our relationship (or any relationship, for that matter). Perhaps I've learned unconditional love, or just the capacity to take care of myself. Iktome's lances have passed through me, leaving only the silvery traces of their scars. I understand now how I wronged you a year ago. I know now how hard it has been for you. So I approach you with an open heart, and a renewed spirit, saying, it is time for the horse and bear to run together again.

Love,

Medicine Horse

This was my last session with Dr. Hammerschlag before I would go up the mountain to complete my healing. As usual, he lit the sage quietly and we smudged ourselves. He offered a short prayer, and then it was time to talk.

"Remind me of all the terrible things that have happened to you," he said.

I giggled. "No! I don't feel like crying today!"

"Why not?"

"Because it's over. I am content. I'm done with the struggle. I accept. Everything that happened to me, I accept."

"It's a good thing to accept and to thank the Creator for your newfound acceptance." He stretched out his long arms toward heaven, looked up, and yelled, "CREATOR, THANK YOU." The room shook. And then melodramatically lowering his voice (I laughed again), he said, "But you must not give up the struggle for truth. Do you know the story of Jacob and Esau? Jacob and Esau were brothers. Esau, the older brother, rough and curly haired, was heir to the land. But Jacob was most favored by his mother. When Abraham, their father, lay dying, she wrapped Jacob in a sheepskin so that he would be mistaken for Esau, and receive his father's blessing as his heir. When Esau returned, he found to his fury that Jacob was master. His anger was so great that their mother sent Jacob to live twenty years with his uncle, where he worked hard and married. He longed to return, but feared his brother's wrath. He prayed to God, who assured him that he would help him. On the night before his return, he was awakened by a stranger attacking him and forcing him to wrestle. Jacob struggled with the stranger all night long, and by morning, Jacob had prevailed. When as the sun began to rise, the stranger called out to him to let him go. Jacob had a glimpse of his face, and knew that he had seen the face of the Angel of God. He had wrestled with God and he had survived. God's Angel said to him, 'Henceforth, you will be called Ysrael and your children shall cover this land.' He turned to go home, exhausted and tattered, and saw his brother coming over the hill, greeting him with forgiveness and love."

Carl paused. "I am a Jew," he said. "Do you know what we are called? We are not called the sons of Esau. We are not called the sons of Jacob. We are called the sons of Ysrael." He whispered. "Do you know what that means? IT MEANS STRUGGLES WITH ANGELS! I AM A SON OF YSRAEL!" (Shouting, hands flailing, bushy hair was flying about). Then his eyes grew soft and he leaned forward. "I know that you are not a Jew. But my sister, my friend, you are a daughter of Ysrael, because you, too, struggled with the Angel. You must never stop your struggle, because it is your nature. It is your gift . . ."

"Now take your thousand prayer ties, and when you are ready, sometime before the first day of spring, you will do your all-night vigil surrounded by these ties. After your vigil, you will leave the circle through the ties of spring. You will have a sweat lodge ceremony, and after the ceremony, you will return your ties to the Stone People and the fire. You will then leave your winter behind you and you will be healed."

It happened as he said, but not exactly in that order. I didn't know how the sweat lodge would happen, or when all this would occur. Perhaps the last week in January, I thought when I am done with my seminar . . . but it rained a freezing rain that weekend, and I didn't feel like an all-night vigil. Perhaps my birthday, I thought. But my birthday came and went, with so many festivities that there seemed to be no time for such a long ceremony. Late in February, Roseann called. "May I come for my birthday? And can our friends have a slumber party at your house? And can we do a sweat lodge? I need to find the still place I found in Ten White Bears' lodge. I know I can find it in yours."

Her birthday was the weekend that would be the anniversary of my disintegration and separation from Ten White Bears. I knew the dangers of the "anniversary effect," the possibility that my depression could be re-engaged by the memories, the date, even the slant of light that matched that of my zero hour. I had planned to spend it quietly, taking really good care of myself, although I always disliked people who take really good care of themselves. It always seemed to me to be the height of narcissism to pamper oneself just to get through a mood. Nevertheless, that had been my plan. But I didn't hesitate long; what could be better than a houseful of my dearest friends to help protect me from the Panther?

So on the first Friday in March, Roseann flew in with her husband Harper. As small and pretty as she is, she still managed to look perfectly ferocious as she strode toward me, high-heeled boots tapping. She snapped, "Look at you! How much weight have you lost? I could kill that medicine man for this!"

"Oh Roseann, I'm just fine. I feel great. And I plan to gain ten pounds this weekend!" Harper gave me a hug and said, "Then let the eating begin!"

Our friend Marsha arrived on a later flight, and Roseann's brother drove up from Tucson. Pipp arrived in her aged brown Toyota with the bumper sticker, "Magic Happens," laden with teas and herbs. She had brought the Pipe with her. That Friday night we sat around my fireplace just as we had two years before when I had confessed my strange attraction to the spiritual life and the medicine man who had brought me to it. All of us had spent some time struggling with the angels in the last two years. Roseann spoke of the depression she was just beginning to name, and Pipp talked about learning to be alone. We made our plans for the sweat lodge, knowing that the words we shared beside the fire were preparing us for our meeting in that sacred ceremony.

I decided that Saturday night I would do the vigil alone at Taliesin and ask my friends to join me Sunday morning at sunrise for the sweat lodge ceremony. Susan, my friend and mentor at Taliesin, would meet my friends at the gate and bring them to the sweat lodge site.

Saturday night came, and it wasn't the solemn affair I had envisioned. A fast wasn't really possible; but Delmar had taught me that many of the orthodoxies of vision quests were just that—orthodoxies, and not necessities. I packed my medicine basket, flashlight, and blankets with a stomach full of birthday cake. Instead of a private preparation, my women friends and I banged around the kitchen preparing the breakfast food for the next day. We were all wearing the matching orange pajamas that Roseann had brought for us. Sandy called several times during the preparation to wish me luck. The men chatted with us, asking constant questions. "What's that stick for?" "Can I try your drum?" "Do you gals really WANT to do this?" My daughter kept waking up and padding into the kitchen to join the excitement. "Mommy, can I have some of these grapes? Can I eat them in bed?"

Finally, everybody settled down and went to their rooms, the women to get a few hours of sleep and then wake each other up before dawn. The men had a plan to sleep late, drink cappuccino and then read the *New York Times*. I went in to kiss Chuck goodbye. He was already fragrant with sleep. "Have a good time, and get well," he murmured, and turned over.

The crescent moon was setting and Venus was rising over Taliesin Mountain when I arrived at the sweat lodge clearing. I stood there and watched the orange horn of the moon slip behind South Mountain. It was cold and breezy, and it seemed very strange to be out alone in the middle of the desert at midnight. I began to remove my prayer ties from my basket, untangling the long strings as I pulled them out. First the red ones. There was number one, made of Delmar's wife's tablecloth, with its big knot and fat pouch of sweet-smelling tobacco. There was the neat knot that Ten White Bears had taught me to make on the day after my healing in the desert with Delmar. And the long string of red ties made throughout November and December when I felt my spirit beginning to stir again. These were followed by yellow ties I remembered making through the holidays and New Year in my parents' house. Then came the black ties made hastily as I prepared my winter seminars and got the children ready for a new semester. Finally, the white ties.

I arranged the ties in a circle around me almost thirty feet across. I sat down facing east, my sleeping bag wrapped around me. I could see the great grandfather saguaro that guarded the sweat lodge in front of me, and the looming outline of the peak of Taliesin Mountain. Above the mountain, the great Star Path lay across the sky. All around me the palo verde trees and mesquites whispered in the wind, and a few early crickets chirped. It was funny that I had come this far to reflect and pray, and after twelve months of obsession with my misery and loneliness for my teacher, I didn't have a thought in my head, except that it was damned cold.

I got chillier as the night wore on, and I trembled each time a gust whipped up the dust in the clearing. I sat there as dumb as a beast, with no visions, no enlightenments, nothing but the quiet and the night. So I brought to mind every family member and friend I had ever known, sort of in chronological order, and sent a prayer up of thanks for what they had given me. I spent some time with my grandmother Barbara. How wonderful to see my Grandma behind me in the mirror as she braided my hair and said in German, "You are my little Brynhilde." Wait . . . wait . . . What was it? "Du bist meine kleine Brynhilde." Her little Brynhilde, the warrior goddess who rescued heroes from battle and took them on her horse Grane to Valhalla. The one who was rescued from a twenty-year sleep by Siegfried's kiss. The one who was betrayed by Siegfried. The one who galloped to her death, leaping into his funeral pyre. The flames had leapt up and destroyed the heavens themselves, and the old Gods along with them. I laughed as I thought of Brynhilde in her braids and horned helmet, galloping around saving guys and working herself up into a rage as one after another disappointed her. It was not the first time that I wondered if we are all programmed to play out some fairy tale script given to us when we were too young to refuse. Perhaps, though, as Carl said, perhaps I was being prepared, even as a child, for the struggle that lay ahead of me. Maybe the story of Brynhilde was not about rescuing men, or a particular medicine man, but about rescuing my own power.

The night continued. The breeze whipped the flames high, snapping sparks into the darkness. The mesquite smoke and dew-soaked creosote bushes entwined their fragrances. Pack rats skipped by me just beyond the firelight, and the distant scuffling of the javelina family feeding on prickly pears could be heard near the road. I yawned and shivered, and kept having the impulse to laugh. What if my self-healing ceremony caused a brush fire and burned down Frank Lloyd Wright's wife's dog shrine, which was perilously close by? Would I be reviled by architecture critics, by dog lovers, by Mrs. Wright's fans? Freezing in my blanket, I remembered that inside the trunks in the archives were Mr. and Mrs. Wright's capes, berets, and furs, and fantasized wrapping myself in them. What if I were found, dead of exposure in the morning, wrapped in Mr. Wright's cape? What would he have thought of my sweat lodge? Would it have fit into his master plan?

Fortunately, these whims gave way to an awareness that the sky had changed from black to indigo. Dawn was coming. What had Carl told me? That I should make a gate right where the medicine ties of spring began. That at dawn, I should walk through that gate into spring. But would spring really be there? Would I feel different outside the medicine circle of my grieving? Would it really be better over there, to the east, where the sun was lightening the sky? Dawn was coming, and I had made no major discoveries. I had reviewed the blessings of all the people of my life. I had remembered Brynhilde, and let her go galloping away. And I had laughed. Perhaps this was enough.

I heard footsteps scattering the gravel on the road. My friends were arriving! Time to leave the circle.

My women friends arrived as the first glow of the dawn lit the sky, with many hugs and excited whispers. Susan, Roseann, Pip, Marsha, old and new friends, crept into the lodge and sat in the four directions, with me by the door. A friend named Barbara, as fire keeper, brought in the first twelve stones, and the ceremony began. The Creation story arose from my lips and I found myself speaking of our First Mother. Suddenly I was she, and she was in me. I spoke in gratitude and love to the women who had seen me through the darkness. We spoke of women things, and I shared the lessons I had learned during my winter. In the east, I told our First Mother's story, and how she gave her body to be our Earth. The lesson of the east was given: All things are sacred. And I shared my personal lesson of the east: Love is the only genuine emotion.

Another twelve stones were brought in, and I told the story of Iktome and the Forty-Nine Warriors. How surprising to hear, as the words fell from my lips, that this time, the littlest warrior who faced the terrors of Iktome was a young woman! The lesson of the south was told: You are the Mystery, and the Mystery is you. Face your most frightening emotions and let their lances run through you. They are nothing but illusions, for you are not separate from the Mystery, which is Love. My friends told the stories of their fears and gave their fears back to the fire.

It was the time of the third round, the time of the west, and now I was lost in the Mystery. I do not know what story was told, but I remember our sweet song:

May the Great Spirit grant you peace of mind.
May the peace be there in all the things you find.
May the peace be there in what you leave behind.

In this round where we honored the time of maturity and womanhood, I heard my friends speak of the joys and sorrows of adult responsibilities. The lesson of the west ended the round: Respect and maintain the differences. Consider, I said, consider that you are exactly where you are supposed to be. And that others are where they are supposed to be.

When the stones of the fourth and final round were brought in, sunlight poured in the door. In the great darkness and heat of that last round, we breathlessly recounted our stories of north, and the losses of winter. "Only the earth and the sky last forever. Make each day a good day to die." Medicine Swan's words, given to me in my winter rang out, seemingly in her voice: "You will have everything you need. Stay strong and beautiful and loving and you will be ready." We sang loudly, we drummed, and we reached out to one another, joining hands in the darkness and closing the Hoop. We were cleansed, and made new.

After the sweat lodge, as my friends lay peacefully steaming on the cool desert floor, I knew it was time to burn my thousand prayer ties and return them to the Mystery. So I quietly moved on my knees toward the glowing embers of the fire that had heated our stones, bringing my bundle of ties. I heard a slight stirring coming from the sparse shadows of the creosote bush to my left. Roseann was lying there on her side. I saw her face turn toward me, her black eyes glistening watchfully. She smiled. I smiled back.

As I gathered up the red ties, I thought of the first spring-time of my soul, when my spirit was newly awakened. I thought of my fearful first sweat lodge and the joyful second one. I remembered the April evening four years before when I had yield-ed to the call of the Spirit for the first time, and I gave thanks for that miracle. I lay the ties on the stones. They hissed and were gone.

Next I held the yellow ties of summer over the fire, remembering the great bloom of knowledge during my appren-ticeship, the songs and stories, the visits to the Spirit land, and my learning the language of dreams. I threw the yellow ties in a heap, and they too turned to white smoke.

Then came the bittersweet black prayer ties of autumn and early winter, and I remembered Ten White Bears' gentle grieving and my efforts to bring him from between the wind. I remembered the love that settled over me as the snow fell, the Creator's blessing before sleep. The black ties smelled like burn-ing leaves as they disappeared.

Now it was time for the white ties of winter. I remembered my possessiveness and desperate attempts to hold on to my teacher, but this time without shame. After the strawberries and the candlelight, the well-worn manuscript and the wooly medi-cine blanket, the snow and the dawn, the bubbling greetings and the bundled goodbyes . . . after all of this, was it such a terrible thing to have wanted it to go on? Was it so terrible that I should have wanted this good and kind man, this keeper of a great soul, to remain by my side? Only an angel could have been indifferent to his awakening life force, and I was only an ordinary woman. I remembered my rage against him when he separated from me, but this time the Panther had no power over me. I had struggled with her and I had prevailed. I remembered the passing of the Little Horse into the arms of Medicine Swan as I lay sick in the cold waves of Lake Michigan. I knew now that the Little Horse had borne within her the certainty of her own death, because she was incomplete. The separation was necessary to help me become complete. It was the wisdom of the Spirit that made this happen. Remembering the kindness and love that had surrounded me through my winter, I clutched the white ties to my heart. Remembering the great mystery of healing, I kissed the bundle. Oh, the ties of winter were hard to give up! I held them to me again, and heard once again a rustling next to me. Roseann's eyes filled with tears, and she smiled encouragingly. She nodded, and her lips formed the words, "Go ahead." I lay the white ties upon the now white ashes with a sigh, and they formed a lovely column of white smoke, spiraling up into the bright blue sky.

So it was that I gave up my sadness and was healed, and became Medicine Horse of the White Hand Clan, the one I am now.

Only a few weeks later, when the wildflowers on mountains around our Valley burst into bloom, Ten White Bears surprised me with a visit. We climbed Taliesin Mountain. We received the Pipe in ceremony, both of our hands outstretched, from our friend Susan, who bade us to work together in peace and friendship.

How has life been different since that time four years ago when I ended the journey into darkness? Mostly, it has been an ordinary life. I help my little girl get ready for school; I drive into the university, perhaps meeting Chuck for coffee before work. I go to meetings, teach classes, and meet with students. I go home, shop on the way, fix dinner, help Gracie with her homework, relax with Chuck, email my son at college and my friends, and go to bed.

Recently, I found a beautiful retreat house on several acres in the desert, and bought it to have a place for a sweat lodge, and for my students, colleagues, old friends and new to come together to learn about spiritual intelligence. It is called Cascabel, which means "little bell." It is also what the Mexican people call the rattlesnake, the symbol of transformation. It is a busy life, managing a university career and a vocation as a teacher of the medicine ways. On the best days, I am aware of the sacredness of each moment. On the worst days, I'm tired and distracted, like everyone else.

What is different about my life is how, even on a tired and distracted day, I might hear the call, the call to go There, and to heal or teach not from my intellect, but from my connection to the Mystery. A student comes in with tears in her eyes because she cannot finish her thesis; I begin the usual platitudes about filing for an extension, and then hear the call. I go There, and somehow know the source of her pain, and speak the words that need to be spoken. Often those words are a person's great secret: "You cannot work because you are still grieving for the loss of your child. Take your time to grieve." After the initial surprise, "How did you know that about me? How did you know I lost a child?" there is relief and a little healing.

It is in my teaching that I most often hear the call. When that happens, the ordinary classroom with its uncomfortable chairs and fluorescent lighting suddenly becomes a nonordinary place. Through stories of my apprenticeship, and stories of medicine men and women and their work, I transport my students along with me to the places I have been, and challenge them to make the same journey.

My students often ask, "Was it real? Did your teacher dematerialize? Did you really change into a panther?" These questions now have a different meaning for me. It was real to me. It was not like being a panther. It was being a panther. I was in the Spirit World, and the rules are different there. Here in the ordinary world, no, I'm sure that these events appear differently. In the sweat lodge, people are liberated from time and space; the ceremony takes them into the sky and down below the earth, and seems to them to take about twenty minutes. To the fire keepers outside, the voices in the lodge are muted but all present and accounted for, and the ceremony takes about four hours. However, the effects of these events in the ordinary world are indeed real. The people who enter the sweat lodge emerge with observable behavior changes that last often for a lifetime. My teacher was able to disappear and evade a well-meaning hospital staff so that he could perform the final rites for our dying friend. My ulcer was healed, and stayed that way. My heart was healed and stayed that way. Spiritual intelligence involves understanding that there is not a distinction between real and not real, rather that there are layers of realities, with different ways of knowing at each level. This is how I try to answer my students' questions about reality.

My students are also full of questions about how these experiences fit into the scientific paradigm in which I still participate. Because my work involves training both psychological researchers and therapists, I have had to think carefully about what science means to me now. Unlike many scholars who experience a spiritual transformation, I didn't turn my back on science. Despite all that has happened to me, I still love to help a student figure out a way to get a really clear confirmation of a hypothesis he or she holds dear—using a research design that will rule out as many answers as possible besides yes, you're right, or sorry, you're wrong. I still love the spirit of skepticism and the love of data that protects us from ideologues. I still use the experimental method to study such aspects of spirituality as "the effects of ceremony on anxiety states." But I also use the shamanic states of consciousness to seek visions about what scientific paths to explore. I know it would be funny to many of my colleagues to think that I use prayer and visioning to decide what topic to investigate next! But it seems to work for me.

Now I have more ways of knowing. Science is one of the disciplines, like meditation or the sweat lodge, for accessing knowledge. Science gives specific details with probabilities attached; religious meditation and ceremony give broader truths, with many possible interpretations. I like to think in and to use the languages of both science and spirit. Thinking back on the events of my apprenticeship, I could construct a natural explanation for every extraordinary happening. That intellectual exercise would make none of it any less magical to me. That we humans should be created in such a way as to be able to have these experiences seems to me a miracle and a gift of the Mystery. To think about these experiences analytically, even to study them scientifically, might be just another way of honoring the Mystery, if we do these things in a sacred way.

In my introductory counseling class, I created a ritual to open the class and to welcome the new counselors to the helping profession. I hold a printout of research data in one hand, and I hold a bundle of burning sage in the other. I display the printout. "This is Science," I say. "Science teaches us to carefully observe the people we help; to withhold our assumptions; and to respect the accumulated learning of the scholars who have gone before us. It teaches us independence of mind and the value of a rational search for the truth." Then I display the sage, smudging myself and passing it around the class to do so with one another.

"This is the Spirit," I say. "The Spirit teaches us to be humble about the limits of our knowledge; to recognize that those we help are our brothers and sisters; and that we heal through our connectedness with them and the great web of being of which we are a part. The science of psychology and the spiritual basis of the traditions of healing are the two pillars of psychotherapy; they are both sacred, and you will learn a respect for both in this class."

My students also ask, "Did you really have to go crazy? Did you really have to *die* like that?" I give the answer that every medicine person has ever given me: Yes, you have to experience your own death. It is the only way. Anyone can learn the songs and stories of the healing traditions of another culture. Anyone can buy a pipe, and wear ghost beads, and learn to build a sweat lodge. But to allow yourself to be completely vulnerable, to be willing to lose everything, even your sanity—this is what is required.

An anthropologist who has studied shamans around the world has said it better than I can say it. Wade Davis (1998) says,

> . . . unlike the priest who is a socially inducted and initiated member of a recognized religious organization, the shaman is one who as a consequence of a completely personal psychological crisis has gained a certain power of his or her own. Whereas the priest is concerned with integrating the individual into a firmly ordered and well-established social context, the shaman seeks the release of his or her own wild genius, wherever that may lead. Almost invariably, an overwhelming mental crisis is part of the vocational summons. Indeed, for the seeker of shamanic wisdom, it is a fine line between mystical initiation and psychological breakdown. Yet though this crisis may resemble a mental breakdown, it cannot be dismissed as one. For it is not a pathological, but a normal event for the gifted mind in these societies, the realization and intuition of a level of spiritual depth that gives the world a sacred character. By following a solitary vision, the shaman breaks not the other traditions of this tribe, but with the comparatively trivial attitude toward the spirit realm that seems to satisfy the majority. In seeking this most difficult path, the shaman becomes the master of death and resurrection, of health and well being. (p 145)

I was never a wild genius, or a "master of resurrection" and I was a clumsy apprentice. I went kicking and screaming though my own journey into darkness, and it took a lot of people's time and energy to pull me out. However, the result was the same as for my teacher, and his teacher before him, and his teacher before him: I was given the capacity to use vision, prayer, and ceremony to honor the Mystery and to help others in their healing.

Wonderful opportunities arise all the time to practice my newfound skills, and I take them when I can. Delmar and I teach a course in shamanic healing at the university—probably the first course taught by a professor and a medicine man. I am learning Apache and its sister language Navajo, and that has led to many new friends and new experiences among the Native American people of Arizona.

I am also called to do ceremonies to mark passages in peoples' lives or in organizations. Word gets around, and I end up blessing new homes or new offices. I might help friends who are getting married to say the words that they want, or if a friend has a new baby, I might be called to make a medicine bundle and do ceremony to honor the new life. I get out of balance, and the call comes and tells me to do ceremony for my own healing, and I obey. Occasionally I am approached by a group of people who ask me to do a sweat lodge. This is a great honor, and I try to oblige.

The sweat lodges in Michigan have now been returned to the Earth and another Hoop closes. The center of my spiritual life is now Cascabel, where a white sweat lodge rises from the Arizona desert in a grove of fragrant sage. In the morning, my horses nicker nearby, and coyotes surround the lodge with song all night. In the crown of the lodge is woven a small twig from the Michigan lodge, symbolizing the continuity of the sweat lodge's medicine power. People come from all over the world to teach and learn the traditional ways of healing of the Four Great Nations in the peaceful adobe house and in the surrounding saguaro forest.

Many of the fire keepers are young people who come to learn the medicine ways. Many of the teachers are friends I met along my path toward wholeness. One of them is an experienced medicine man who comes to Cascabel often, who teaches the young ones their tasks, and who wraps me in my medicine blanket when my ceremonies in the sweat lodge have ended. He is my friend Ten White Bears.

We travel to many conferences and retreats to tell our story. We work with scholars to encourage a new understanding of spiritual intelligence, and we show professional people how to integrate medicine ways into their practice of health care, psychology, or education.

Often when we have been together, we have had the powerful sense of being watched, guided, and provided for. A silvery whisper in the next room as we bend our heads over a manuscript. Twigs snapping around us and a crackle in the wind when, after the sweat lodge, we stand on a wooded dune watching the young people splash in the lake below. "The Spirit World is taking an interest in our work," says Ten White Bears. And I think of a phrase from Dante I learned in college. I didn't fully comprehend it, but I used to say it over and over to myself because it was so beautiful. "E'n la sua volontade e nostre pace": "And His will is our peace." Like Ten White Bears did before me, I have given my will back to the Mystery, trusting, like a proud horse, that I will be carefully led.

The story of the letters, the apprenticeship, and the journey into the shadows now recedes into the past, and present events create a new story. I am so happy that these things happened to me. As we close this Hoop to begin a new one, I think of the story of Creation, how our first Grandfather prepared the Turtle for our First Grandmother to ride upon when he went away to the end of the Star Path; how she lay herself down for her children and yielded herself up; and how our First Grandfather was there to meet her when she returned to the heart of the Mystery. And when savoring the richness of this life, I remember to give thanks for my First Teacher, who showed me the way along the Star Path, who watched over me as I traveled through darkness, and who was there to greet me when I found my way Home.

Epilogue

In a sense we are all Native to this Earth. All of us that live on Turtle Island have not only the right, but also the obligation to love and nurture our Mother Earth and Father Sky. It is a gift of the Great Mystery. The four great nations of people were given the responsibility by the Great Mystery to protect and care for the Earth, Water, Wind, and Fire. According to the legends the Red People were given the earth, the Yellow People were given the water, the Black People were given the wind, and the White People were given the air. Beginning here, we can understand the strength of living in harmony on the great hoop of the Medicine Wheel.

Ten White Bears always tells stories. When he tells stories he begins with the creation story he loves so much. He believes the story has so much meaning for people of today. He encourages people to talk about the stories and the meaning of them. He admonishes people to recognize and celebrate their differences of interpretation. He has a profound belief that each story has a special meaning for each individual, and that if each of us will take the time to share our understandings of the stories he tells, we will begin to sustain our communities and our world.

The last story that Ten White Bears tells is at the end of the Sweat Lodge, at the end of his story telling, and at the end of all of the gatherings where he is a participant. It is the story of the Raven.

I want to tell you a story. This comes from the Abenake people who live in the north, on the Laurentide plateau, in the Mistassini Forest, in northern Canada. It is the story of Raven. I have changed it a little bit just for you.

The Raven was born the son of the Thunderbird. He was born with white feathers. The Thunderbird was sent to the Mother Earth to rid it of all evil and bad things. The Thunderbird would fly around the earth and destroy all that was bad. Like his father, Raven took up the task of ridding the earth Mother of all evil. He grew into a smart and courageous warrior.

One day the Raven was flying around the forest and he saw a long house. He had never seen a long house before so he didn't know if it was good or evil. So the Raven flew down to the top of a tree that was near the long house and waited and watched.

The long house spoke to Raven and invited him in through the open door. Being smart and courageous, Raven watched with curiosity, but did not move from the tree. The long house again spoke to the Raven and invited him to enter. Raven spread his wings and flew up into the sky and circled the long house. He was still not sure if the long house was good or evil. Then he flew down to the long house and perched himself on the peak above the door. The long house spoke again, "Raven come into me. It is warm in here and you will be comfortable."

The Raven just sat on the peak of the long house wondering what to do. The long house spoke to the Raven for the fourth time and invited him in. Raven jumped off the peak of the house and with all of his courage flew through the door into the long house.

Inside the long house Raven found a fire in the very center. It was a good fire. It was the fire of life. As Raven approached the fire it began to pulse with his heartbeat.

The fire spoke to the Raven and told him the four great lessons of life.

The fire spoke the first lesson. "You are the Mystery and the Mystery is you. You cannot change this and if you think of yourself as separate you will have a hard life full of sickness, difficulty and disease."

Then the fire of life told Raven the second great lesson of life. The fire said, "All things are Sacred. They are sacred because they are created by the Great Mystery."

As Raven watched the fire it started to get bigger and told the third lesson. "Respect and maintain the differences."

The fire got bigger again and spoke the fourth and last lesson, "Remember, only the earth and sky last forever, make every day a good day to die."

The fire of life got even bigger and reached up to embrace the raven. When the embrace ended, the Raven's feathers had been singed black. Next to the Raven's feet was a small medicine bag. It was a gift from the fire. The fire of life spoke to the Raven and said, "Inside the medicine bag are the seeds of good. Plant the seeds of good in your life and they will grow like strawberries. Then there will be no room for evil or bad things in your life or on the Mother Earth."

As we complete this book, we close another Hoop and return to the beginning of the Medicine Wheel. We are different, each in our own way, from when it all began on that late summer night eight years ago in the sweat lodge. We have both gone through a transformation to greater awareness and realization of the Great Mystery. We learned many lessons, both great and small on the path around the Medicine Wheel. The greatest, most gentle lesson of our story was at the end, when we closed the hoop, and when we remembered that our relationship was just one of many. We are related to the Earth and Sky, to our families, our communities, nations, and world. The closing of a relationship reminds us of our Oneness with all Creation.

All relationships ebb and flow, begin and end, change and renew. Each relationship comes with the responsibility to care, to nurture, and to love unconditionally. When partners in the relationship live this way, the relationship becomes one of shared being and mutual creation. These kinds of relationships help us live our life vision, because we are continually helping our partners to remember who they are. We are helping one another to remember the vision given to us by the Great Spirit. We are helping one another remember all the ways in which we are all related.

Respecting and caring for all of our relationships is the measure of our character. Understanding that all relationships end, that we must eventually close the Hoop, helps us to do this. Anticipating the closing of the Hoop leaves us little time for behaviors or thoughts that do not enhance the relationship. There is no need for guilt, fear, or jealousy. A relationship of shared being, carefully tended, helps us mature in the heart of the Creator and broaden our realization of the Great Mystery.

When it is time to close the Hoop, you will know. Read the signs on the trail of life and you can anticipate the best moment. Close the Hoop carefully with awareness and close it gracefully. Know that the more intense the relationship, the more difficult it may seem to change and make the end happen. When this occurs, you may feel a resistance to closing the Hoop. The reluctance is born from illusions of uncertainty and self-concern. The Great Spirit provides our relationships only so that those involved can increase their knowledge of their relatedness to all things and their awareness of the Mystery. These realizations happen only when the Hoop is closed. Experience the ecstasy of the closing of the Hoop.

The only relationship that lasts forever is the one we have with the Great Spirit. This is the road of life. It is a good road.

And so it is with us. The Hoop is closed. We begin again. A relationship of mutual creation and shared being. Planting the seeds of good.

Ten White Bears   Medicine Horse

References

Andrews, I., (1983). *Medicine woman.* San Francisco: Harper San Francisco.

Boyd, D. (1974). *Rolling thunder.* New York: Dell.

Bruchac, J. (1993). *The Native American sweat lodge: History and legends.* Freedom, CA: Crossing Press.

Castenada, C., Castenada, C., & Rosenman, J. (1991). *The eagle's gift.* New York: Pocket Books.

Davis, W. (1998). *Shadows in the sun: Travels in the landscape of spirit and desire.* Covela, CA: Island Press.

Emmons, R.A. (1999). *The psychology of ultimate concerns: Motivation and spirituality in psychotherapy.* New York: Guilford.

Frank, J., & Frank, J. (2000). *Persuasion and healing.* Baltimore, MD: Johns Hopkins University Press.

Gardner, H. (1983). *Frames of mind: The theory of multiple intelligences.* New York: Basic Books.

Gordon, R.J., Nienstedt, B.C., Gesler, W., & Gesler, W. (1998). *Alternative therapies: Expanding options in health.* New York: Springer Publishing.

Hammerschlag, C. (1989). *The dancing healers: A doctor's journey of healing with Native Americans.* San Francisco: Harper San Francisco.

Hammerschlag, C. (1994). *The theft of the spirit.* New York: Fireside.

Hoffman, E. (1981). *The way of splendor: Jewish mysticism and modern psychology.* Boulder, CO: Shambhala.

Kiev, A. (1964). *Magic, faith and healing.* New York: Free Press.

Morgan, M., & Garrison, C. (1995). *Mutant message down under.* New York: HarperCollins.

Moyers, B.D. (1993). *Healing and the mind.* New York: Doubleday.

Noble, K. (2001). *Riding the windhorse: Spiritual intelligence and the growth of the self.* Cresskill, NJ: Hampton Press.

Winkelman, M. (1992). *Shamans, priests, and witches: A crosscultural study of magico religious practitioners.* Tempe: Arizona State University Press.

Winkelman, M. (2000). *Shamanism: The neural ecology of consciousness.* Westport, CT: Bergin & Garvey.

Printed in the United States
1427000002BA/1-54